D0471045

ALSO BY DIFFEE

THE REJECTION COLLECTION:
CARTOONS YOU NEVER SAW, AND NEVER
WILL SEE, IN THE NEW YORKER

THE REJECTION COLLECTION VOL. 2:
THE CREAM OF THE CRAP

THE BEST OF THE REJECTION COLLECTION:
293 CARTOONS THAT WERE TOO DUMB, TOO DARK,
OR TOO NAUGHTY FOR THE NEW YORKER

HAND DRAWN JOKES FOR SMART ATTRACTIVE PEOPLE

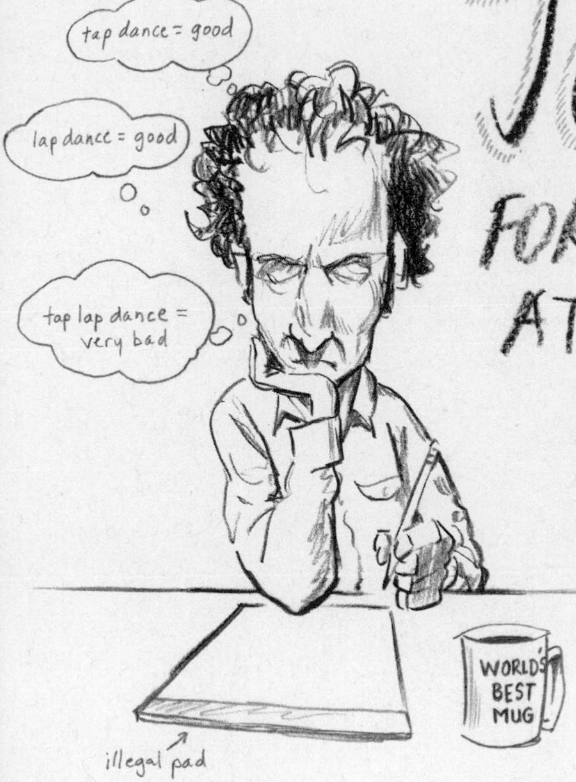

tap dance = good
lap dance = good
tap lap dance = very bad
WORLD'S BEST MUG
illegal pad

by MATTHEW DIFFEE

New Yorker Cartoonist, tallish

SCRIBNER

New York London Toronto Sydney New Delhi

Scribner
An Imprint of Simon & Schuster, Inc.
1230 Avenue of the Americas
New York, NY 10020

This book is a work of fiction. Any references to historical events, real people, or real places
are used fictitiously. Other names, characters, places, and events are products of the author's imagination,
and any resemblance to actual events or places or persons, living or dead, is entirely coincidental.

Copyright © 2015 by Matthew Diffee

All rights reserved, including the right to reproduce this book or portions thereof
in any form whatsoever. For information, address Scribner Subsidiary Rights Department,
1230 Avenue of the Americas, New York, NY 10020.

First Scribner hardcover edition May 2015

SCRIBNER and design are registered trademarks of The Gale Group, Inc.,
used under license by Simon & Schuster, Inc., the publisher of this work.

For information about special discounts for bulk purchases,
please contact Simon & Schuster Special Sales at 1-866-506-1949
or business@simonandschuster.com.

The Simon & Schuster Speakers Bureau can bring authors to your live event. For more information
or to book an event, contact the Simon & Schuster Speakers Bureau at 1-866-248-3049 or visit our
website at www.simonspeakers.com.

Manufactured in the United States of America

10 9 8 7 6 5 4 3 2 1

ISBN 978-1-4767-4874-0
ISBN 978-1-4767-4877-1 (ebook)

FOR MOM,
WHO INSPIRED
ME TO WRITE

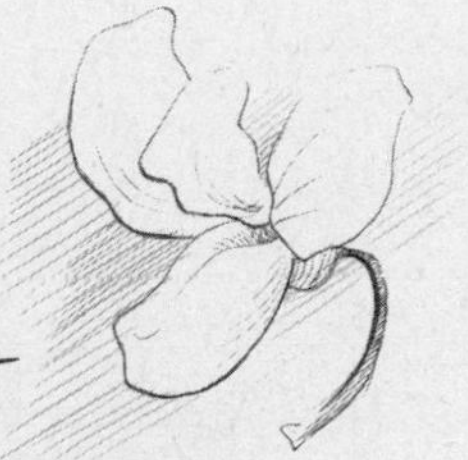

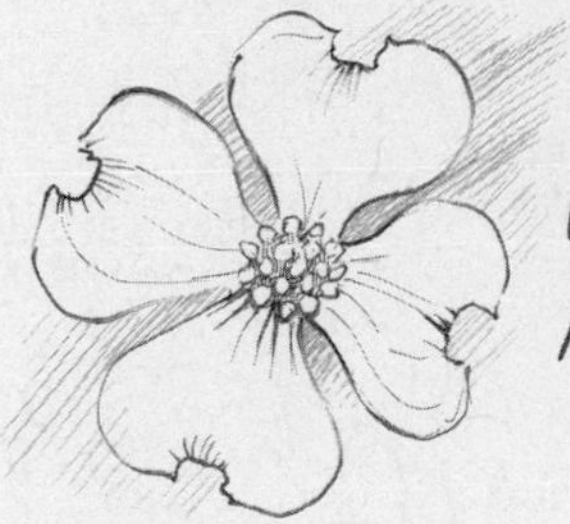

AND DAD,
WHO INSPIRED
ME TO DRAW.

TABLE OF CONTENTS (FOR SMART ATTRACTIVE PEOPLE)

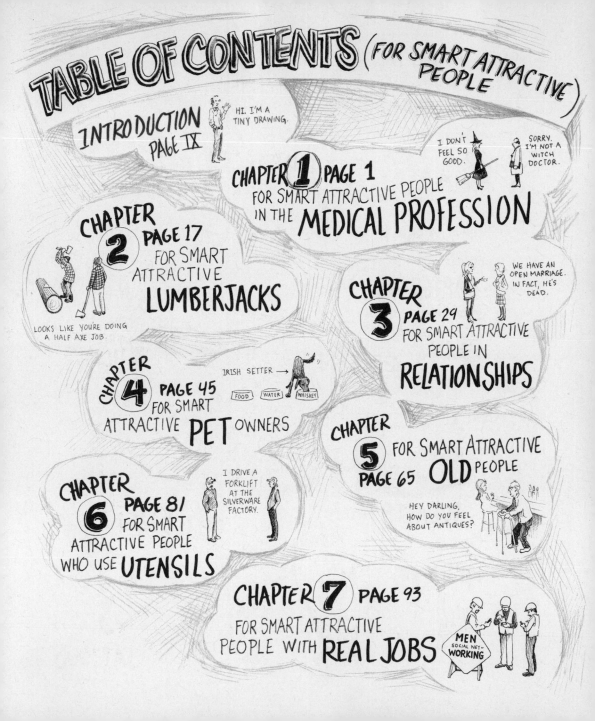

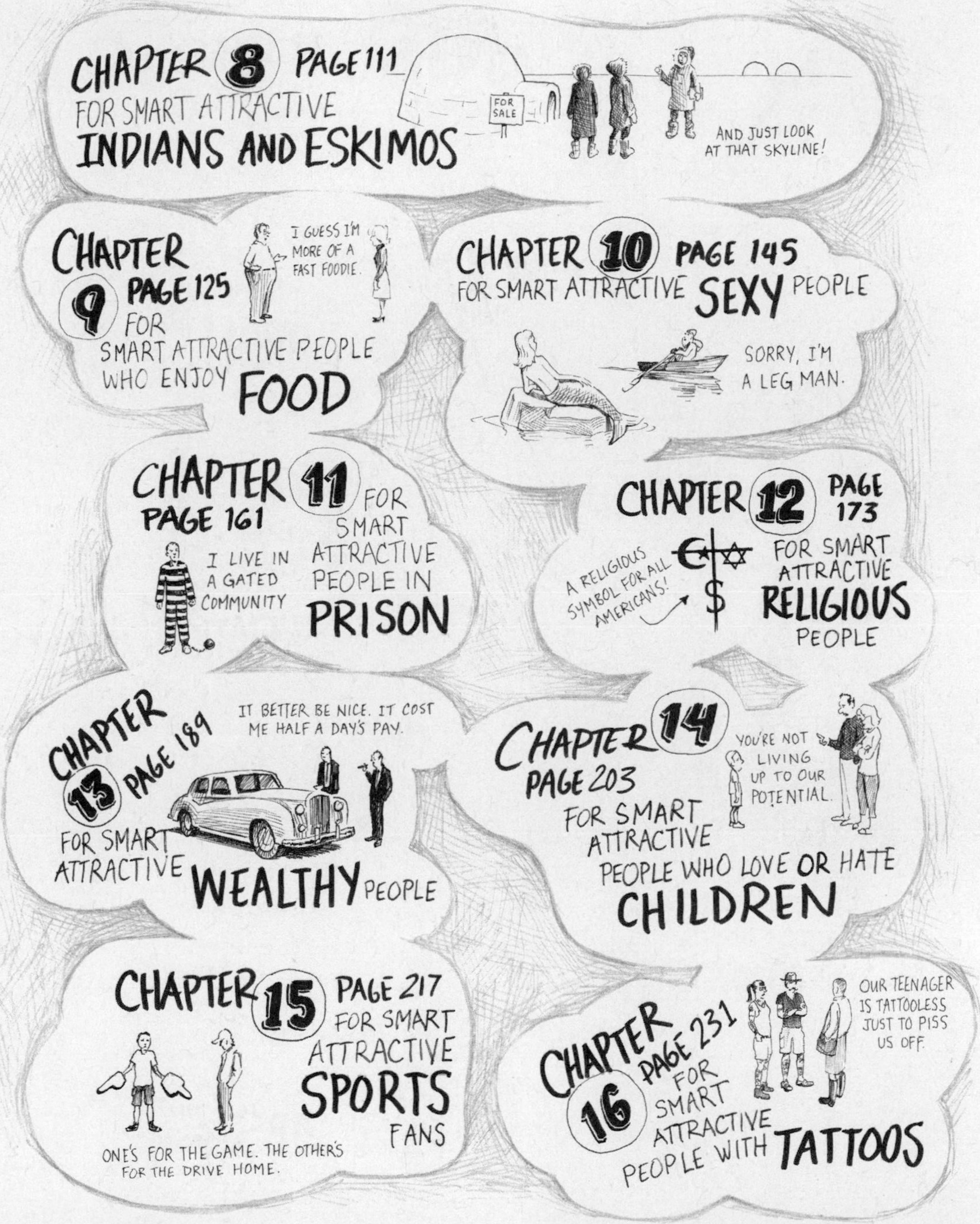
CHAPTER 8 PAGE 111
FOR SMART ATTRACTIVE
INDIANS AND ESKIMOS
FOR SALE
AND JUST LOOK AT THAT SKYLINE!
CHAPTER 9 PAGE 125
FOR SMART ATTRACTIVE PEOPLE WHO ENJOY FOOD
I GUESS I'M MORE OF A FAST FOODIE.
CHAPTER 10 PAGE 145
FOR SMART ATTRACTIVE SEXY PEOPLE
SORRY, I'M A LEG MAN.
CHAPTER 11 PAGE 161
FOR SMART ATTRACTIVE PEOPLE IN PRISON
I LIVE IN A GATED COMMUNITY
CHAPTER 12 PAGE 173
FOR SMART ATTRACTIVE RELIGIOUS PEOPLE
A RELIGIOUS SYMBOL FOR ALL AMERICANS!
CHAPTER 13 PAGE 189
FOR SMART ATTRACTIVE WEALTHY PEOPLE
IT BETTER BE NICE. IT COST ME HALF A DAY'S PAY.
CHAPTER 14 PAGE 203
FOR SMART ATTRACTIVE PEOPLE WHO LOVE OR HATE CHILDREN
YOU'RE NOT LIVING UP TO OUR POTENTIAL.
CHAPTER 15 PAGE 217
FOR SMART ATTRACTIVE SPORTS FANS
ONE'S FOR THE GAME. THE OTHER'S FOR THE DRIVE HOME.
CHAPTER 16 PAGE 231
FOR SMART ATTRACTIVE PEOPLE WITH TATTOOS
OUR TEENAGER IS TATTOOLESS JUST TO PISS US OFF.

INTRODUCTION

Howdy, allow me to introduce myself and this book you're about to read. I can at least explain the title. But first, me. I don't know if you can tell just by looking at me, but I'm incredibly attractive. Maybe not in a leading man kind of way, but in a key grip, possibly stuntman or visual effects supervisor kind of way.

I'M ALSO SMART. THAT'S OBVIOUS. I MEAN, DUH. I'M WRITING A BOOK, ARN'T I?

A LOT OF PEOPLE, ESPECIALLY MY WIFE, ASK ME, "WHAT EXACTLY DO YOU DO ALL DAY?" THE ANSWER IS SIMPLE, BUT APPARENTLY HARD TO GRASP; I THINK UP FUNNY THINGS AND I DRAW THEM. ALL DAY. SOMETIMES, IN ORDER TO DO THAT, I HAVE TO WATCH TV OR NAP.

AND OFTEN I'LL NEED COOKIES.

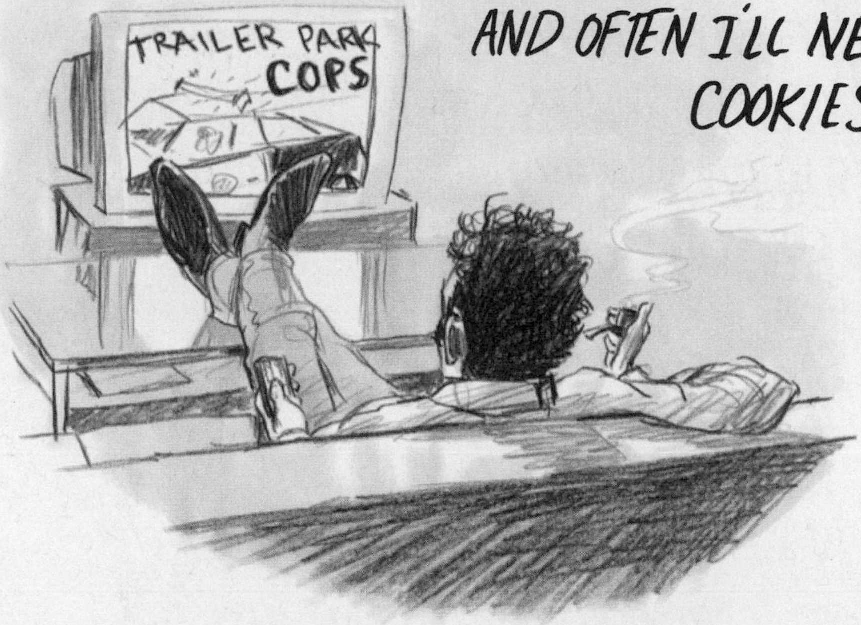
TRAILER PARK
COPS

IN OUR LABEL-OBSESSED CULTURE, MY WORK IS KNOWN AS "CARTOONS," BUT IS THAT REALLY THE BEST TERM FOR WHAT A HANDSOME GENIUS LIKE MYSELF DOES? NO. BESIDES, IT'S AMBIGUOUS. "CARTOON" CAN MEAN WHAT I DO <u>OR</u> IT CAN MEAN AN ANIMATED PROGRAM FOR KIDS OR EVEN A PRELIMINARY STUDY FOR A MEDIEVAL FRESCO. SEE, I TOLD YOU I WAS SMART. THAT'S WHY I PREFER TO THINK OF WHAT I DO AS JOKES THAT I DRAW. AND THAT'S WHY SO MANY PEOPLE COME UP TO ME AND SAY,

You remind me so much of Chris Rock!

YEP, IT'S TRUE. ME AND ROCK ARE BASICALLY THE SAME GUY. I MEAN, APART FROM THE OBVIOUS DIFFERENCES.

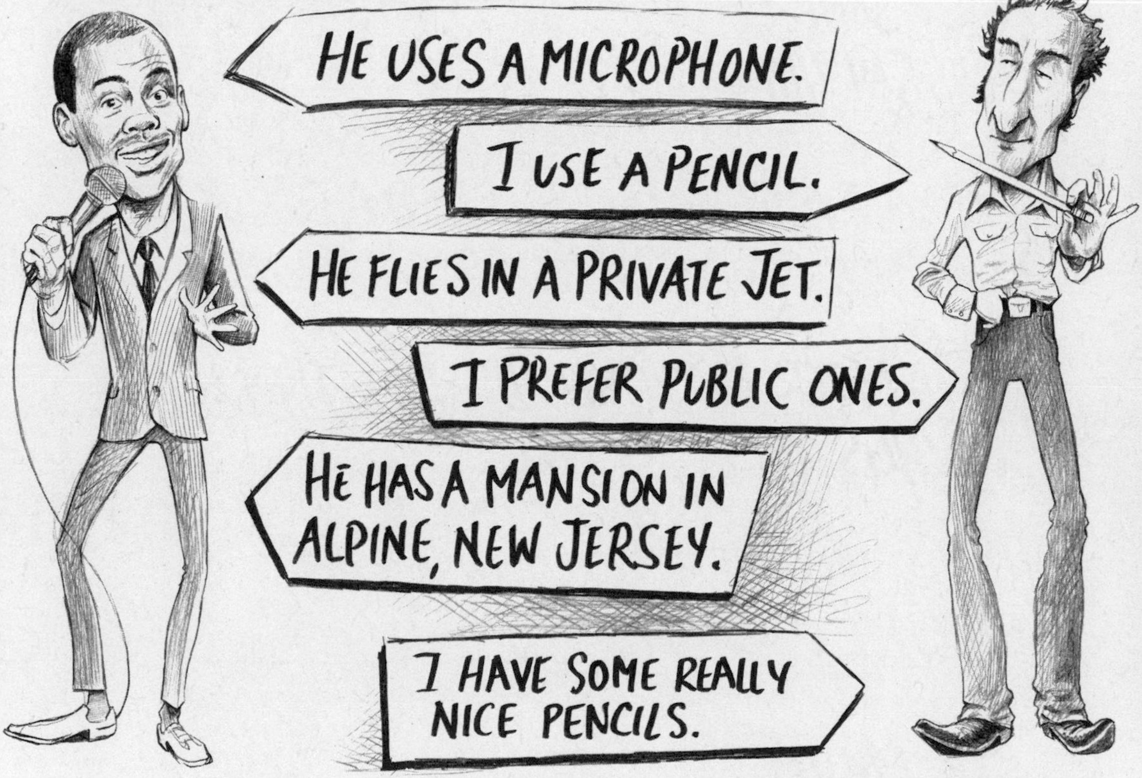

HE USES A MICROPHONE.
I USE A PENCIL.
HE FLIES IN A PRIVATE JET.
I PREFER PUBLIC ONES.
HE HAS A MANSION IN ALPINE, NEW JERSEY.
I HAVE SOME REALLY NICE PENCILS.

OTHER THAN THAT, WE'RE VIRTUALLY IDENTICAL AND I THINK THAT EXPLAINS THE TITLE OF THIS BOOK, AT LEAST THE "JOKES" PART. I'LL MOVE ON TO THE REST.

NOW, YOU'RE GONNA HAVE A HARD TIME BELIEVING THIS, BUT THERE ARE A FEW FOLKS OUT THERE WHO DON'T LOVE MY WORK. I'VE MET SOME OF THEM. THEY COME UP TO ME AND SAY THINGS LIKE,

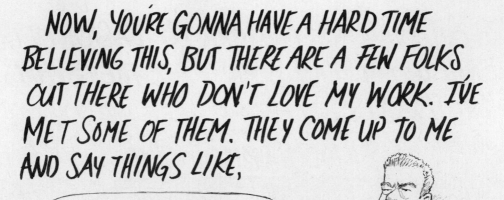

I don't get it.

AND AFTER I EXPLAIN THE JOKE THEY'LL SAY THINGS LIKE,

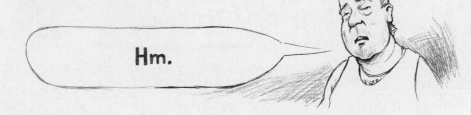

Hm.

OR MAYBE,

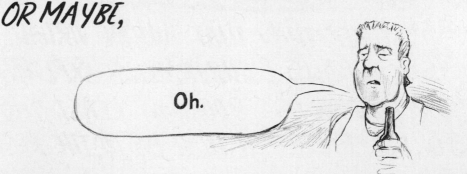

Oh.

OVER THE YEARS, I'VE NOTICED SOMETHING INTERESTING ABOUT THESE PEOPLE. THEY ARE ALL, WITHOUT EXCEPTION, UGLY AND DUMB. THAT'S WHEN I REALIZED THAT MY WORK APPEALS ONLY TO PEOPLE WHO ARE, LIKE ME, SMART AND ATTRACTIVE. IN FACT, THE MORE BEAUTIFUL AND INTELLIGENT A PERSON IS, THE MORE THEY TEND TO ENJOY MY STUFF. GEORGE CLOONEY AND NATALIE PORTMAN CAN'T GET ENOUGH OF IT PROBABLY. SO THAT'S WHY I'M DOING THIS BOOK. FOR THEM AND PEOPLE LIKE THEM, LIKE CATE BLANCHETT AND MAYBE YOU.

I HOPE YOU ENJOY IT. BUT IF NOT, YOU REALLY SHOULDN'T TELL ANYONE, BECAUSE THAT WOULD BE EMBARRASSING. FOR YOU, I MEAN.

CHAPTER ONE

FOR SMART Attractive PEOPLE IN THE MEDICAL PROFESSION

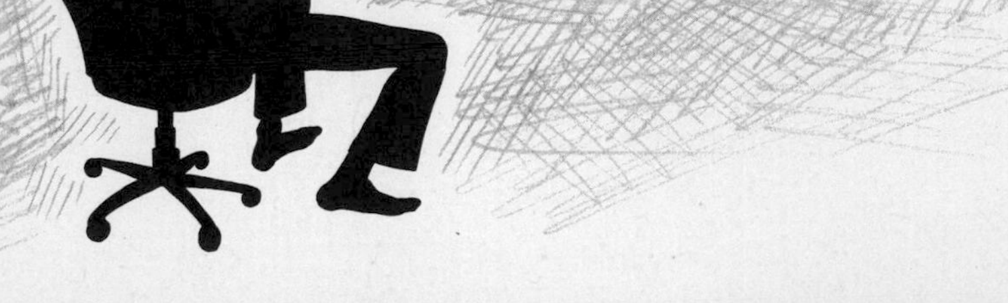
You'd think a snack food that rhymes with a fungal anomaly of the metatarsophalangeal joint would be unappetizing and yet, Funyuns!

I HAVE A LOT OF FRIENDS WHO ARE MEDICAL PROFESSIONALS, WHICH IS A GOOD THING BECAUSE I HAVE A LOT OF OTHER FRIENDS WHO DRINK TOO MUCH AND OWN CROSSBOWS. →

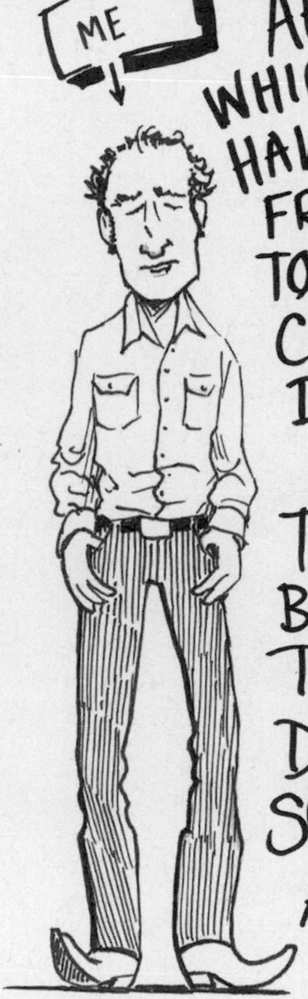

ME

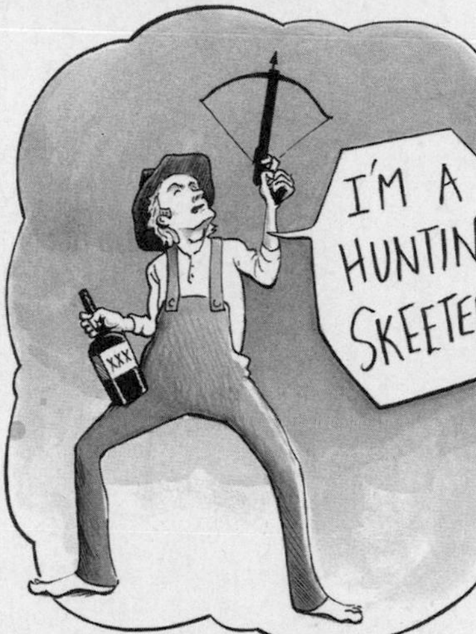

XXX
I'M A HUNTIN' SKEETERS!

IT'S FUNNY, BUT, I NEVER EVEN THOUGHT ABOUT BEING A DOCTOR. THE TROUBLE WITH BEING A DOCTOR IS YOU HAVE TO GO TO SCHOOL FOR A REALLY LONG TIME AND EVENTUALLY YOU HAVE TO STICK YOUR FINGER UP OLD PEOPLE'S BUTTS. I DON'T KNOW ABOUT YOU, BUT I DON'T REALLY ENJOY SCHOOL.

IF I WERE A DOCTOR, I'D PROBABLY BE SOME SORT OF SURGEON: PLASTIC, TREE, OR MAYBE HEART. THEY MAKE A LOT OF MONEY AND, LET'S BE HONEST, IT AIN'T ROCKET SURGERY. ONE THING I KNOW IS I'D KEEP THINGS FUN IN THE OPERATING ROOM BY SHOUTING THINGS LIKE...

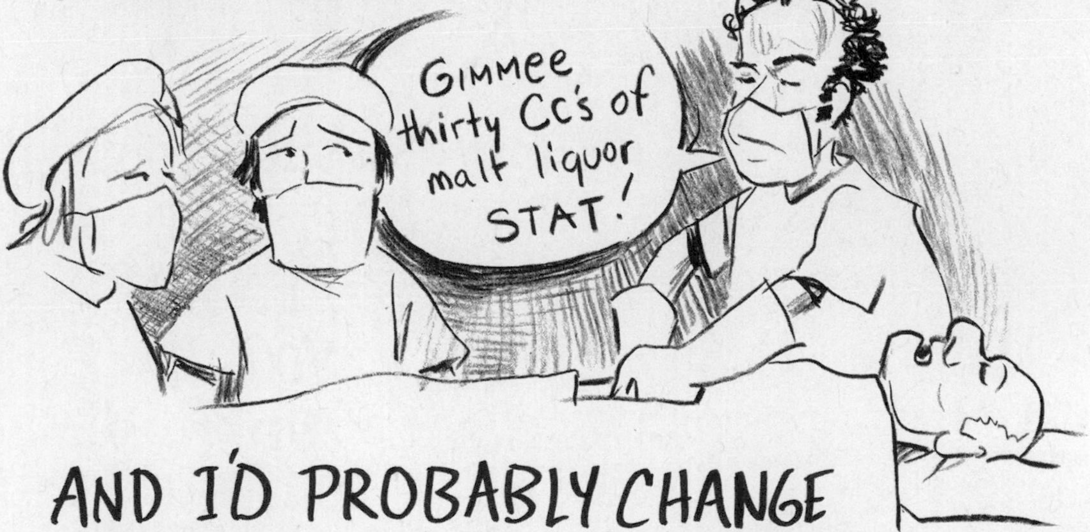
Gimmee thirty Cc's of malt liquor STAT!

AND I'D PROBABLY CHANGE MY LAST NAME TO PEPPER.

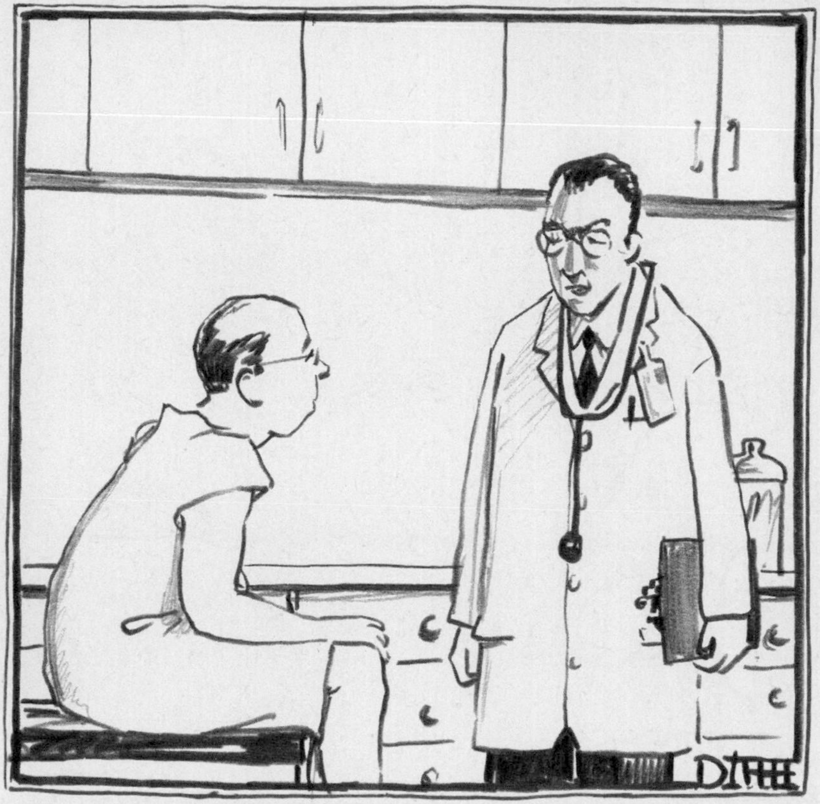
DIFFEE

"It's your ear, nose, and throat."

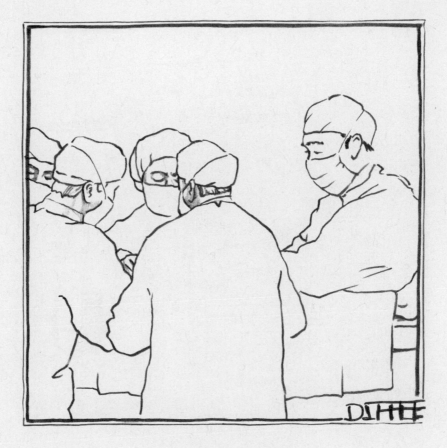

"Try jiggling the liver."

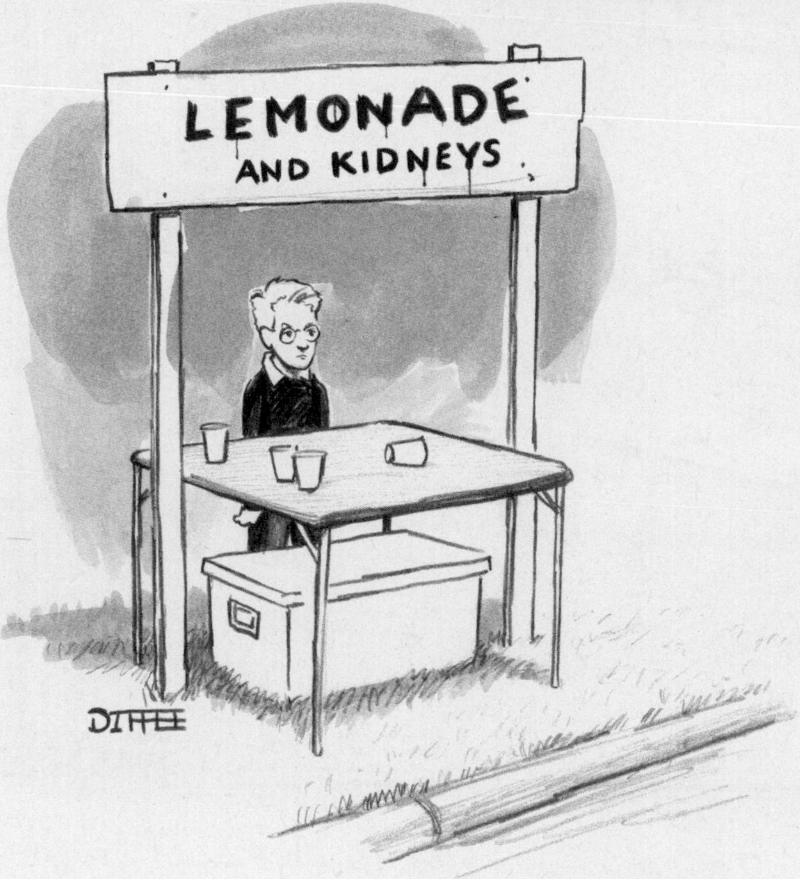
LEMONADE
AND KIDNEYS
DIFFEE

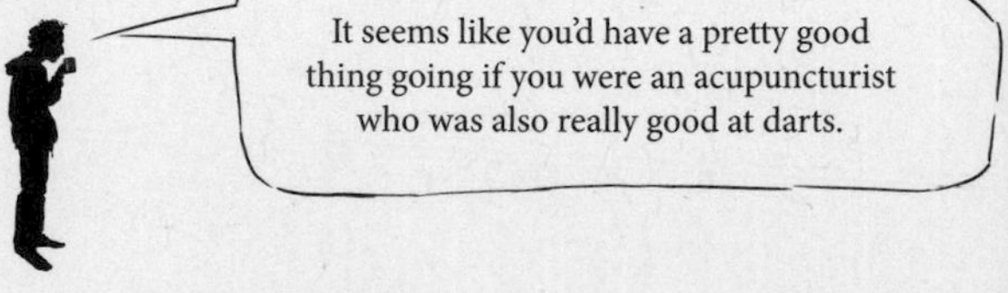
It seems like you'd have a pretty good thing going if you were an acupuncturist who was also really good at darts.

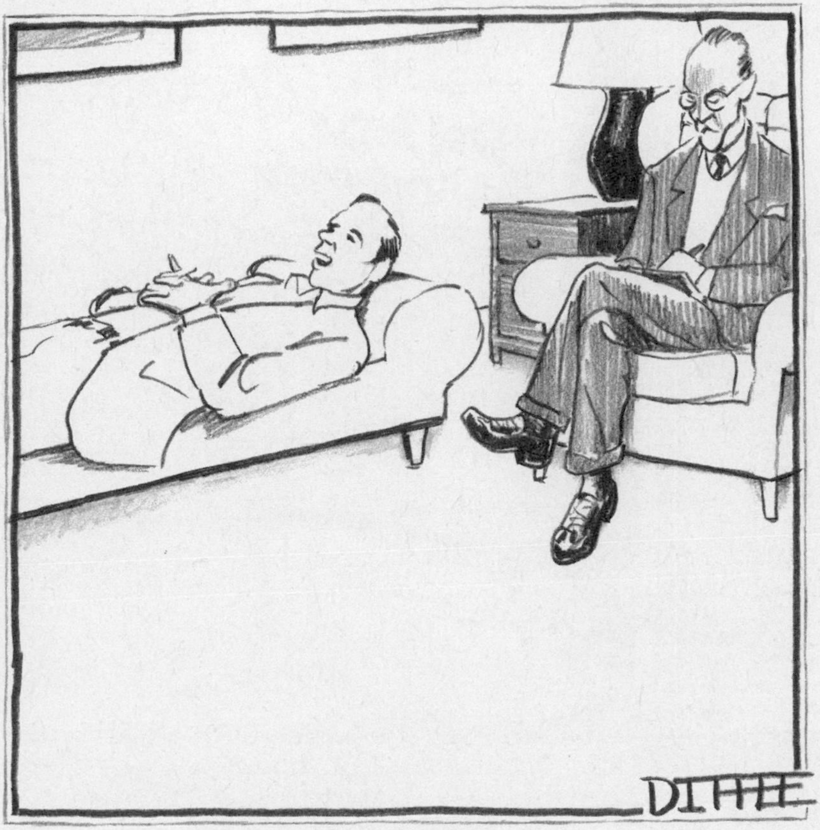
DIFFEE

"I have an imaginary friend. He's a real person—he just isn't really my friend."

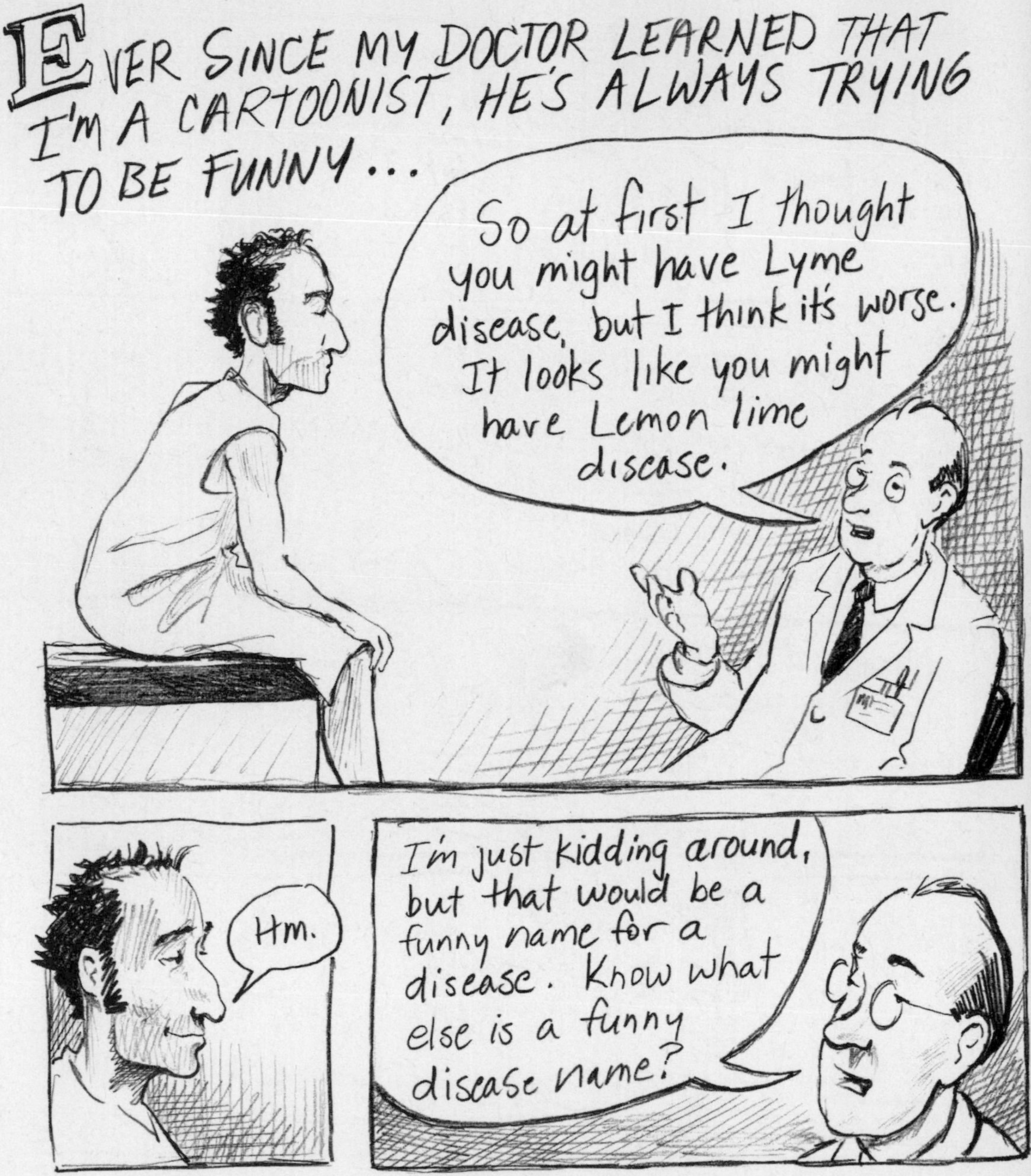
EVER SINCE MY DOCTOR LEARNED THAT I'M A CARTOONIST, HE'S ALWAYS TRYING TO BE FUNNY...
So at first I thought you might have Lyme disease, but I think it's worse. It looks like you might have Lemon lime disease.
Hm.
I'm just kidding around, but that would be a funny name for a disease. Know what else is a funny disease name?

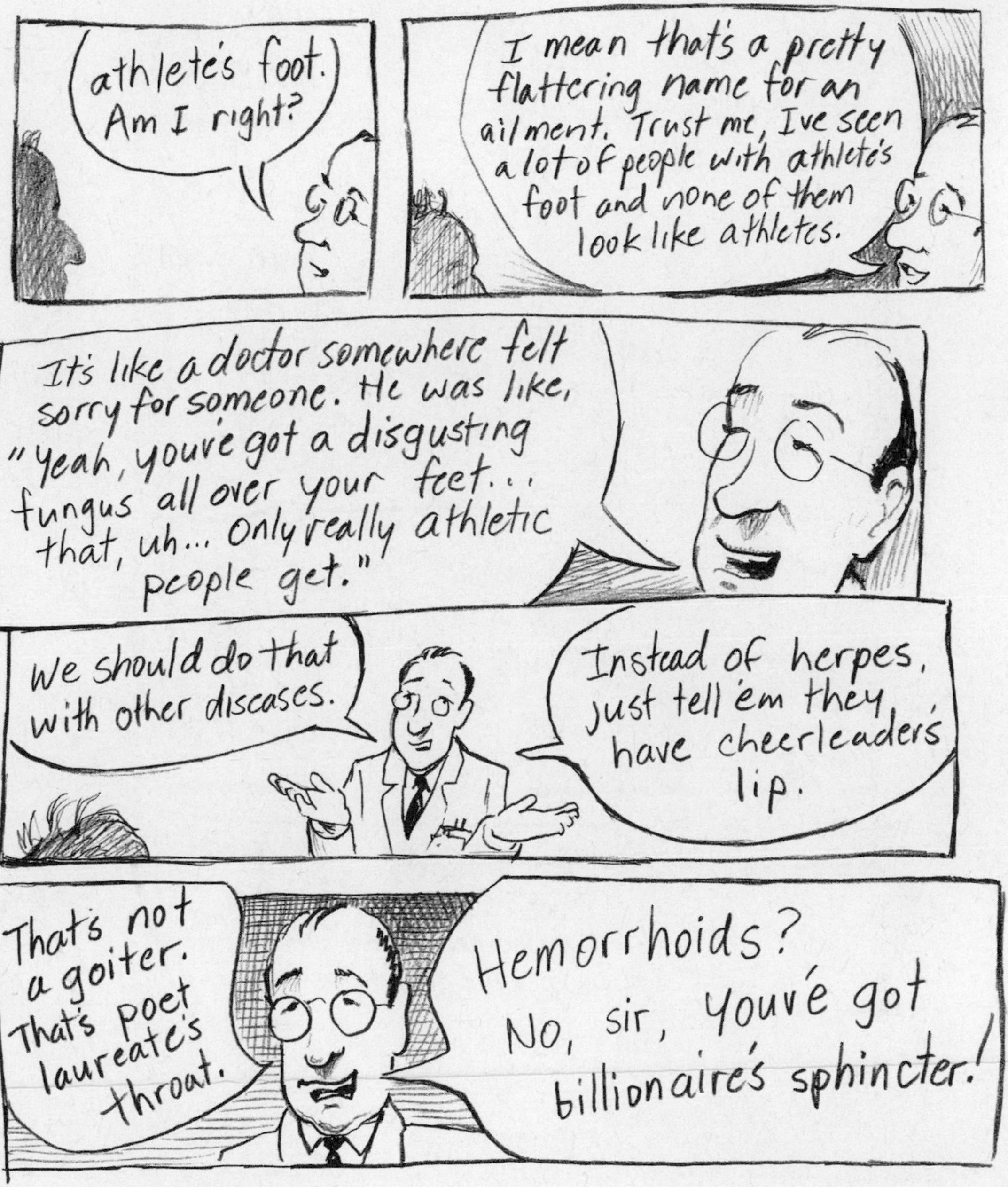
athlete's foot. Am I right?
I mean that's a pretty flattering name for an ailment. Trust me, Ive seen a lot of people with athlete's foot and none of them look like athletes.
It's like a doctor somewhere felt sorry for someone. He was like, "Yeah, you've got a disgusting fungus all over your feet... that, uh... only really athletic people get."
We should do that with other diseases.
Instead of herpes, just tell 'em they have cheerleader's lip.
That's not a goiter. That's poet laureate's throat.
Hemorrhoids? No, sir, you've got billionaire's sphincter!

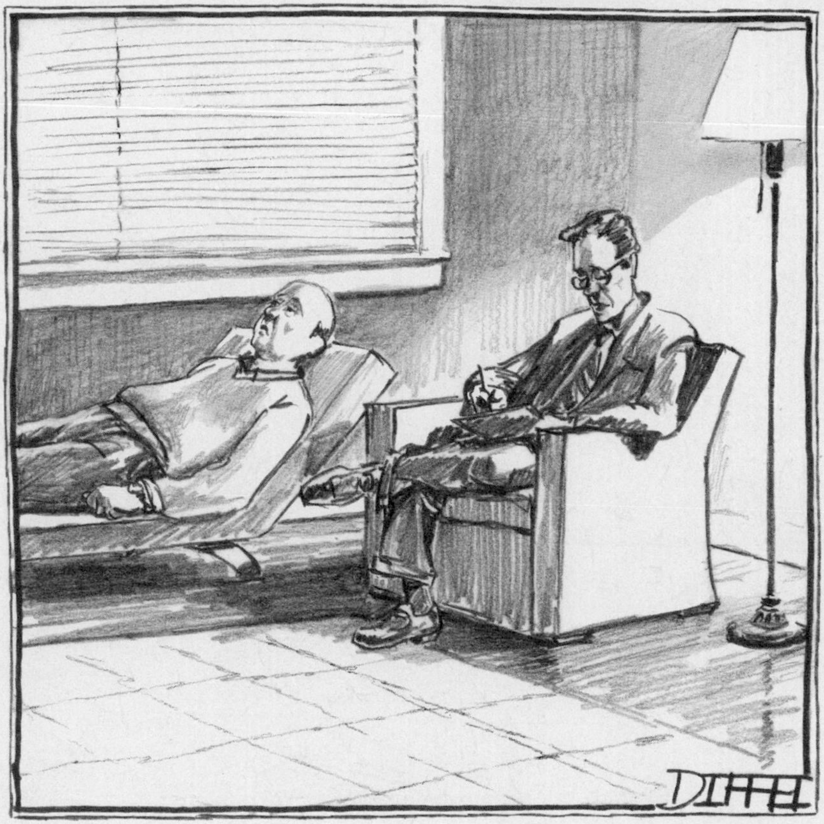
DIFFEE

"These feelings of inadequacy are common among the inadequate."

"I'm afraid Mr. Bickles has some bad news."

What the heck happened to you?

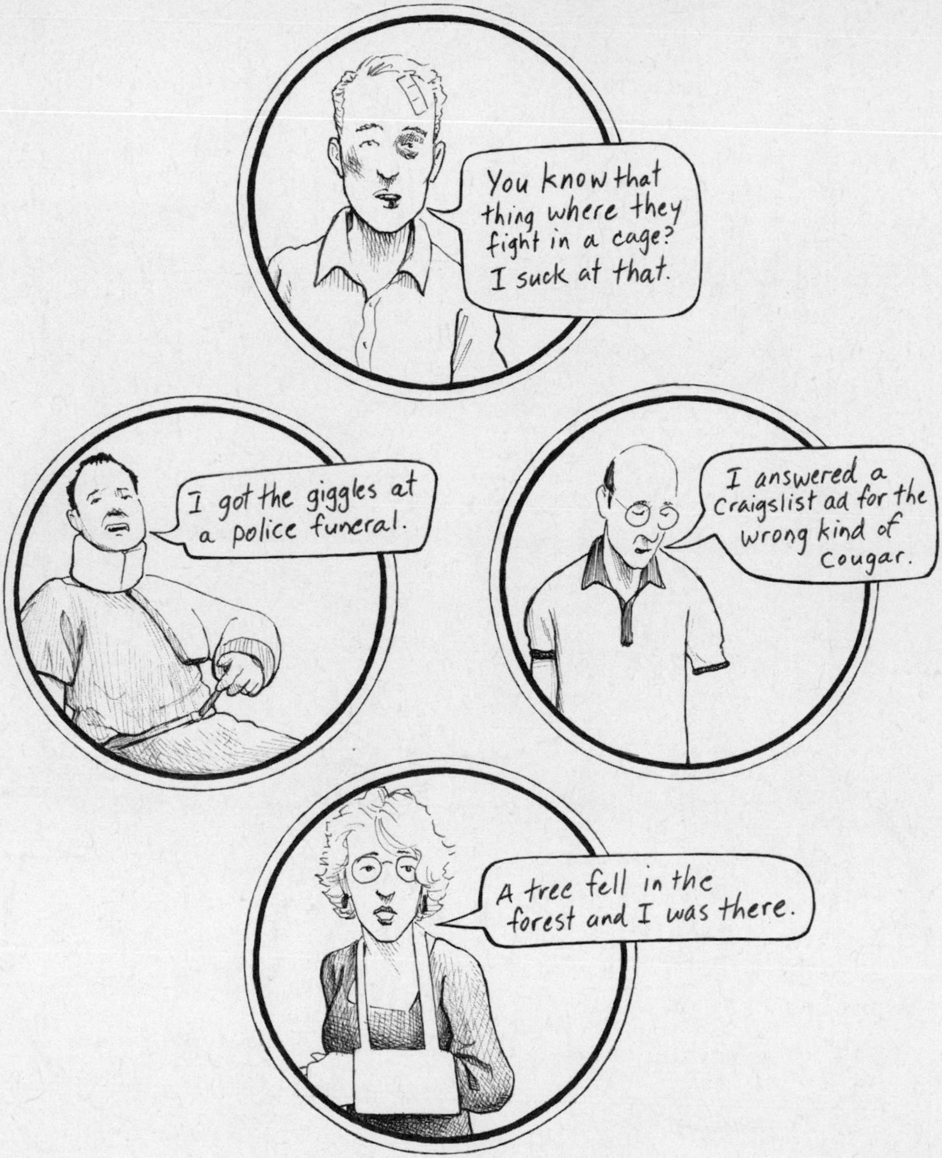
You know that thing where they fight in a cage? I suck at that.
I got the giggles at a police funeral.
I answered a Craigslist ad for the wrong kind of cougar.
A tree fell in the forest and I was there.

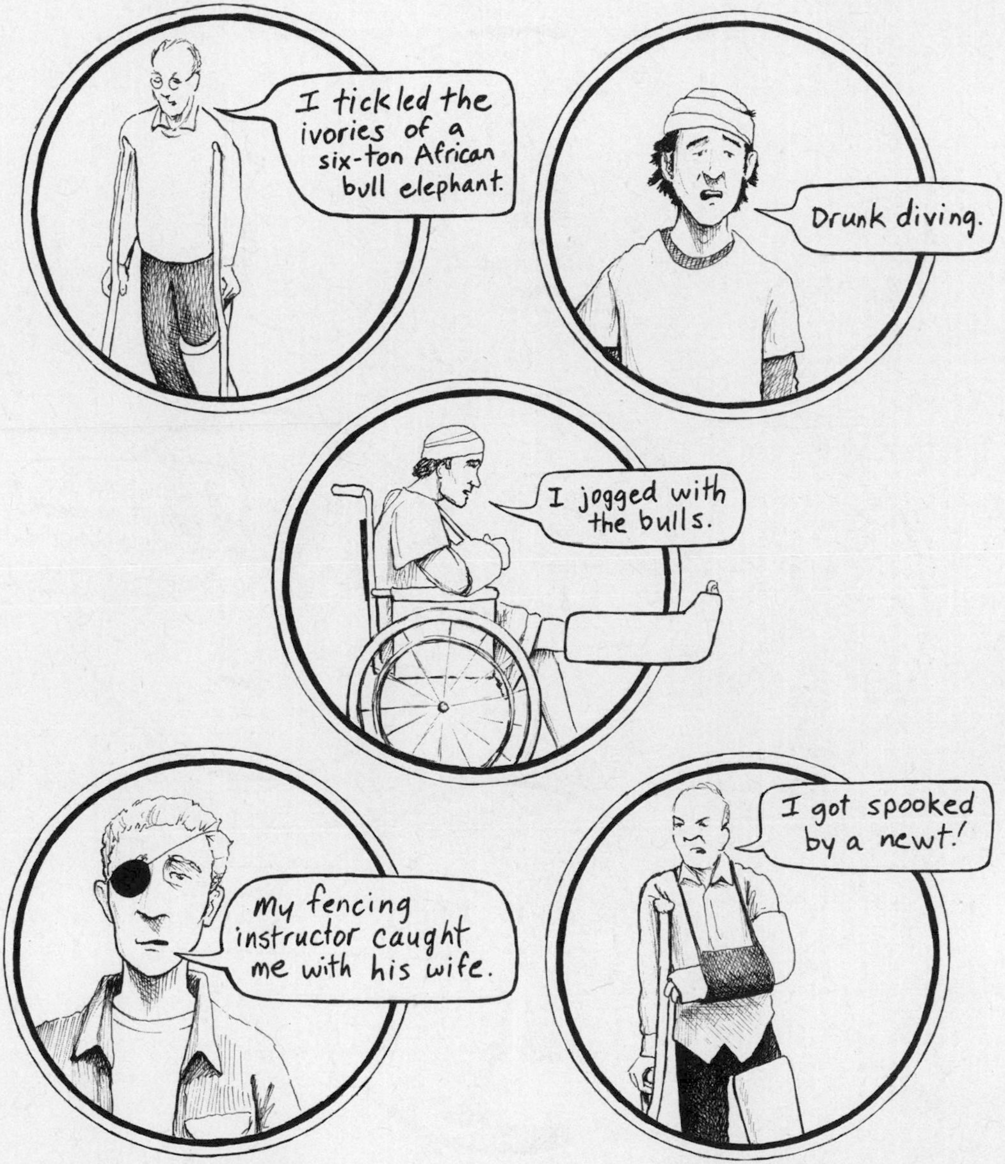
I tickled the ivories of a six-ton African bull elephant.
Drunk diving.
I jogged with the bulls.
My fencing instructor caught me with his wife.
I got spooked by a newt!

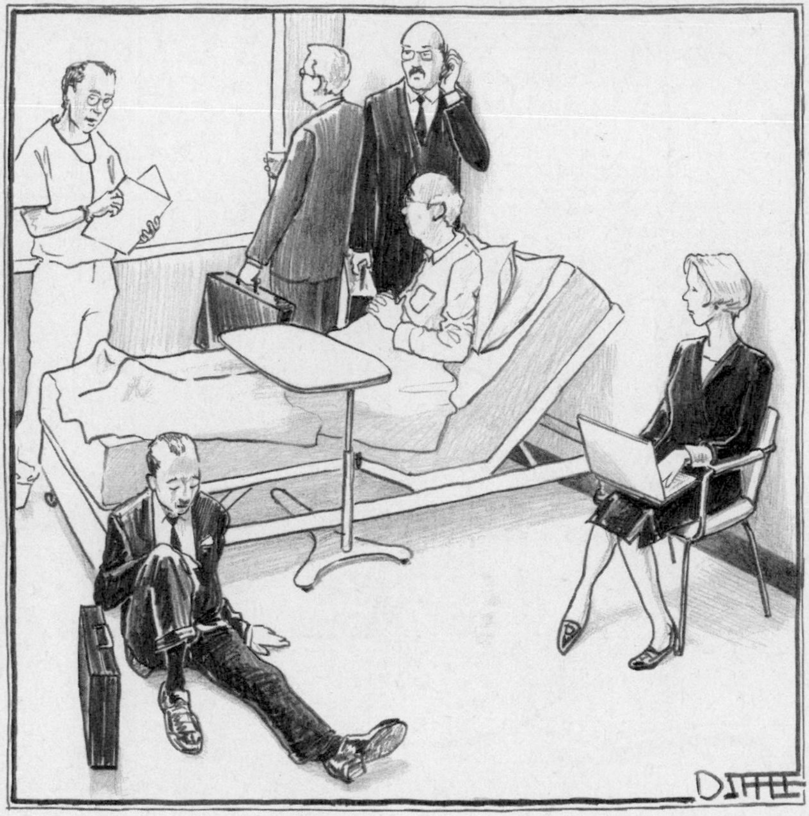
DIFFEE

"I'm afraid you're retaining lawyers."

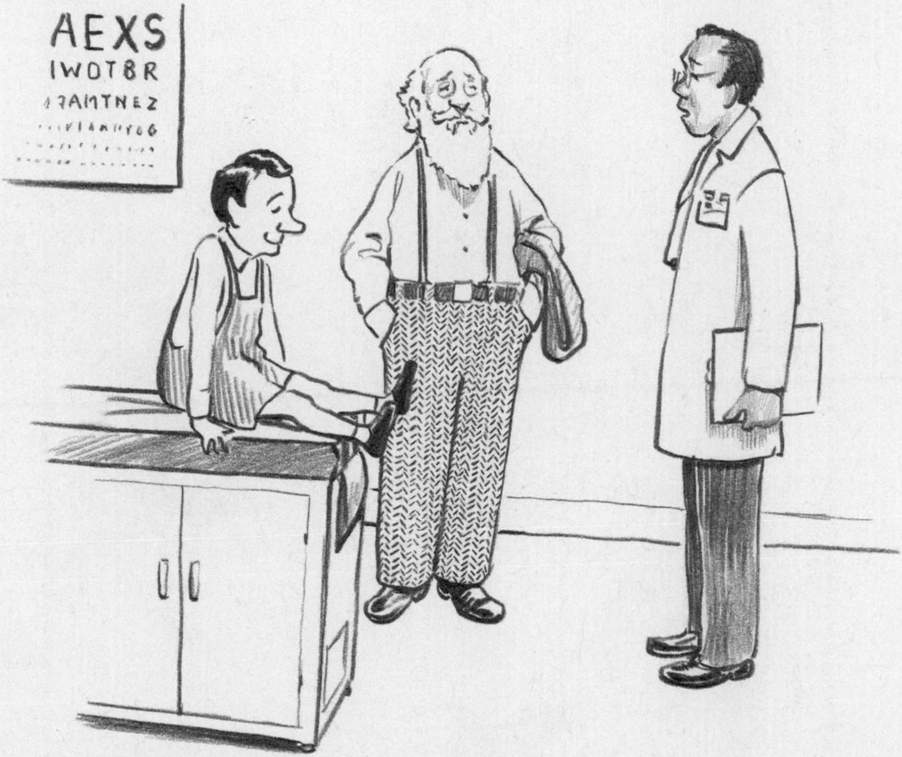
AEXS

"The good news is he's a real boy. The bad news is he has termites."

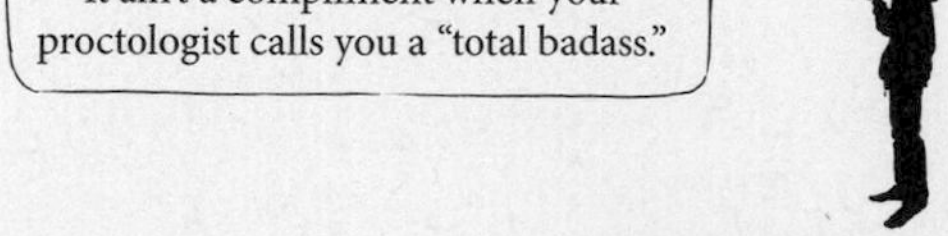
It ain't a compliment when your proctologist calls you a "total badass."

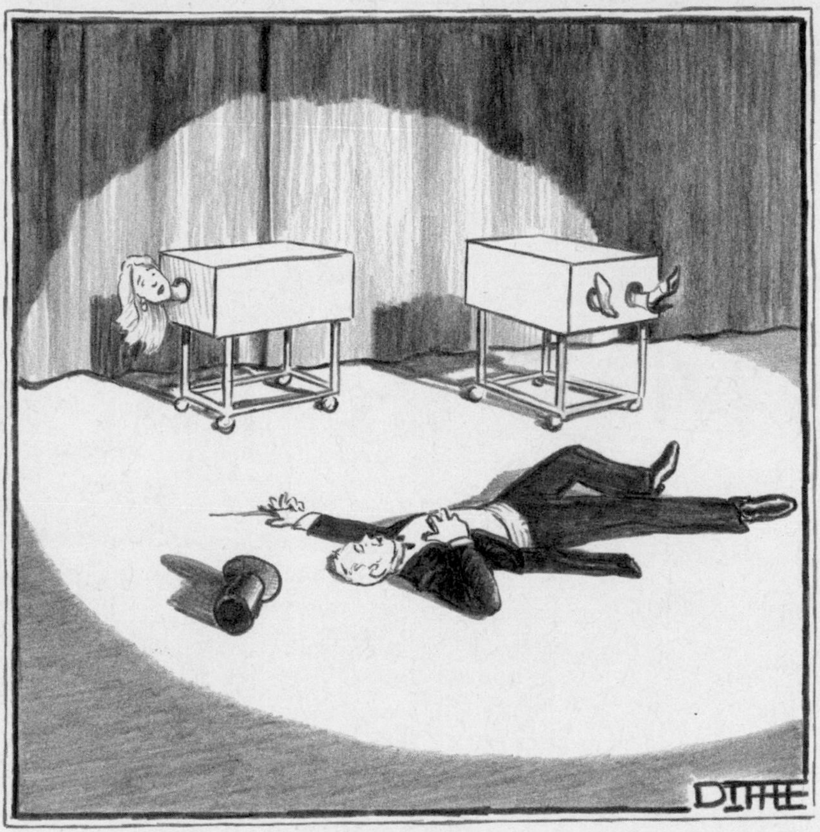
DIFFEE

"Is there a doctor in the house, and more importantly, another magician?"

CHAPTER TWO

FOR SMART ATTRACTIVE LUMBERJACKS

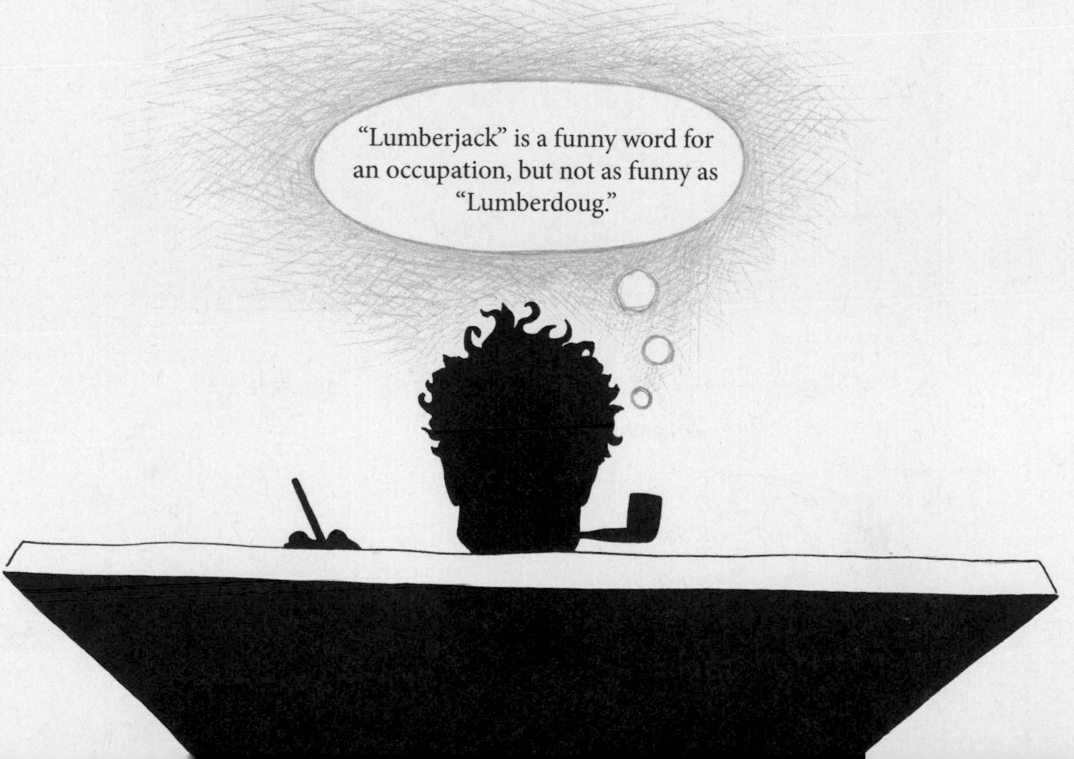
"Lumberjack" is a funny word for an occupation, but not as funny as "Lumberdoug."

WHENEVER I SUCCESSFULLY RIDE A LOG RIDE, WHICH IS FORTNIGHTLY, I ALWAYS THINK, "SHOOT, I SHOULD'VE BEEN A LUMBERJACK!" I ENJOY THE WOODS, I'M NOT AFRAID OF HEIGHTS, I OWN A RED FLANNEL SHIRT, AND I LOVE OVEREATING IN THE MORNING! THE ONLY PROBLEM I SEE IS I DON'T REALLY KNOW HOW TO SWING A SAW BUT I'M SURE I COULD LEARN.

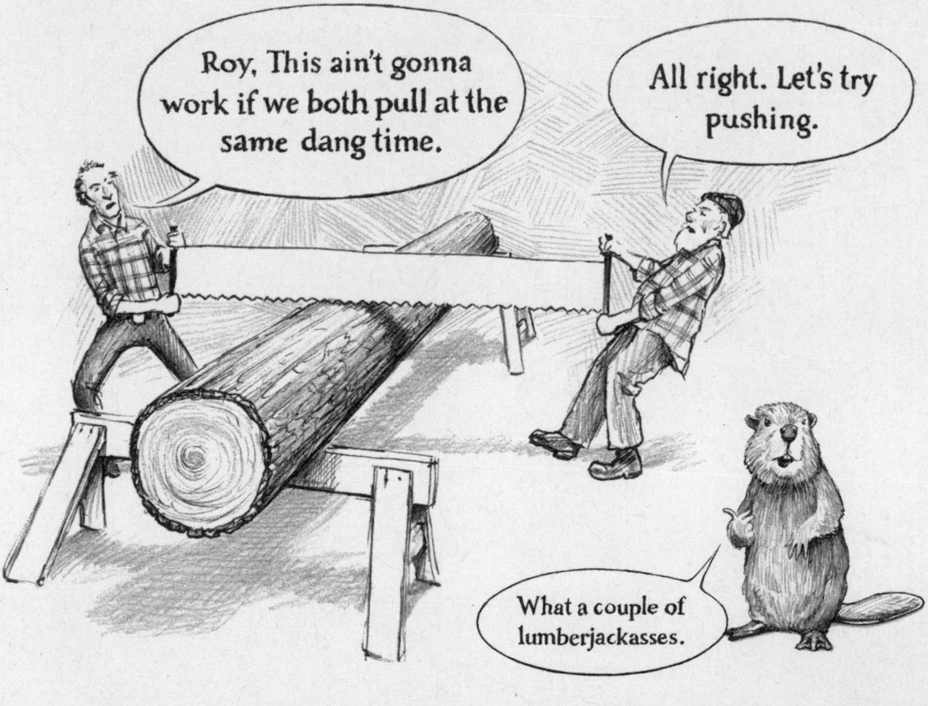
Roy, This ain't gonna work if we both pull at the same dang time.
All right. Let's try pushing.
What a couple of lumberjackasses.

I PROBABLY HAVE A ROMANTICIZED VIEW OF IT ALL BECAUSE I GREW UP IN TEXAS, WHERE YOU'LL SEE A TALL TREE ABOUT AS OFTEN AS YOU'LL SEE A DEMOCRAT, OR A GROWN MAN DRIVING SOMETHING OTHER THAN A PICKUP TRUCK. I GOT PULLED OVER ONCE FOR NOT HAVING

A WEST TEXAS LUMBERJACK ↵

THE REQUIRED GUNRACK. I HAD A SPICE RACK AND THEY FROWN ON THAT SORT OF THING. IT MIGHT BE THAT I WOULDN'T EVEN ENJOY MODERN LUMBERJACKING. THEY PROBABLY USE LASERS NOW AND EAT SENSIBLE BREAKFASTS. I GUESS I'LL JUST HAVE TO BE HAPPY DOING WHAT I'M DOING NOW: QUIETLY WHISPERING "TIMBER" AS I CLIP THE HEDGES.

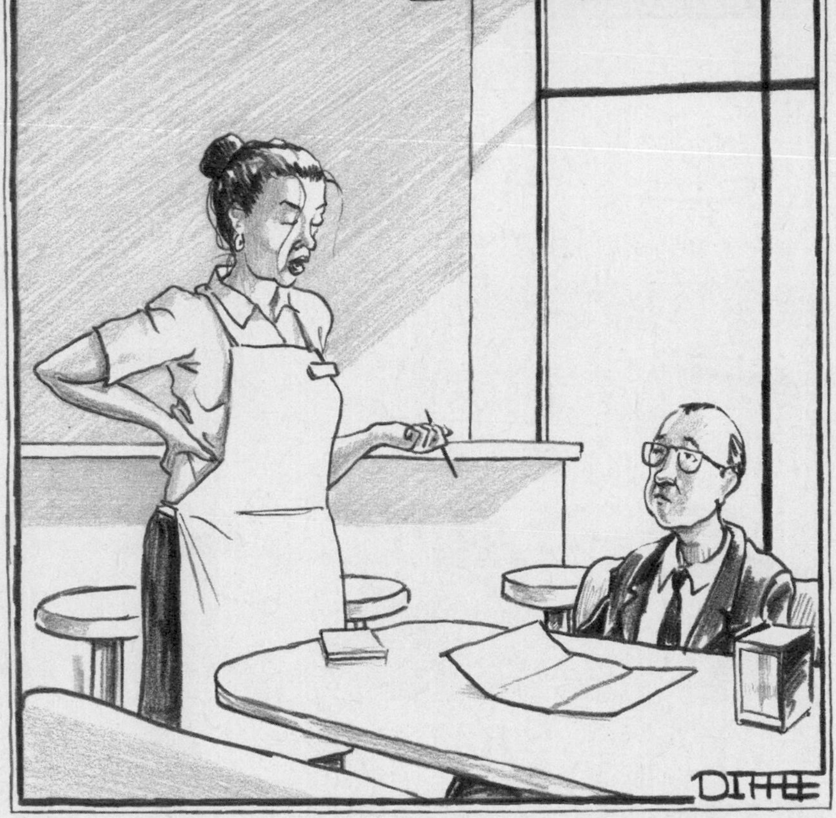
DIFFEE

"Sorry, we don't serve the Lumberjack Breakfast to accountants."

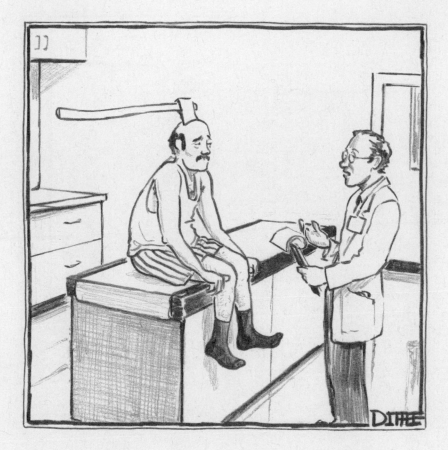

"It could be one of two things; an axe or a maul."

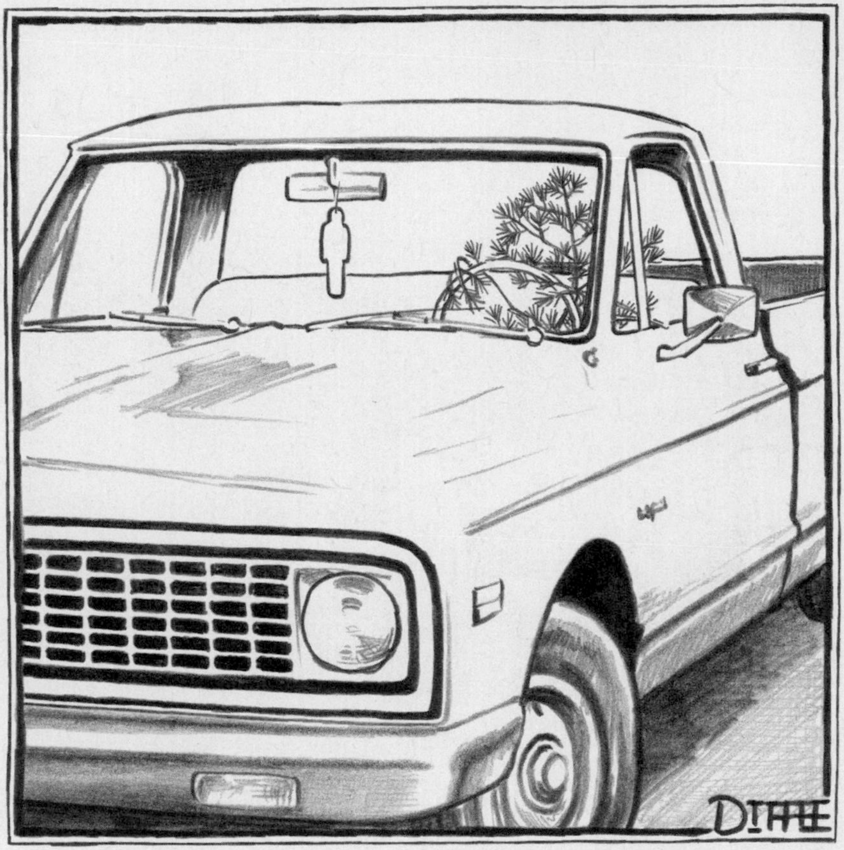
DIFFEE

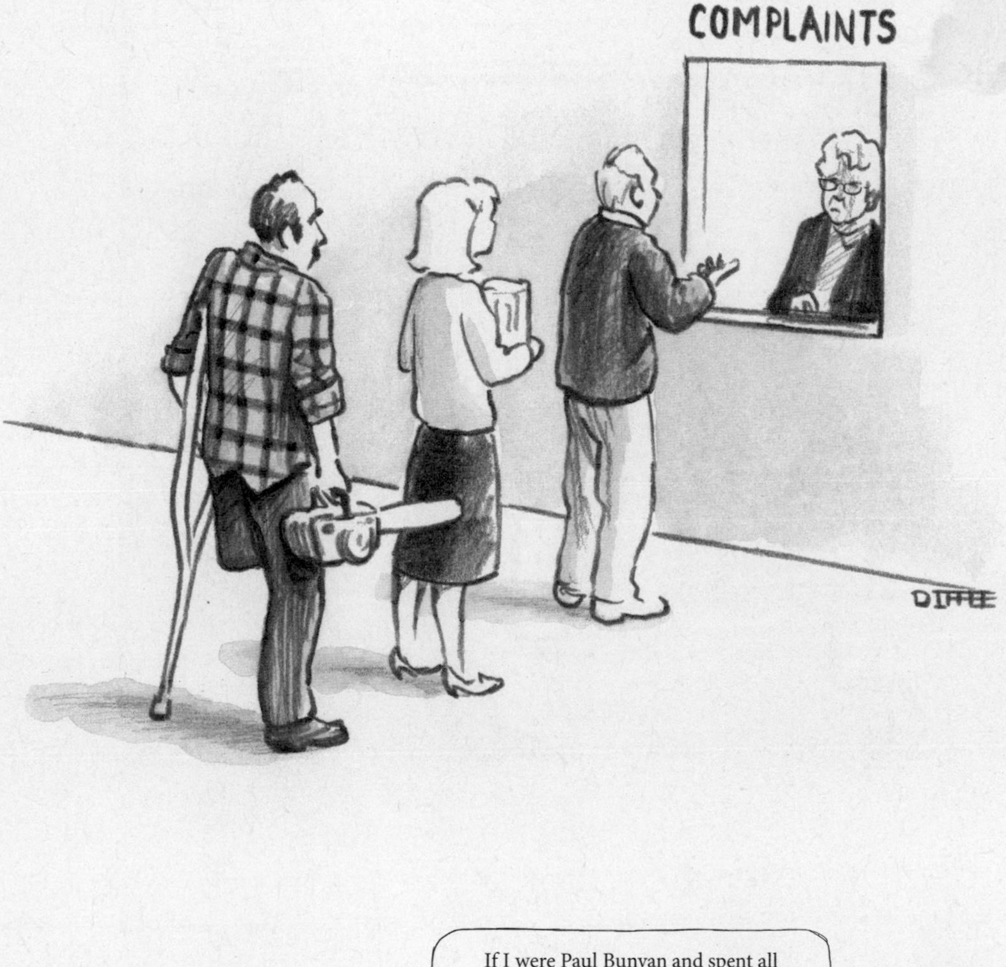
COMPLAINTS

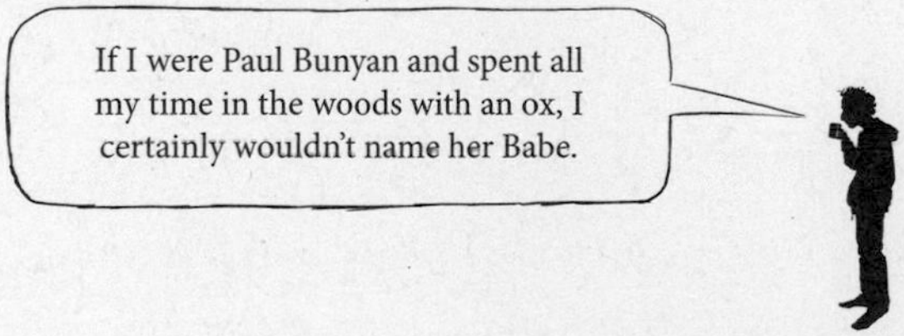
If I were Paul Bunyan and spent all my time in the woods with an ox, I certainly wouldn't name her Babe.

KINDS OF PINES

I don't know who the guy was who came up with the names for the different kinds of pines but I'm pretty sure he was a little bit racist.

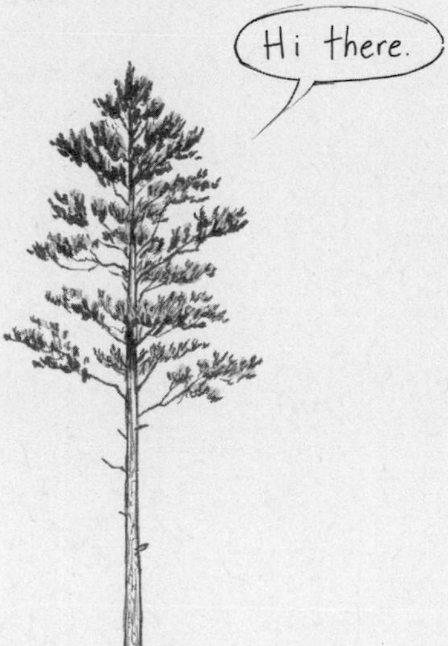
Hi there.

Eastern White Pine

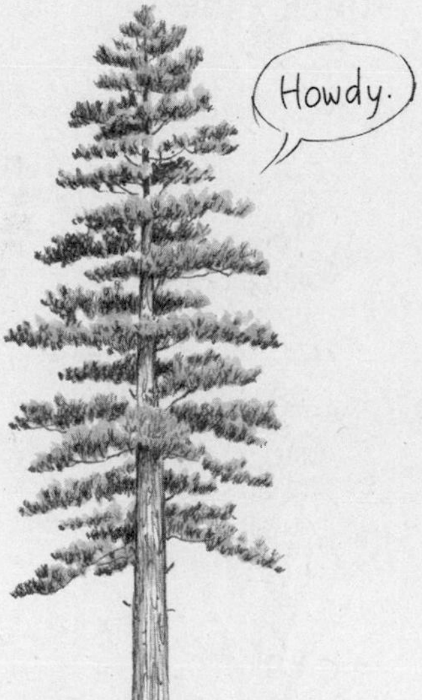
Howdy.

Western White Pine

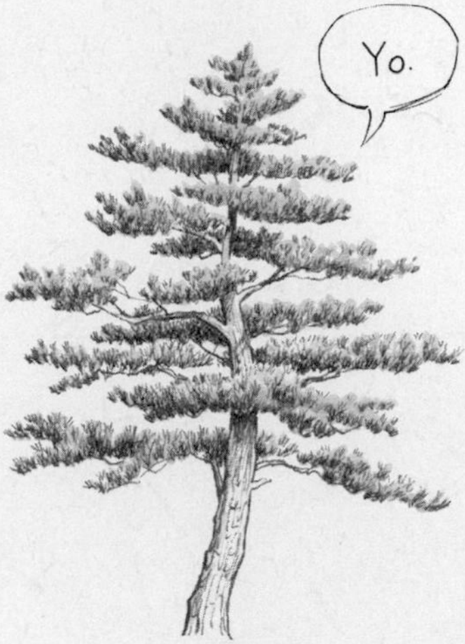
Yo.

Black Pine

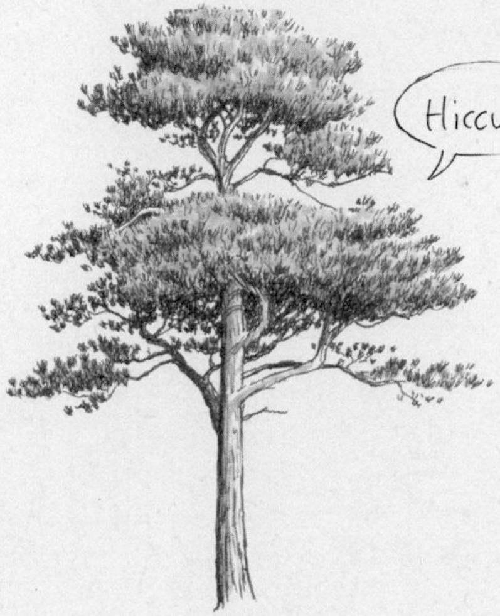
Hiccup!

Scotch Pine

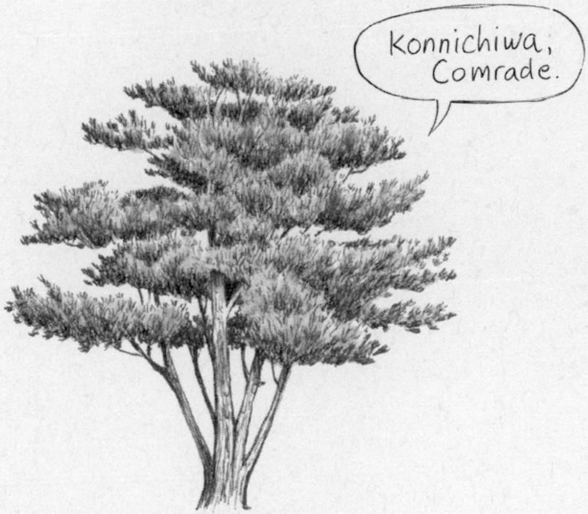
Konnichiwa,
Comrade.

Japanese Red Pine

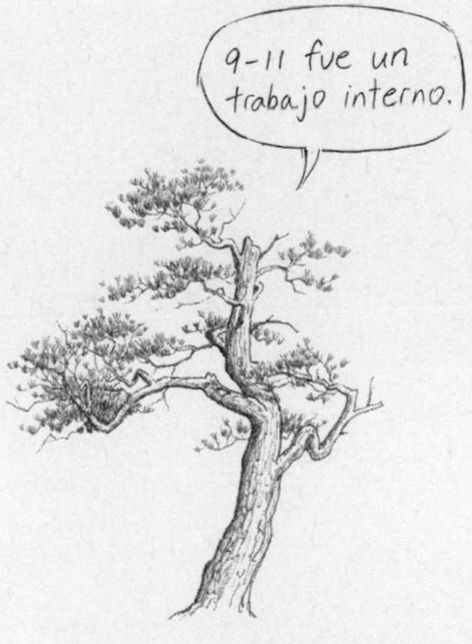
9-11 fue un
trabajo interno.

Mexican Nut Pine

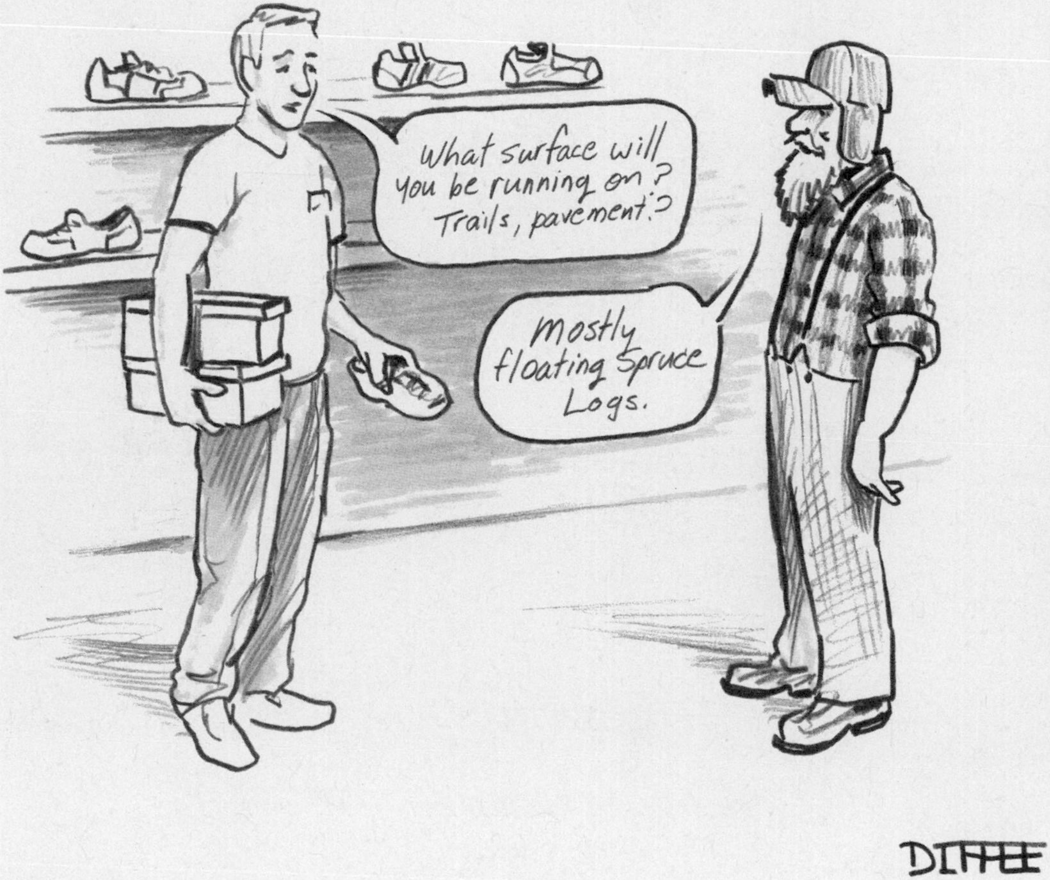
What surface will you be running on? Trails, pavement?
Mostly floating Spruce Logs.
DIFFEE

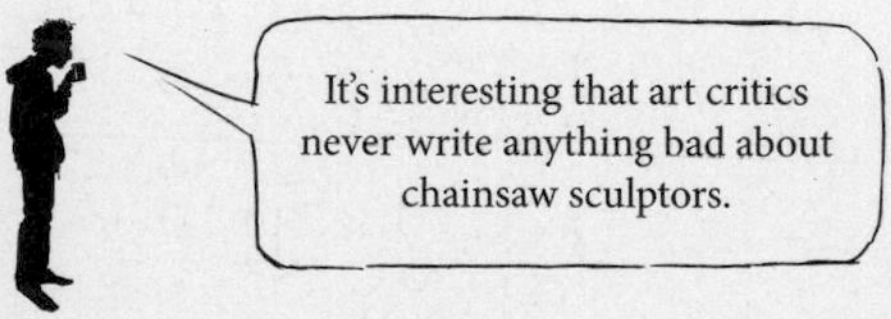
It's interesting that art critics never write anything bad about chainsaw sculptors.

"Please tell me Jedediah and I aren't wearing
the same exact suspenders."

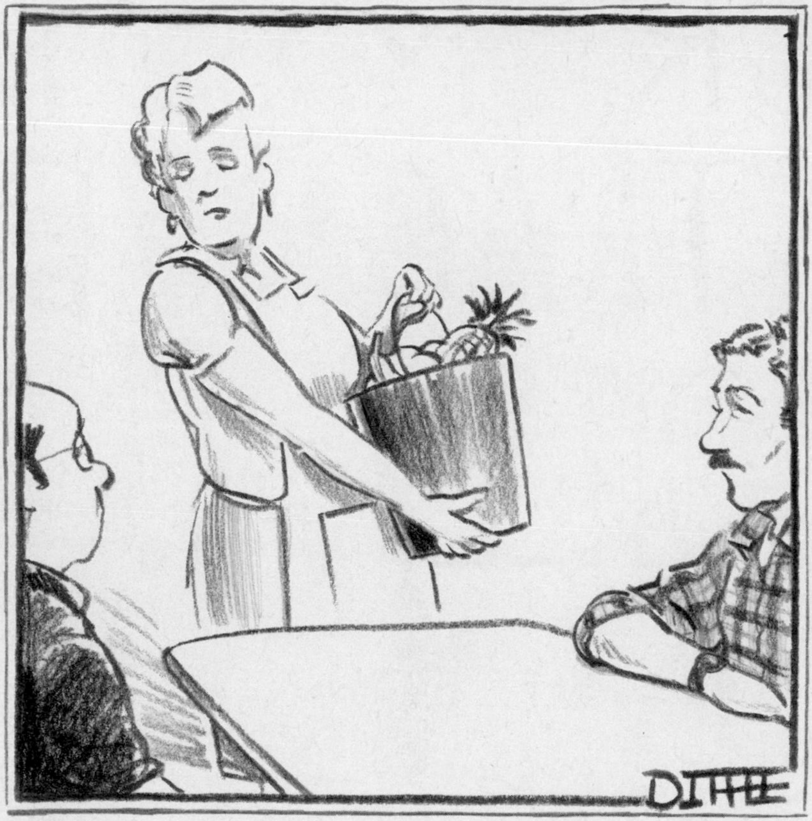
DITTEE

"Who had the Lumberjack fruit cup?"

Chapter Three

FOR SMART ATTRACTIVE PEOPLE IN RELATIONSHIPS

A worrying statistic: one out of every two marriages in America ends in matching velour sweatpants.

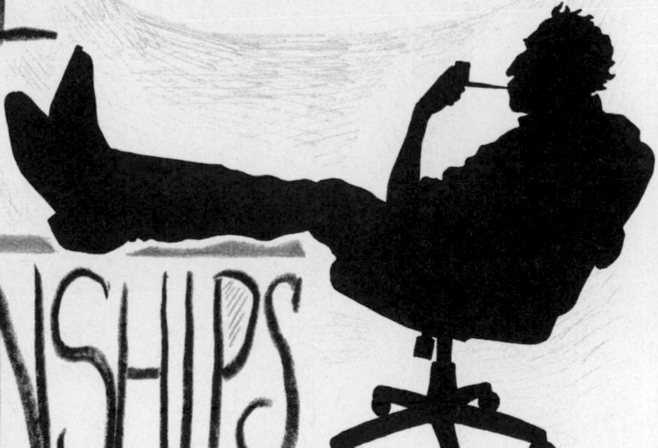

THREE RELATIONSHIP TIPS FOR THE FELLAS OUT THERE. ONE, DON'T FORGET YOUR ANNIVERSARY OR YOU'LL BE CELEBRATING TWO ANNIVERSARIES: YOUR NORMAL ANNIVERSARY AND THE ANNIVERSARY OF THE ONE TIME YOU FORGOT YOUR ANNIVERSARY. TWO, ALWAYS HAVE FLOWERS BEHIND YOUR BACK. YOU'LL HAVE TO RELEARN TO DO EVERYTHING WITH ONLY ONE HAND BUT IT WILL BE WORTH IT. THERE ISN'T A SITUATION THAT CAN'T BE FIXED BY FLOWERS. SHE COMES HOME TIRED AND CRANKY FROM A LONG DAY OF MENTALLY LISTING YOUR FAULTS, BAM! YOU WHIP OUT SOME DAISIES. PROBLEM SOLVED. SHE PULLS YOUR HEADPHONES OFF AND SHOUTS, "ARE YOU EVEN LISTENING TO ME?" BOOM! PANSIES! SHE STAGGERS IN FROM THE GARDEN GASPING, "I THINK I MIGHT BE DEATHLY ALLERGIC TO LONG-STEMMED PERENNIALS." KAPOW! LILIES!

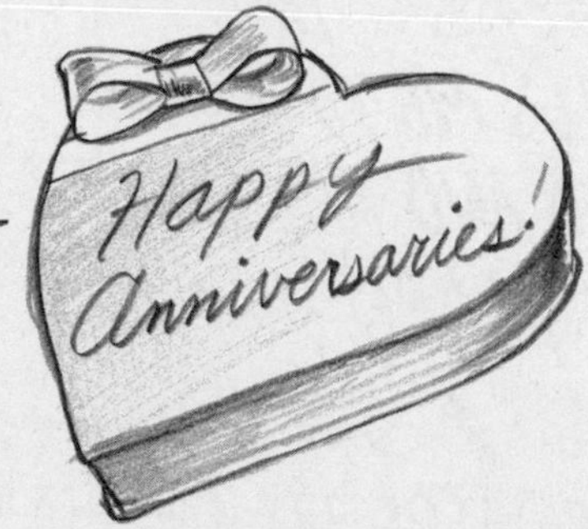
Happy Anniversaries!

BUT WHAT IF YOU RUN OUT OF FLOWERS? THAT BRINGS ME TO MY THIRD AND FINAL TIP: LEARN HOW TO FAKE A SEIZURE. THERE ARE TIMES

I WANT SOME FLOWERS THAT SAY, 'HERE, HAVE SOME FRIGGIN' FLOWERS.'

WHEN NOTHING ELSE WORKS. LET'S SAY SHE ASKS YOU A QUESTION THAT YOU CAN'T POSSIBLY ANSWER WITHOUT MAKING HER ANGRY. SOMETHING LIKE, "WHAT ARE YOU DOING?" DON'T EVEN TRY TO ANSWER. THAT'S WHAT SHE WANTS YOU TO DO. JUST STOP, DROP, AND DROOL. SHE'LL SPRINT TO HER PHONE TO CALL YOUR LIFE INSURANCE COMPANY AND YOU CAN GO BACK TO WATCHING THE UFC. AND LADIES, THESE TIPS WILL WORK FOR YOU, TOO. BUT INSTEAD OF FLOWERS, USE BOOBIES!

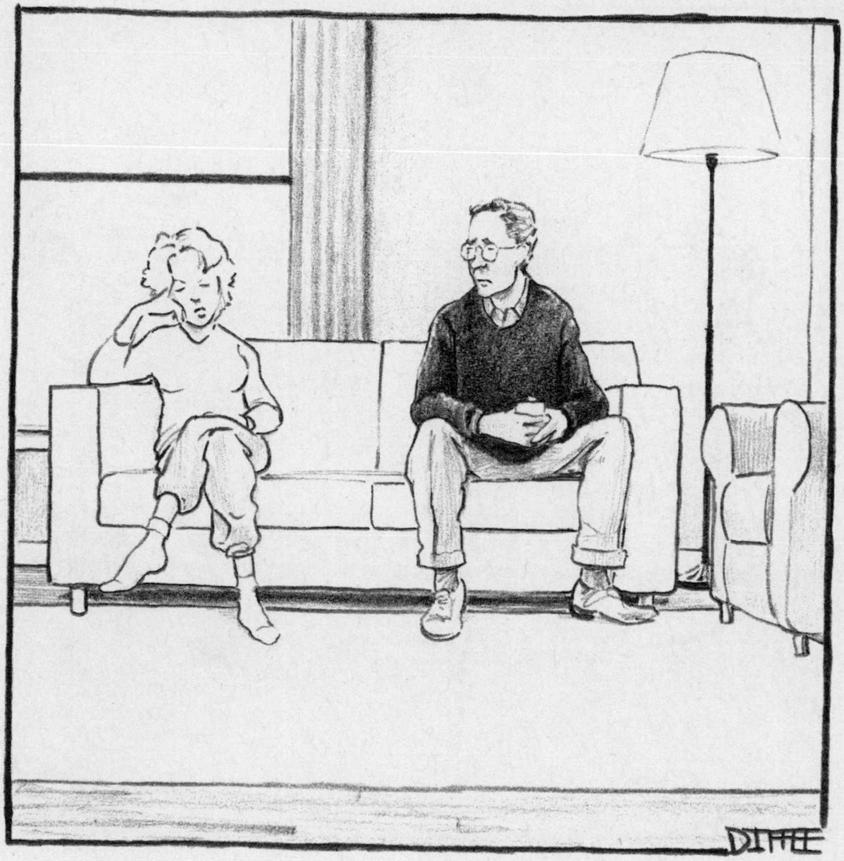
DIFFEE

"It's like you haven't heard a single word I've thought."

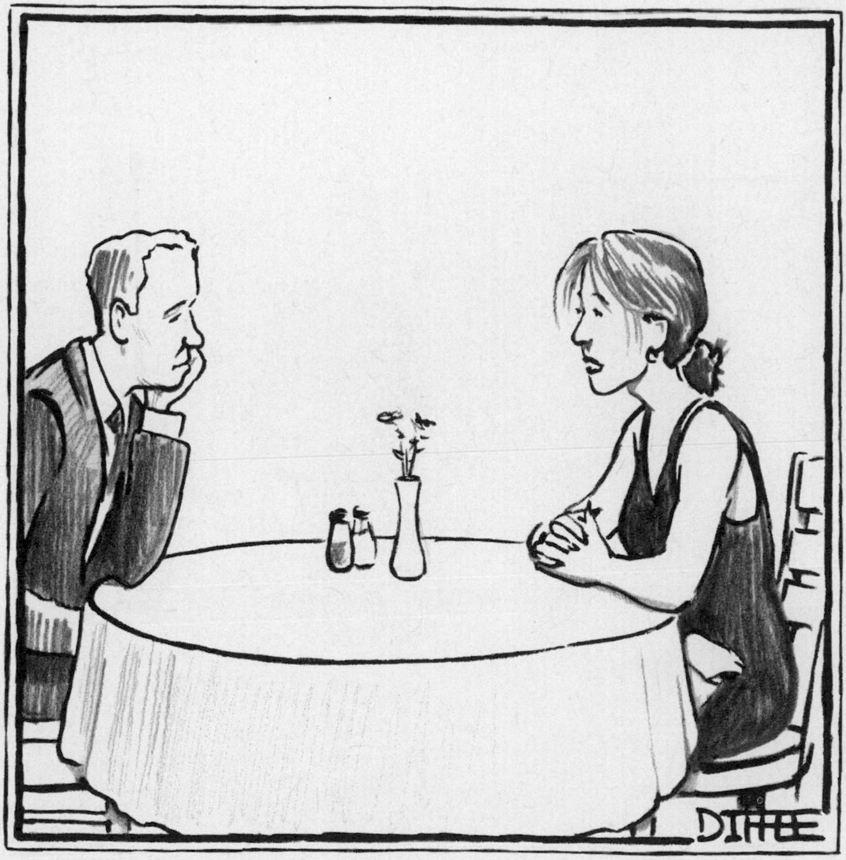
DIFFEE

"You and I are just too different. You say 'tomato' and I'm sleeping with your best friend Marcus."

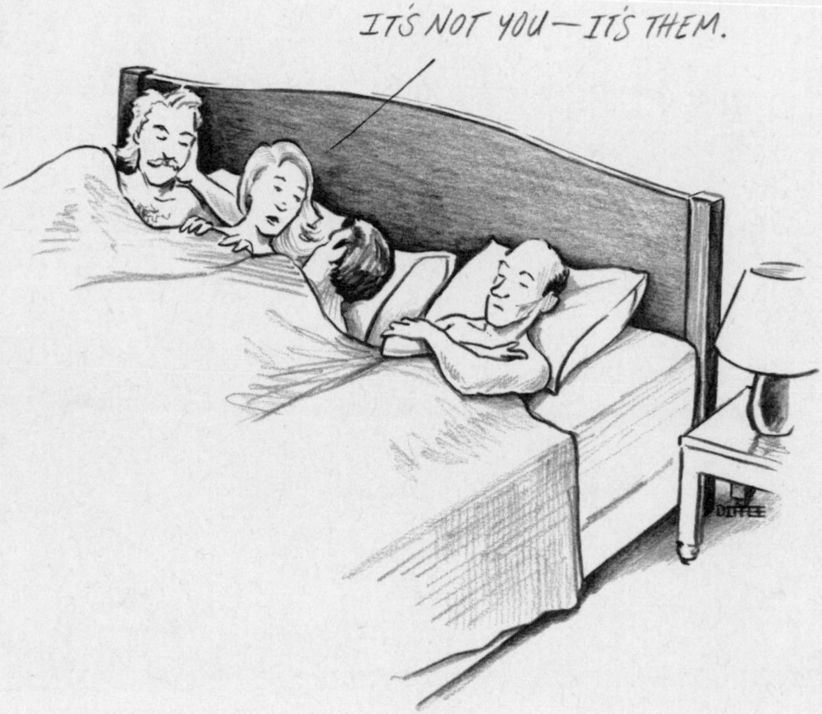
IT'S NOT YOU—IT'S THEM.
DIFFEE

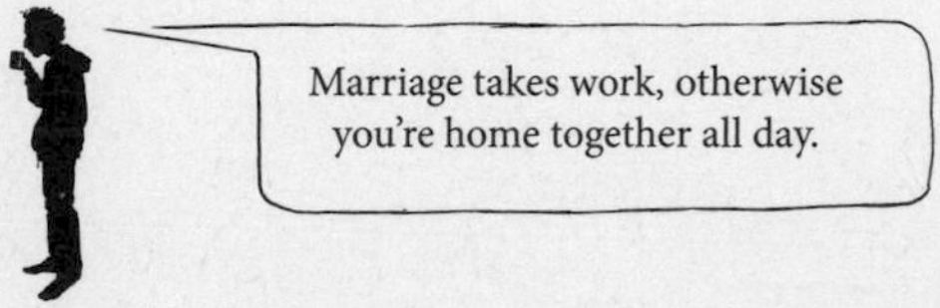
Marriage takes work, otherwise
you're home together all day.

A BICYCLE BUILT FOR TWO DORKS

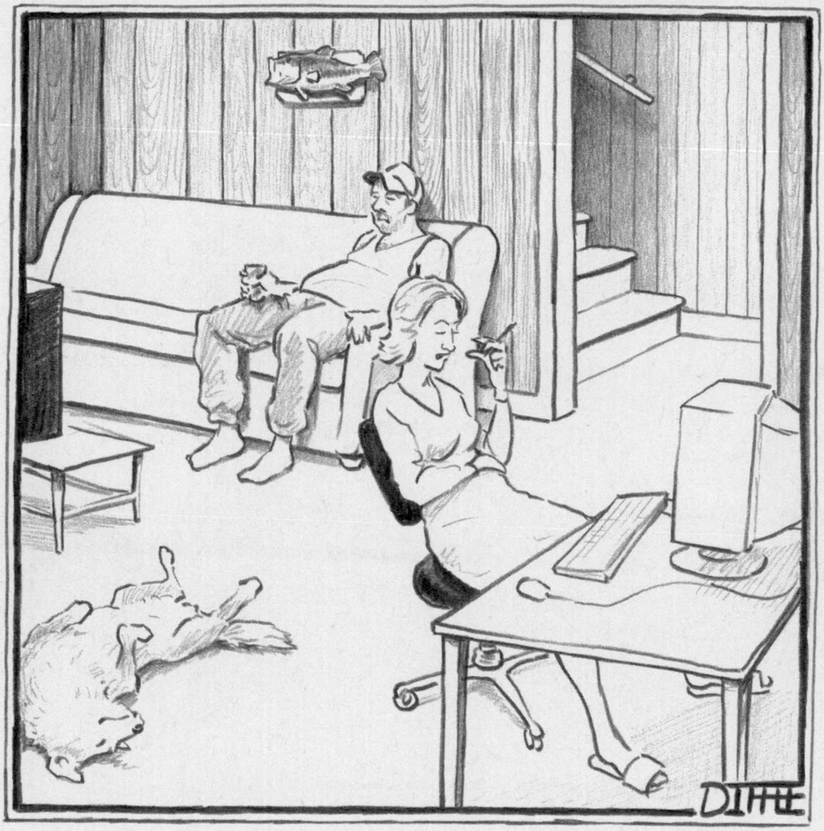
DIFFEE

"Hmm—says here that people who bought books about hunting and fishing also bought books about coping with divorce."

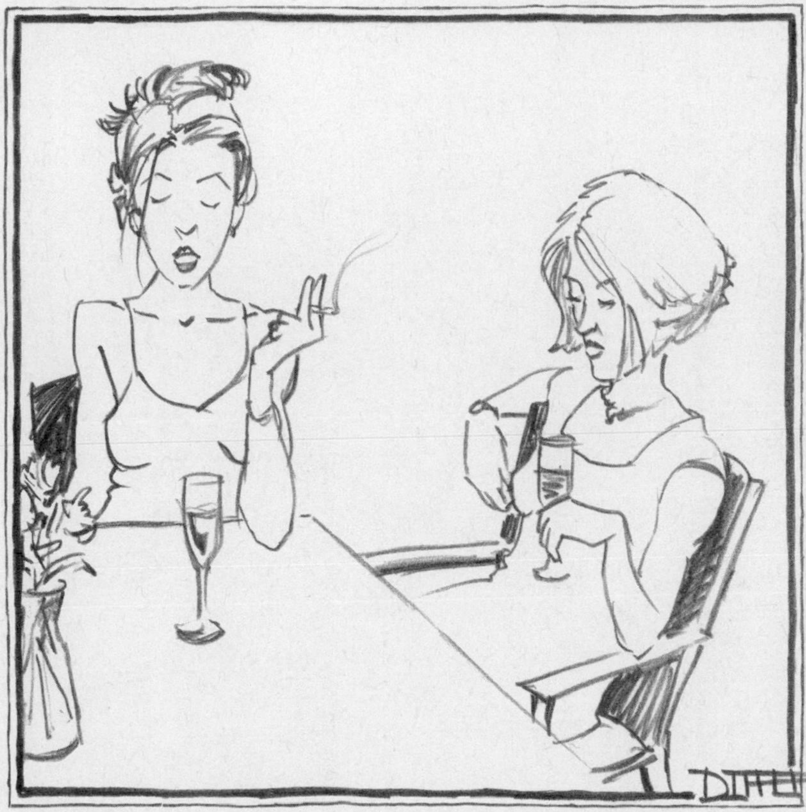
DIFFEE

"I married for love. I divorced for money."

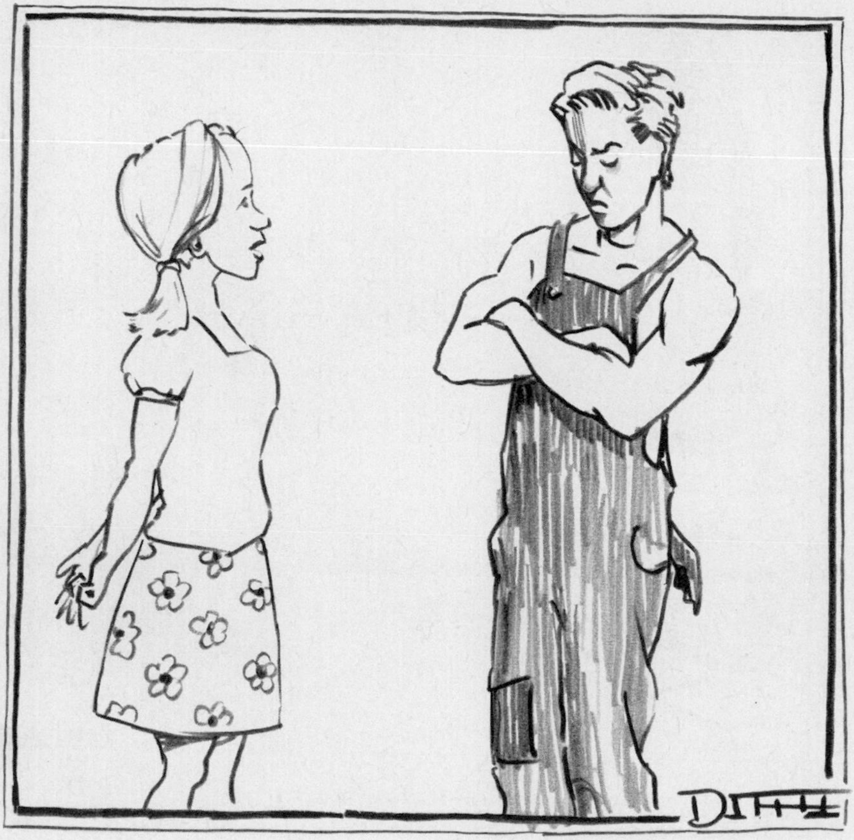
DIFFEE

"I hope we can still be cousins."

"*Whoa, someone's been doing some gathering.*"

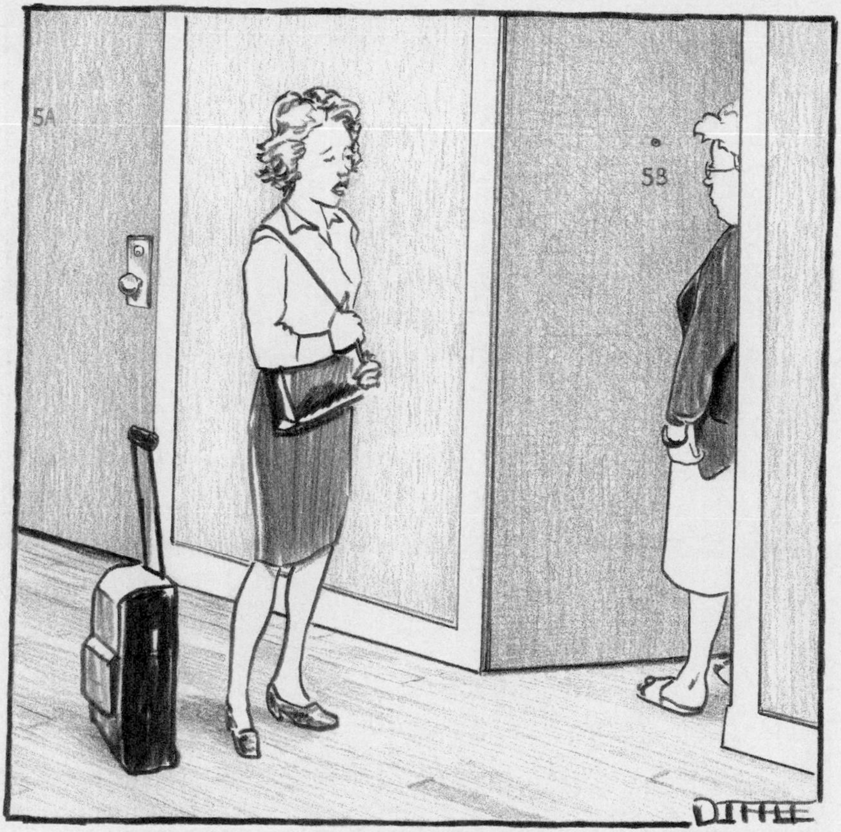
5A
5B
DITTLE

"I'm going away for the weekend. Would you mind feeding my husband?"

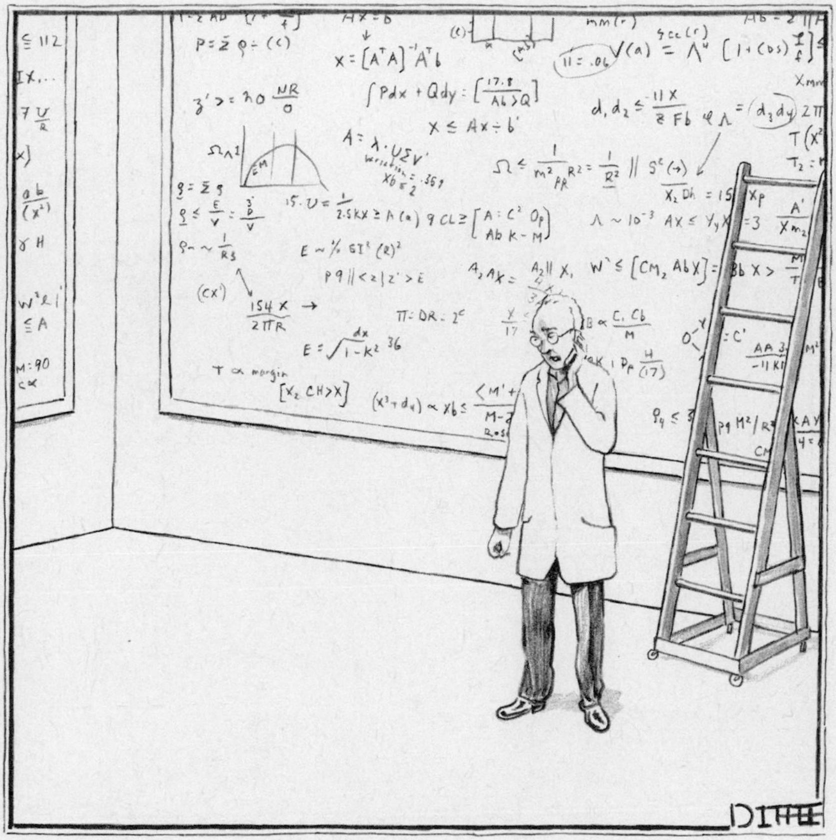

"I just figured out why we've never had girlfriends."

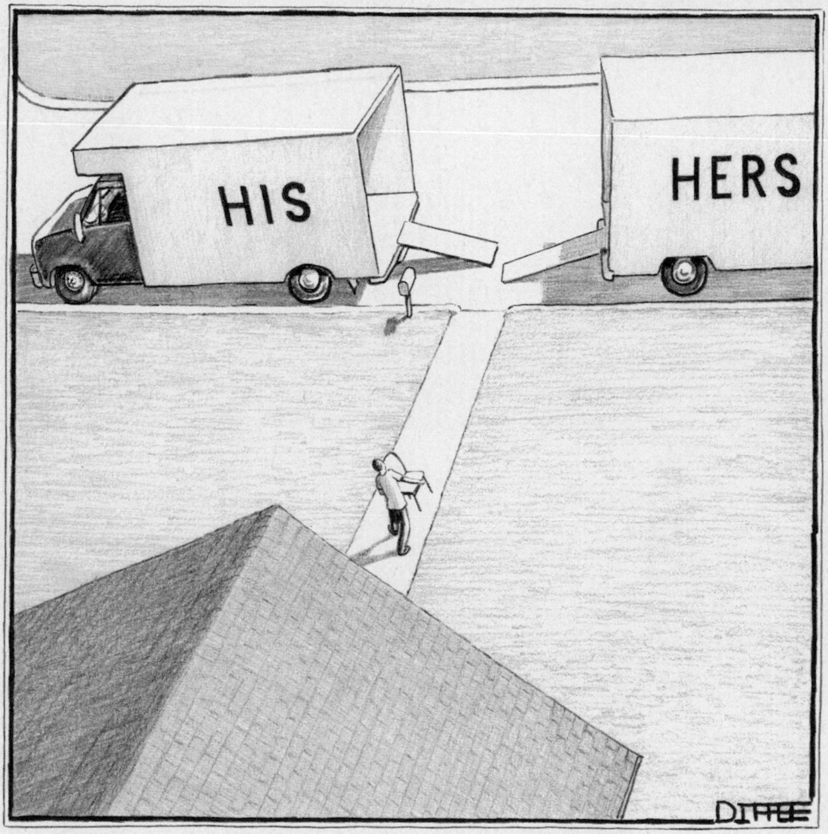
HIS
HERS
DIFFEE

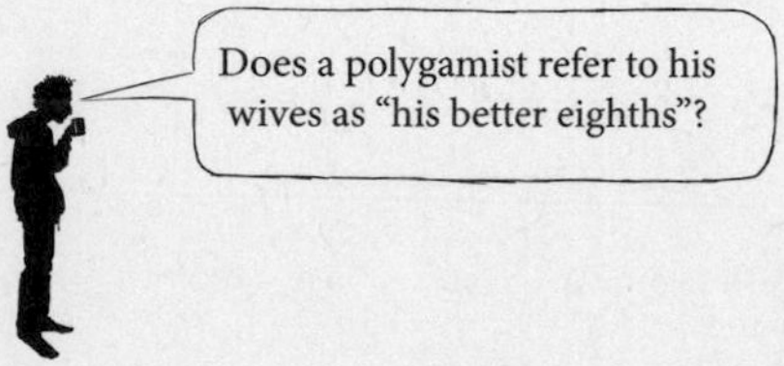
Does a polygamist refer to his wives as "his better eighths"?

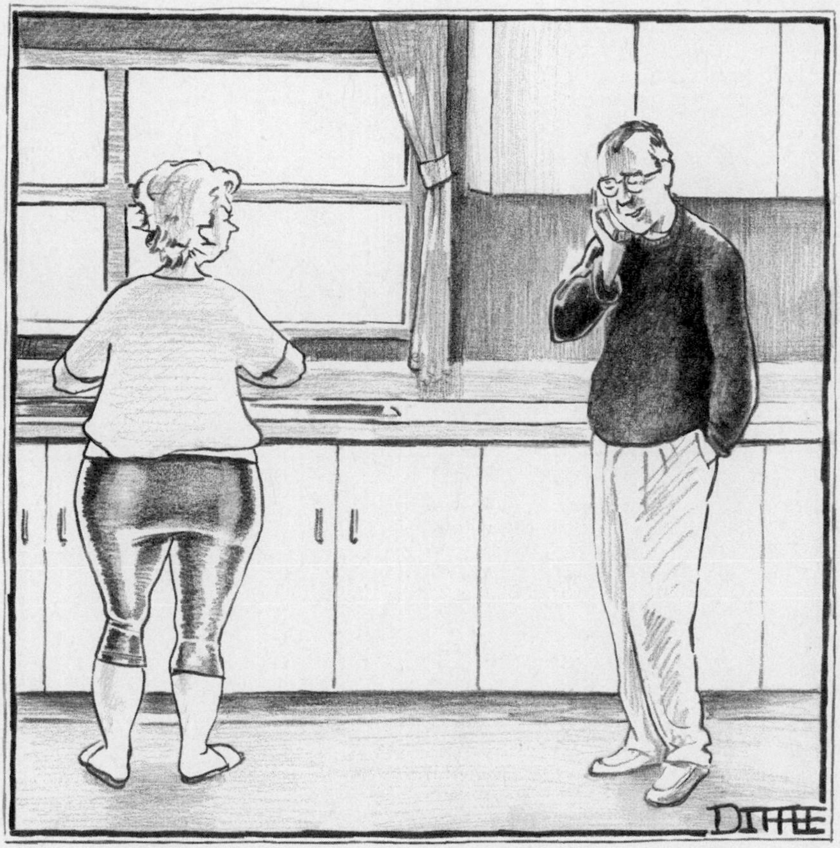
DIFFEE

"She's right here. She's doing some dishes and testing the tensile strength of Lycra."

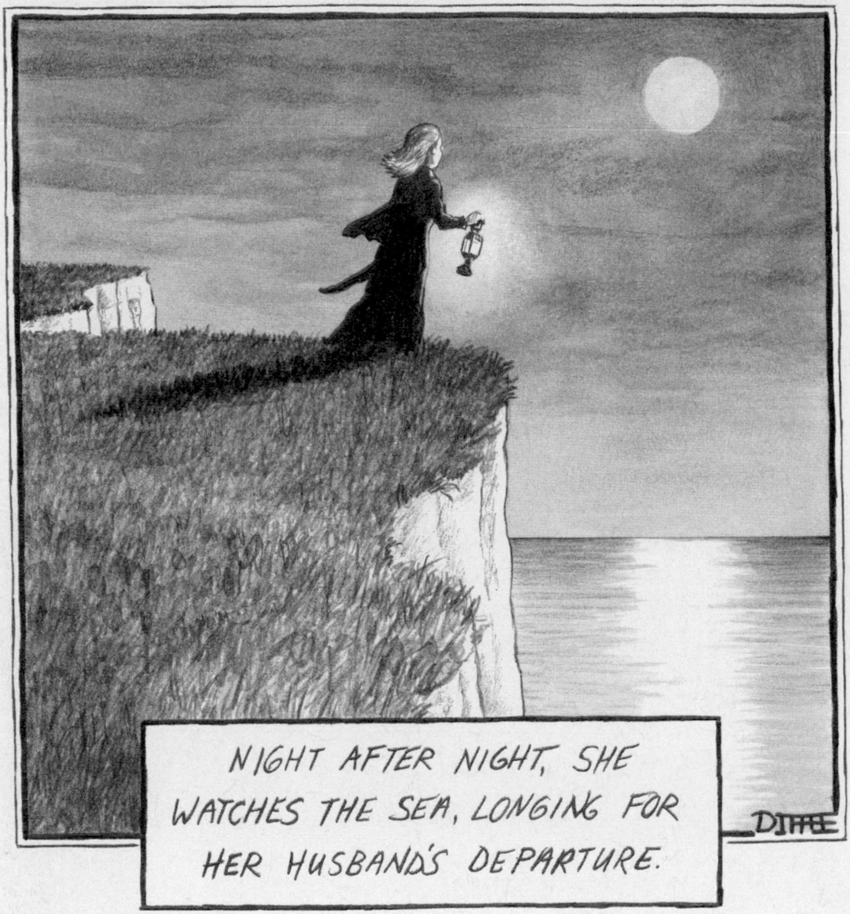
NIGHT AFTER NIGHT, SHE WATCHES THE SEA, LONGING FOR HER HUSBAND'S DEPARTURE.
DIFFEE

CHAPTER FOUR
FOR SMART ATTRACTIVE PET OWNERS

If you name a dog Marco, you should be prepared for a lifetime of hilarious people shouting "polo."

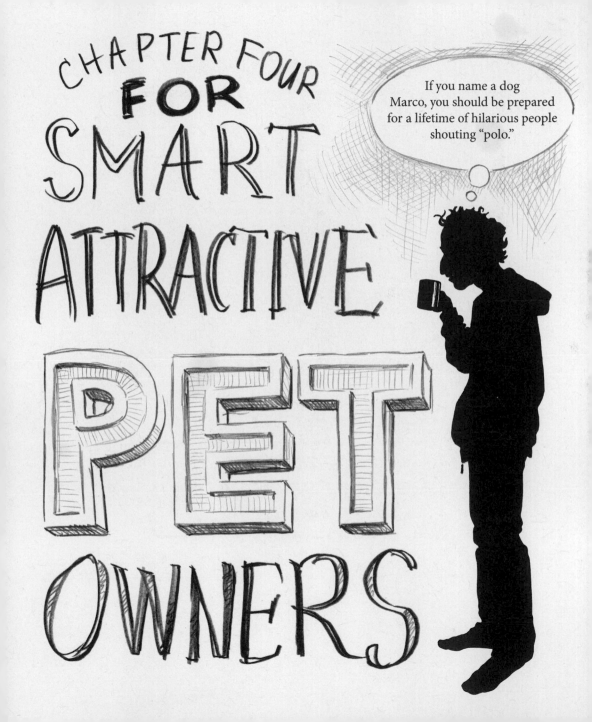

WHENEVER I SEE A GUY WALKING AROUND IN PUBLIC WITH A SNAKE WRAPPED AROUND HIS NECK I ALWAYS THINK THE SAME THING: "SQUEEZE HARDER!" I SUPPOSE I JUST DON'T GET THE WHOLE REPTILE-OWNING THING. I MEAN WHAT KIND OF PERSON WANTS A PET THAT YOU HAVE TO FEED OTHER PETS TO?

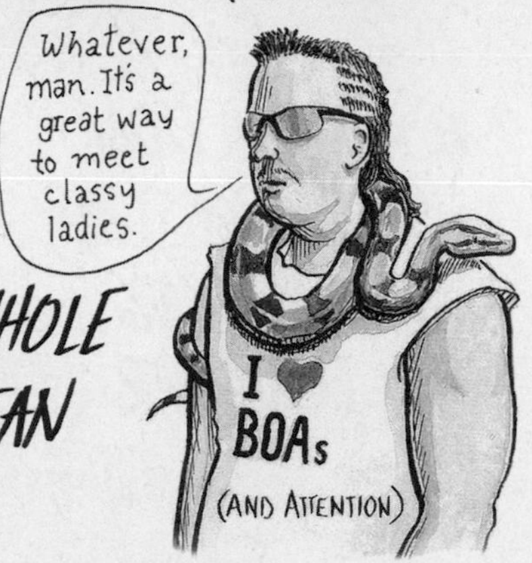

Whatever, man. It's a great way to meet classy ladies.
I ♥ BOAs
(AND ATTENTION)

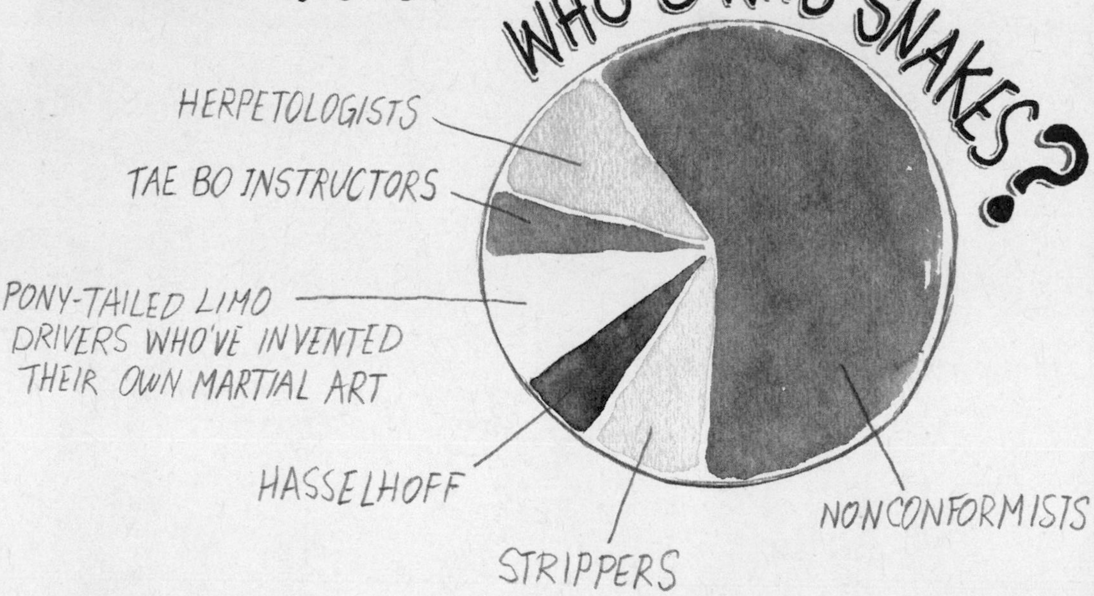

WHO OWNS SNAKES?
HERPETOLOGISTS
TAE BO INSTRUCTORS
PONY-TAILED LIMO DRIVERS WHO'VE INVENTED THEIR OWN MARTIAL ART
HASSELHOFF
STRIPPERS
NONCONFORMISTS

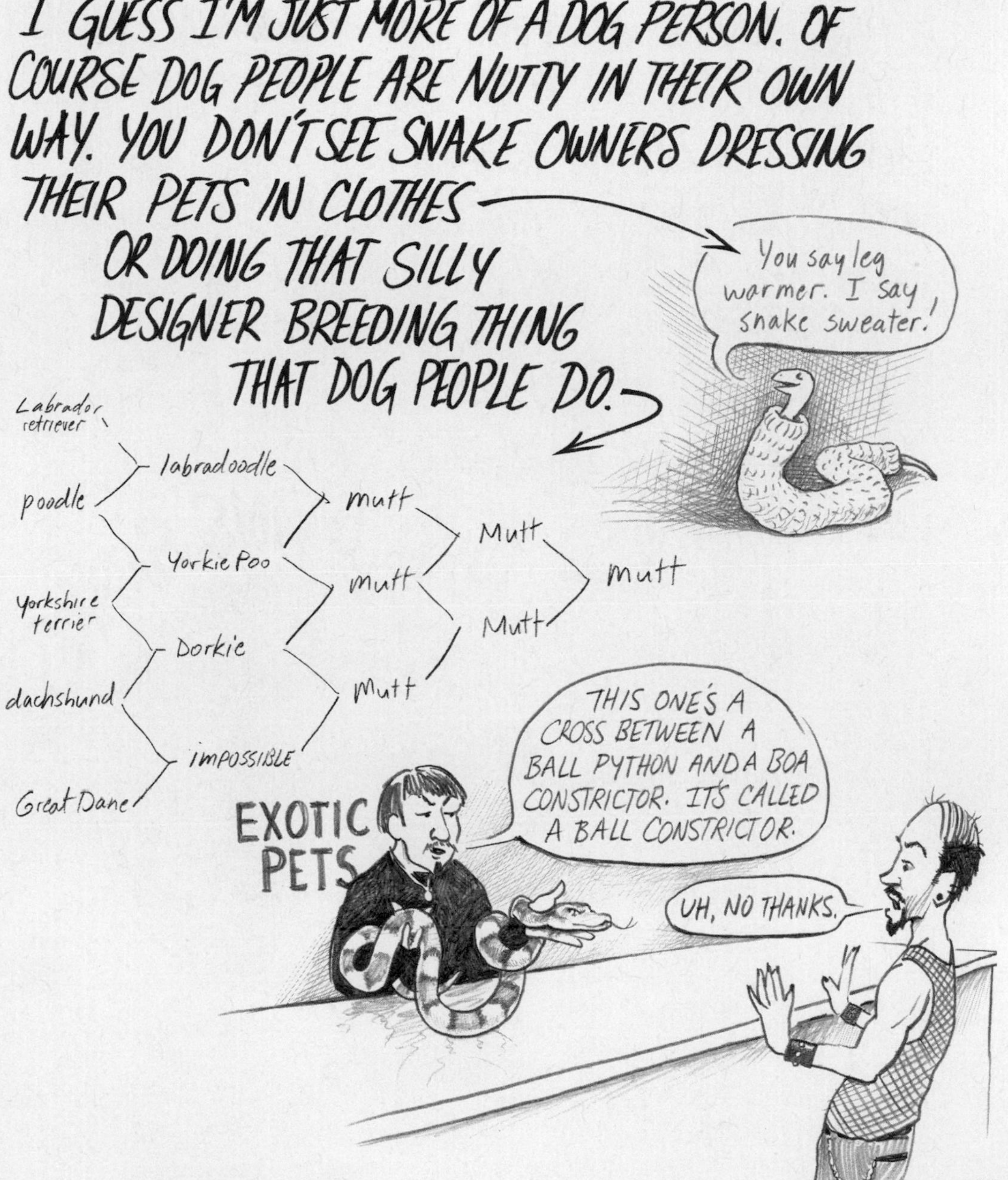
I GUESS I'M JUST MORE OF A DOG PERSON. OF COURSE DOG PEOPLE ARE NUTTY IN THEIR OWN WAY. YOU DON'T SEE SNAKE OWNERS DRESSING THEIR PETS IN CLOTHES
You say leg warmer. I say, snake sweater!
OR DOING THAT SILLY DESIGNER BREEDING THING THAT DOG PEOPLE DO.
Labrador retriever
poodle
Yorkshire terrier
dachshund
Great Dane
labradoodle
Yorkie Poo
Dorkie
impossible
mutt
mutt
Mutt
Mutt
Mutt
Mutt
mutt
EXOTIC PETS
THIS ONE'S A CROSS BETWEEN A BALL PYTHON AND A BOA CONSTRICTOR. IT'S CALLED A BALL CONSTRICTOR.
UH, NO THANKS.

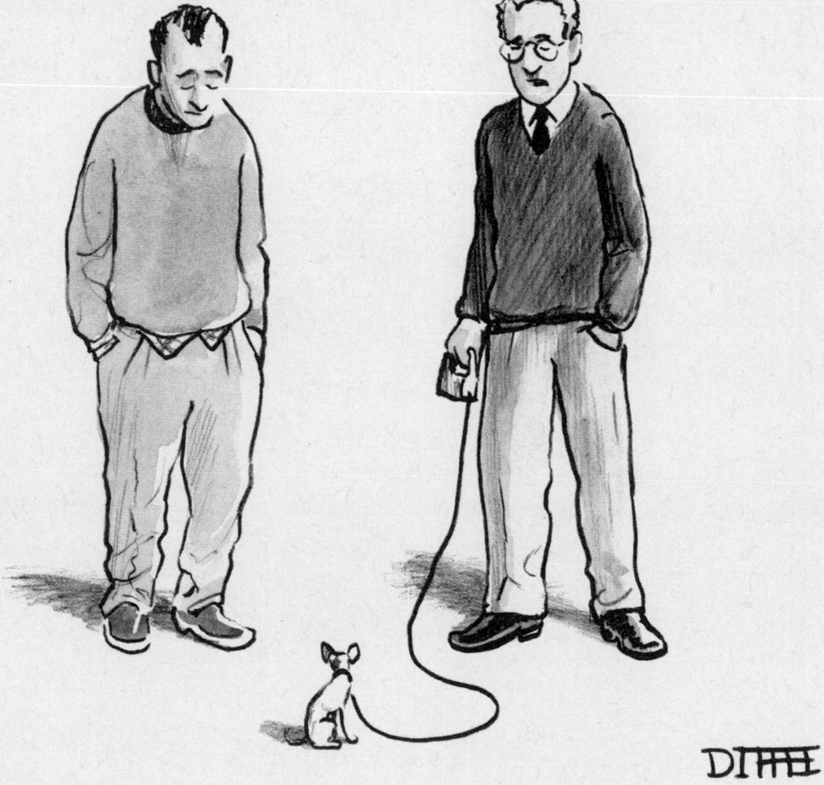
DIFFEE

"They were originally bred as paperweights."

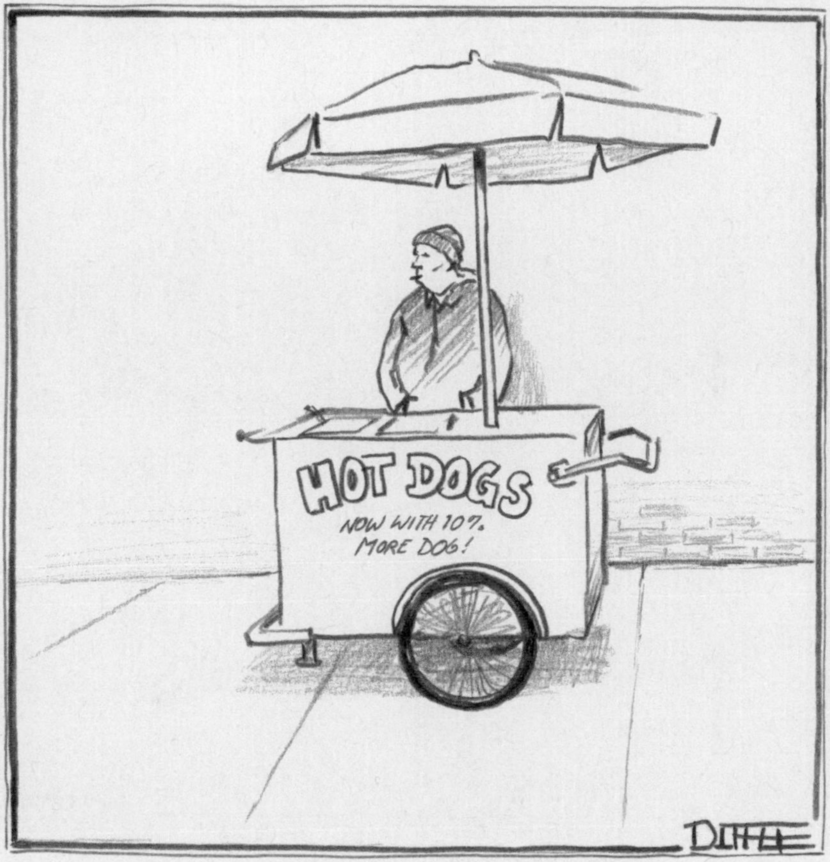
HOT DOGS
NOW WITH 10% MORE DOG!
DIFFEE

"Now, whaddaya say we chase some cars."

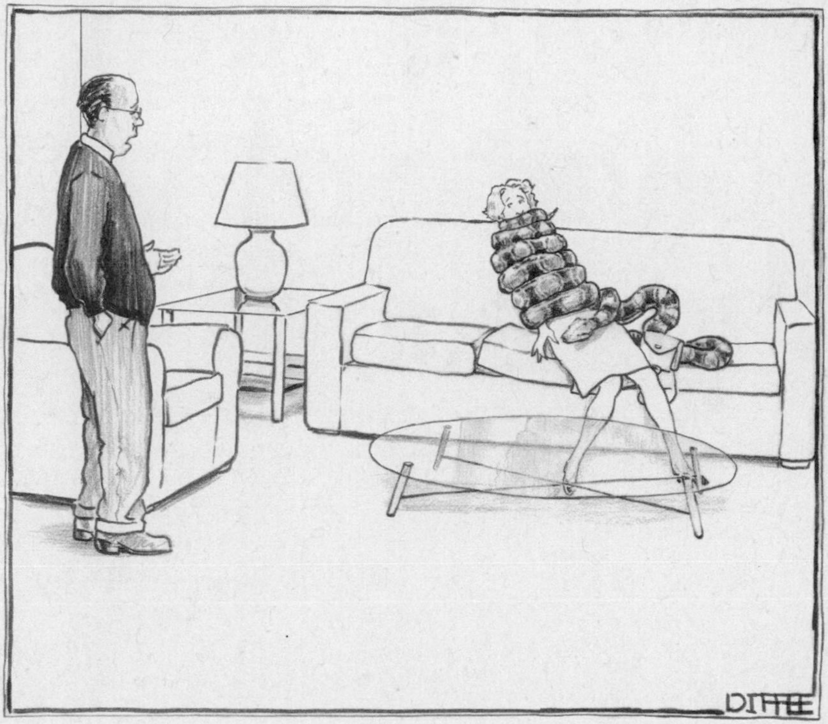
DIFFEE

"Oh, he probably just smells your python."

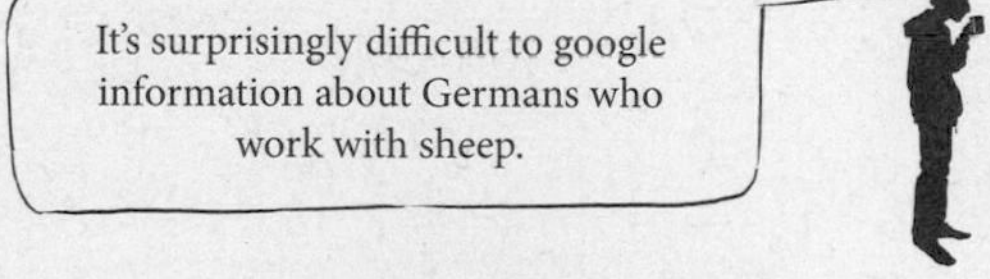
It's surprisingly difficult to google information about Germans who work with sheep.

What your choice of pet says about you.

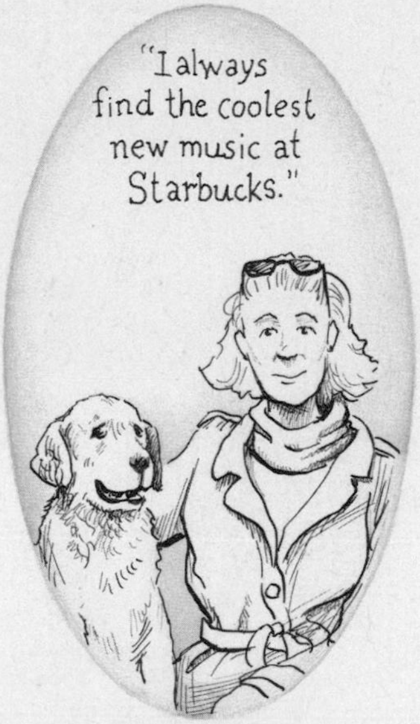
"I always find the coolest new music at Starbucks."

Golden Retriever

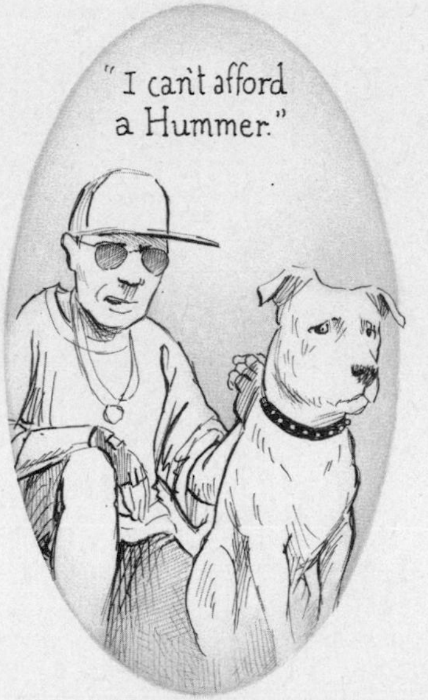
"I can't afford a Hummer."

Pit Bull

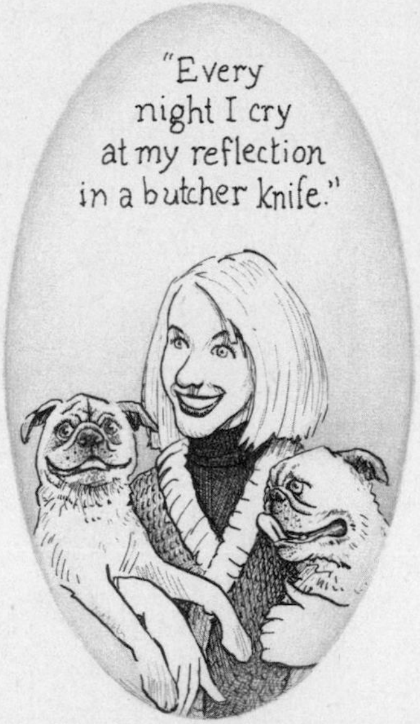
"Every night I cry at my reflection in a butcher knife."

Pugs

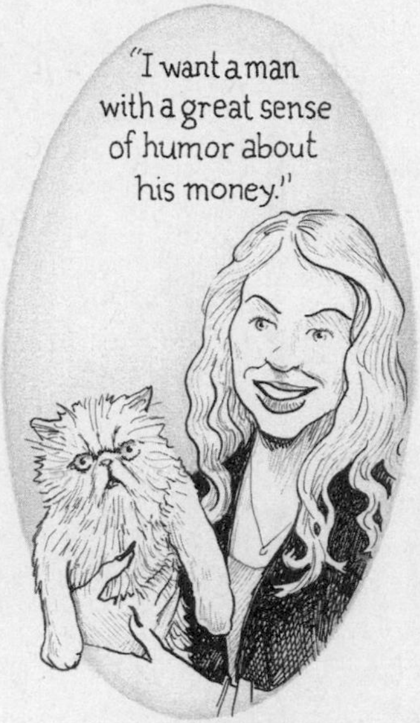
"I want a man with a great sense of humor about his money."

Persian Cat

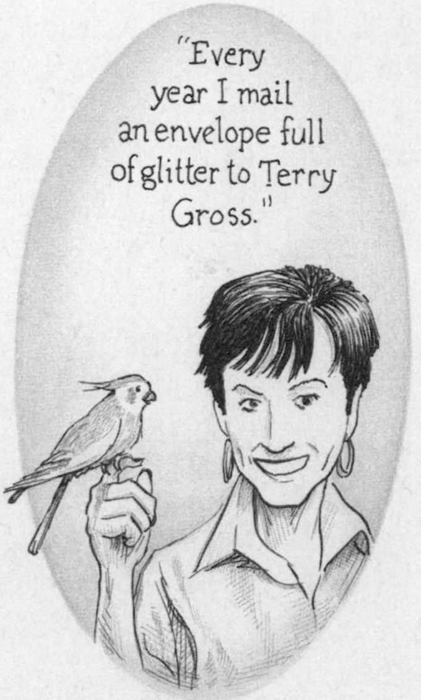
"Every year I mail an envelope full of glitter to Terry Gross."

Bird

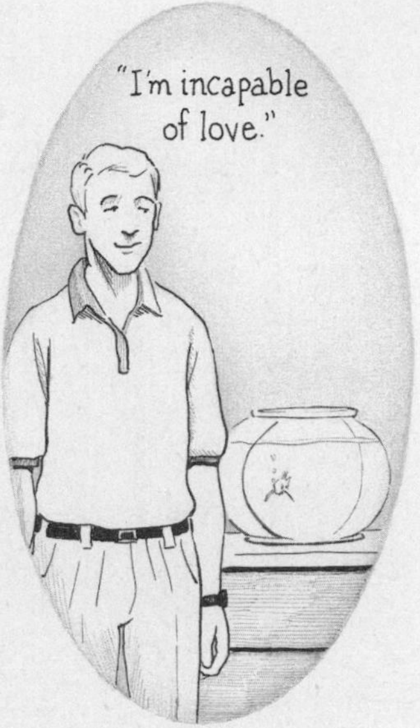
"I'm incapable of love."

Fish

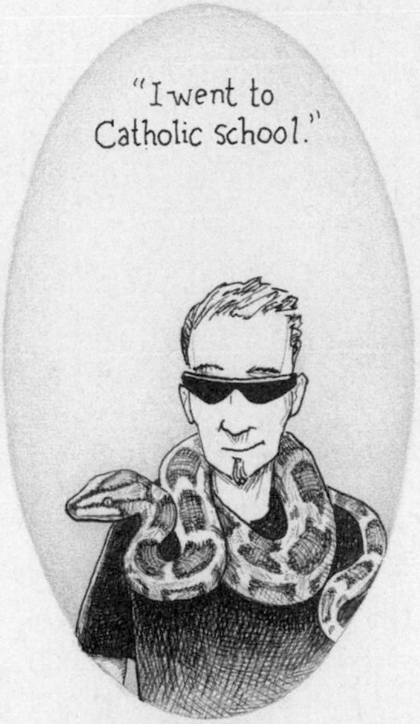
"I went to Catholic school."

Snake

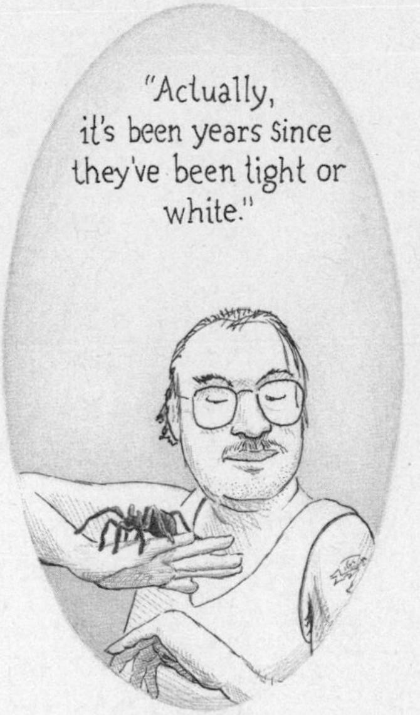
"Actually, it's been years since they've been tight or white."

Tarantula

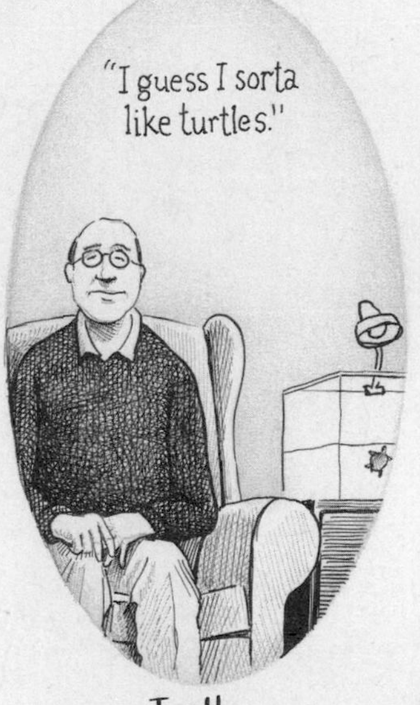
"I guess I sorta like turtles."

Turtle

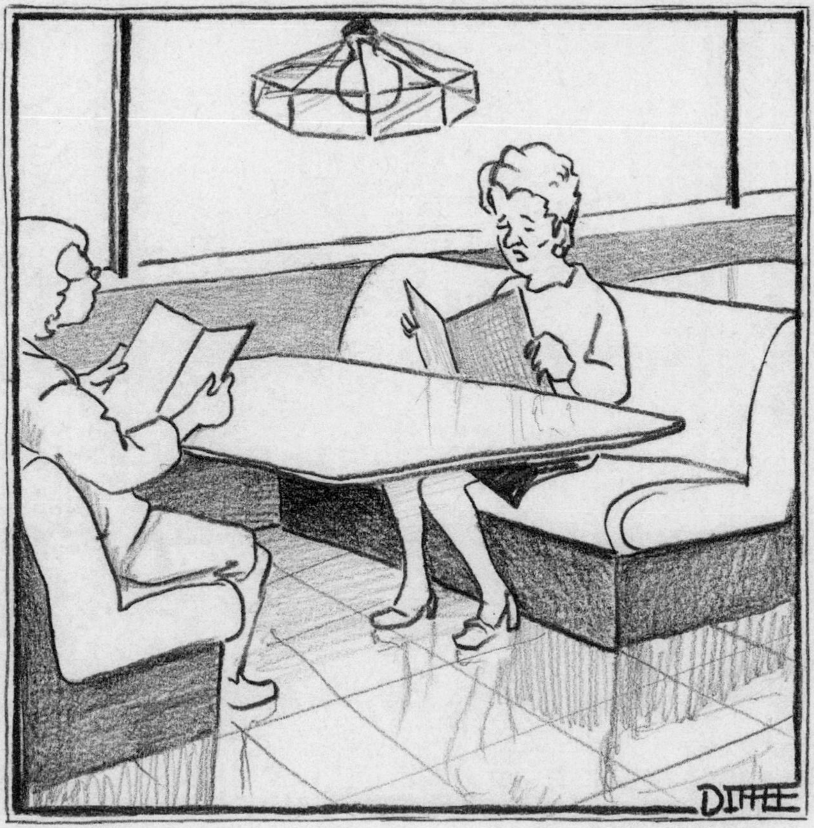
DIFFEE

"What do you think they put on the cat-lover's pizza?"

"Smells like they might have had Cats *here."*

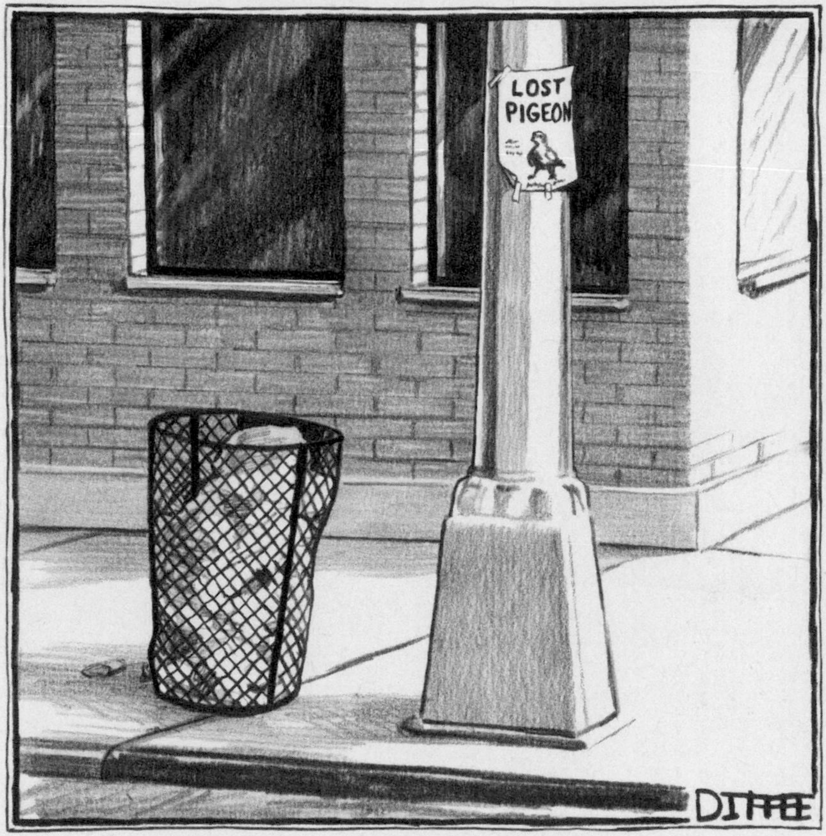
LOST
PIGEON
DIFFEE

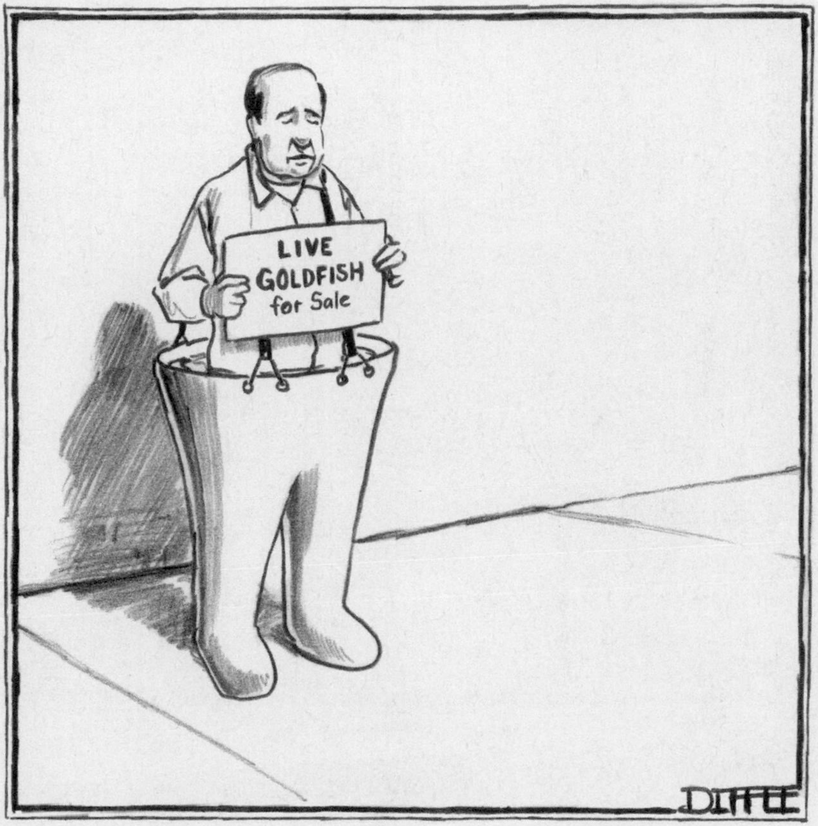
LIVE
GOLDFISH
for Sale
DIFFEE

Honey, look. I bought a chameleon, probably!

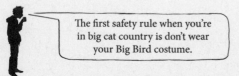

The first safety rule when you're in big cat country is don't wear your Big Bird costume.

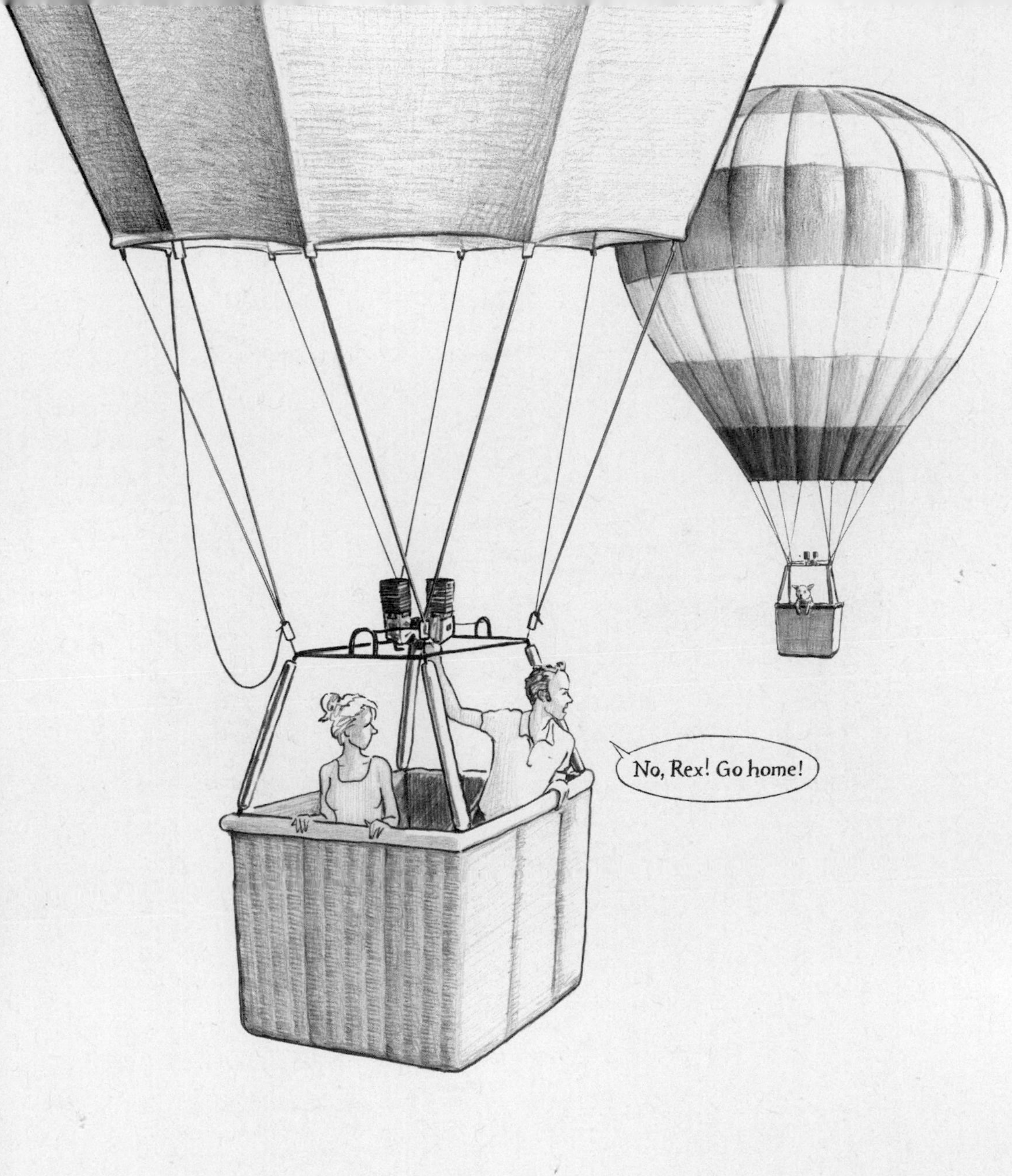
No, Rex! Go home!

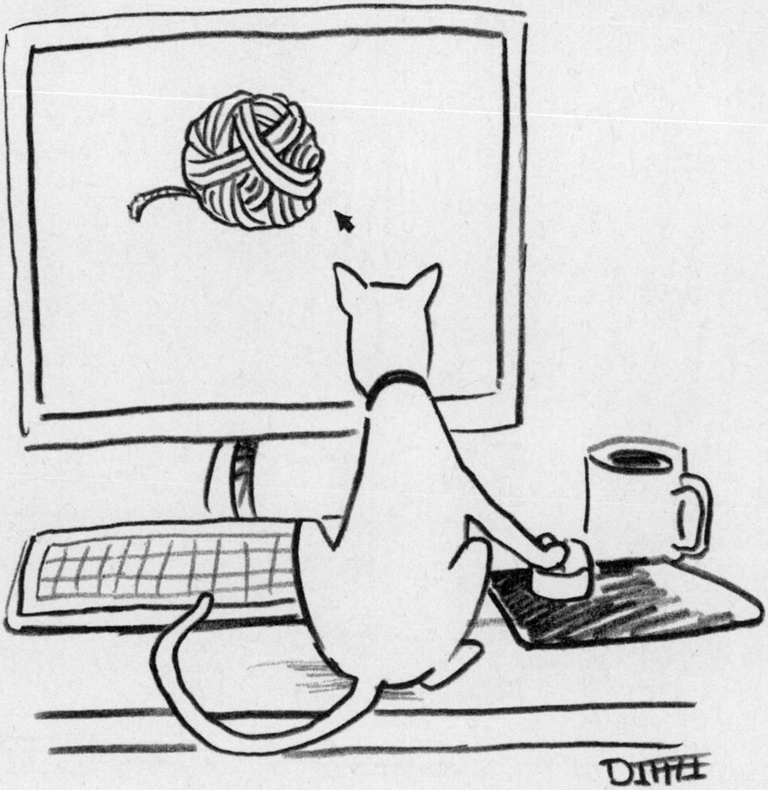

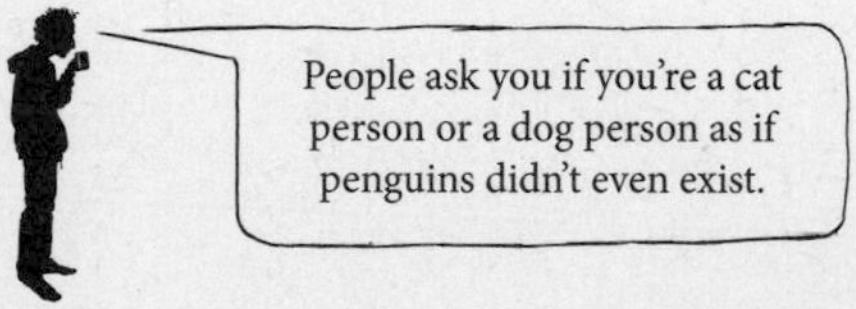
People ask you if you're a cat person or a dog person as if penguins didn't even exist.

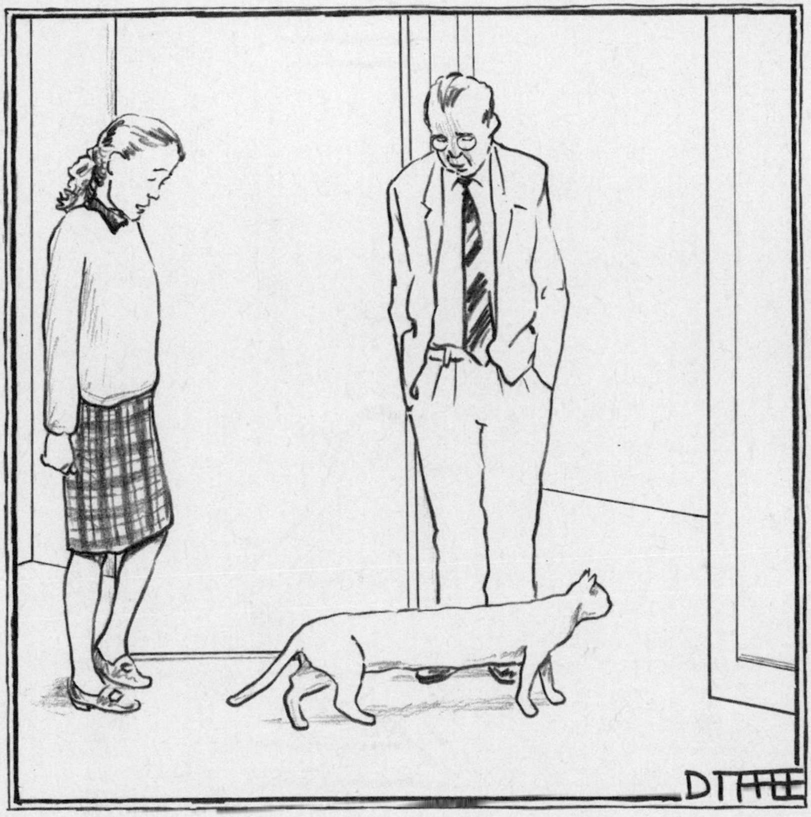
DIFFEE

"She's a wiener cat."

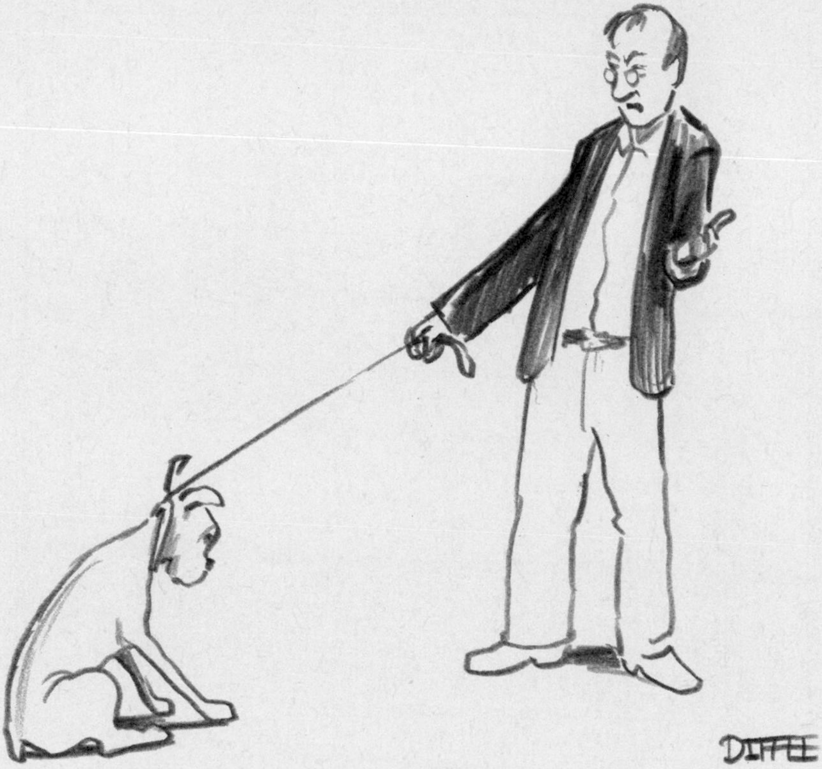
DIFFEE

"Come on, Buster. That was a forty minute walk in dog minutes."

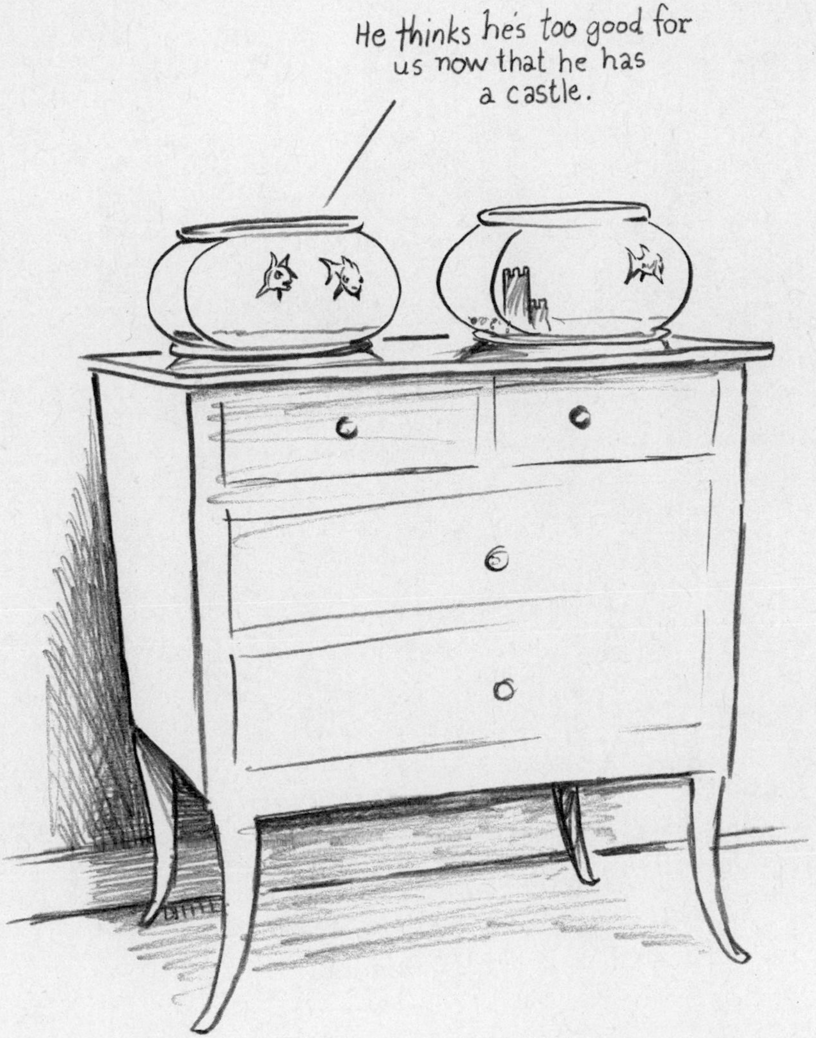
He thinks he's too good for us now that he has a castle.

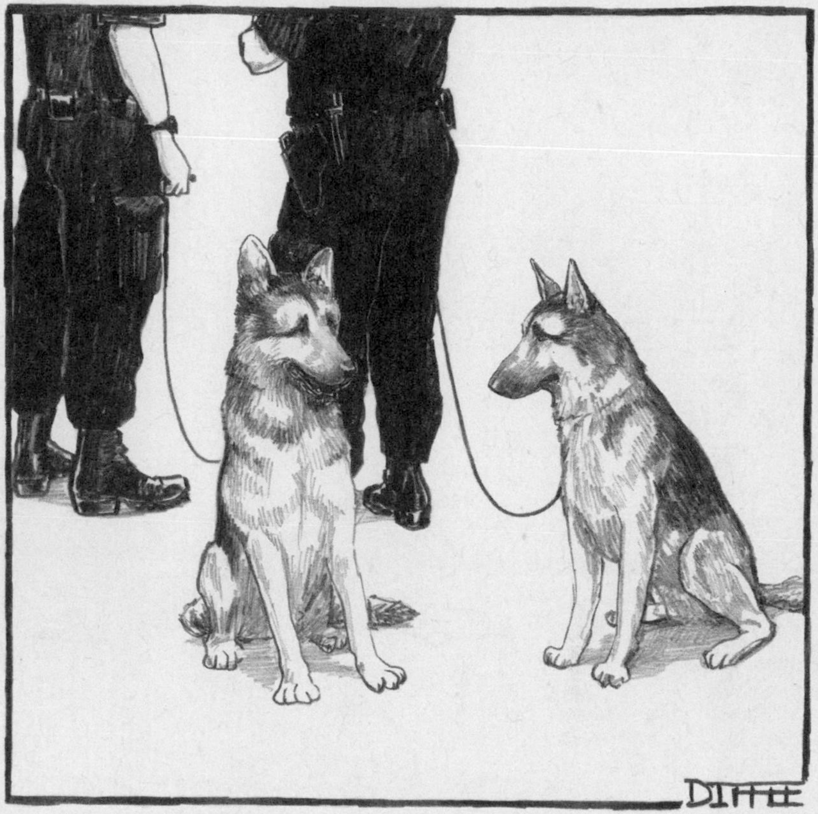
DIFFEE

"I'm starting to really like the smell of cocaine."

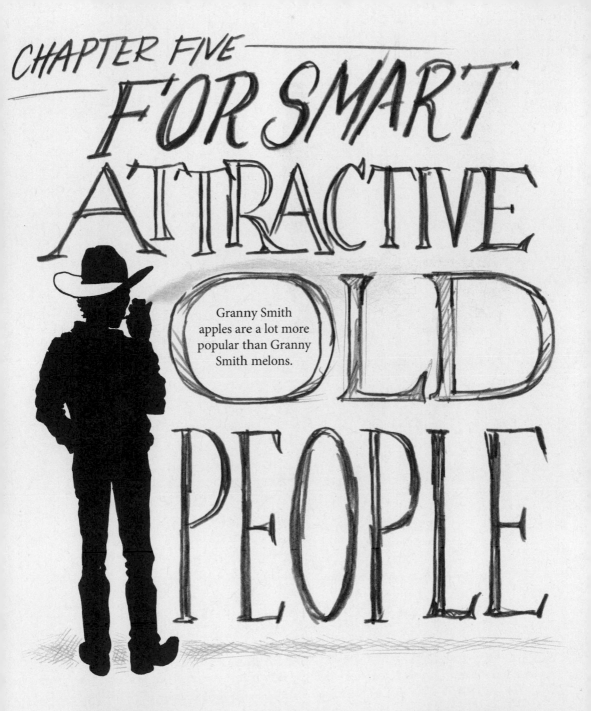

CHAPTER FIVE
FOR SMART ATTRACTIVE OLD PEOPLE

Granny Smith apples are a lot more popular than Granny Smith melons.

WHO SAYS YOU CAN'T TEACH AN OLD DOG NEW TRICKS?

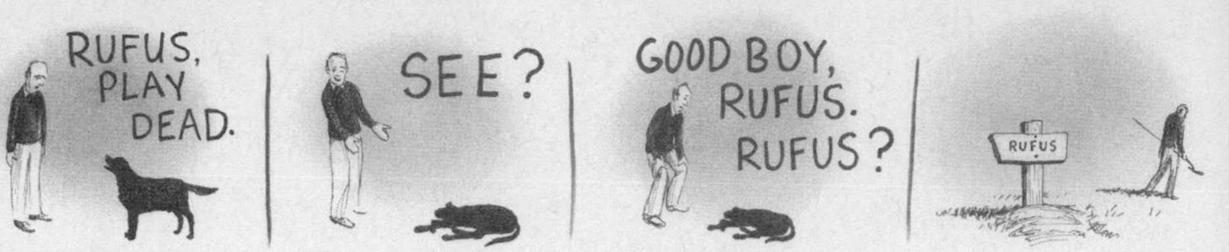
RUFUS, PLAY DEAD.
SEE?
GOOD BOY, RUFUS. RUFUS. RUFUS?
RUFUS

I'M NOT OLD, BUT I SURE HOPE I WILL BE SOMEDAY. NOT IN THE BREAK-YOUR-HIP-SNEEZING KIND OF WAY BUT IN THE NOT-DEAD-YET KIND OF WAY. SEEMS TO ME, THIS LIFE IS LIKE A TETHERBALL MATCH. BIG SWINGS AND CHANGES OF DIRECTION AT FIRST, THEN A SAD INEVITABILITY SETS IN. I DON'T WANT THAT. I DON'T WANT TO FADE. I WANT TO GO OUT ON MY SHIELD, WEARING MY BOOTS, MIXING MY METAPHORS.

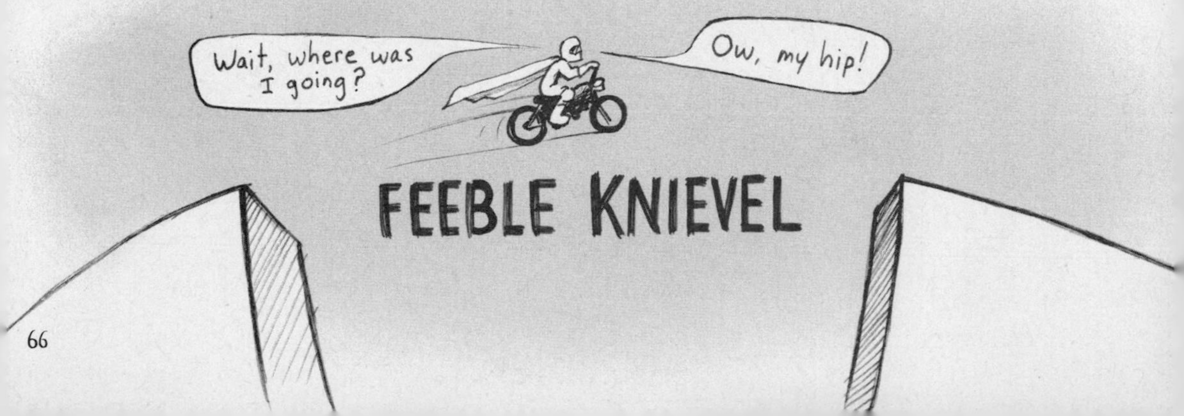
Wait, where was I going?
Ow, my hip!
FEEBLE KNIEVEL

I HAVE A LOT OF RESPECT FOR OUR OLDER GEN-
ERATION. THEY FOUGHT OUR WARS, WON OUR
FREEDOM. THEY ALSO INVENTED FIG NEWTONS,
BUT NOBODY'S PERFECT. ONE THING I LOVE
ABOUT OLD PEOPLE IS HOW OLD AND ODD THEIR
NAMES ARE. ONE OF MY GRANDMOTHERS
WAS NAMED GUSSIE CLYRENE DIFFEE. CRAZY,
RIGHT? ESPECIALLY THAT DIFFEE PART.

NOW.

Myrtle

Percival

Eunice

Lodell

EVENTUALLY.

Heather

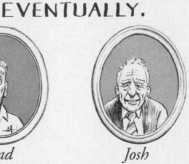
Brad

Josh

Britney

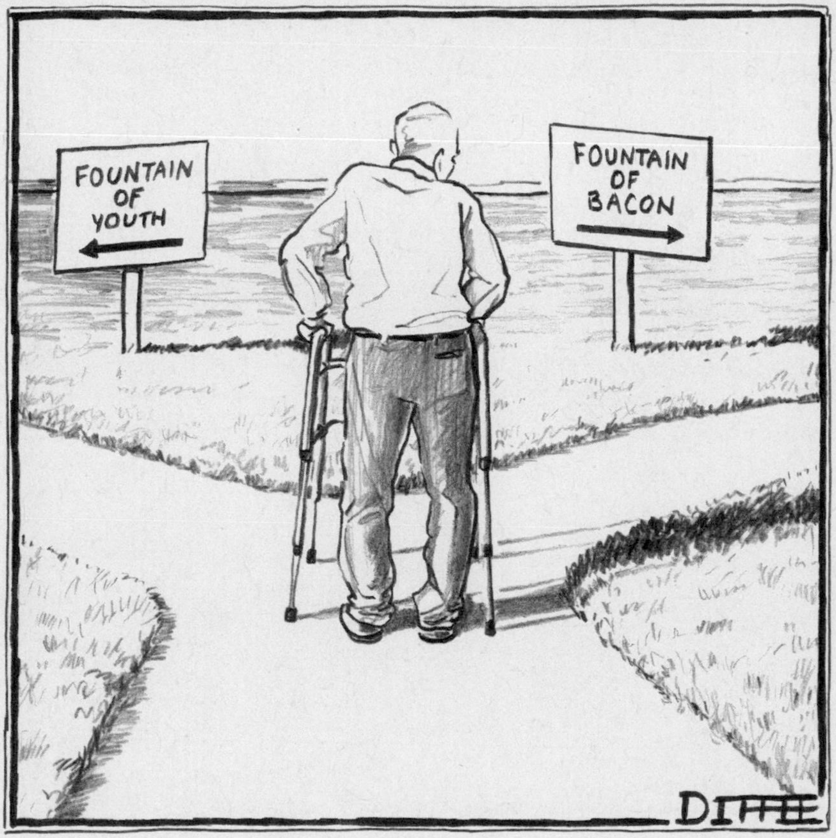
FOUNTAIN OF YOUTH
FOUNTAIN OF BACON
DIFFEE

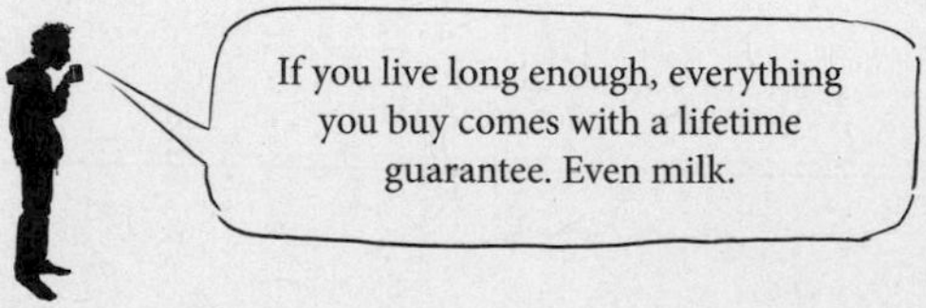
If you live long enough, everything you buy comes with a lifetime guarantee. Even milk.

"They never told us what carrying twenty times our own weight would do to our knees."

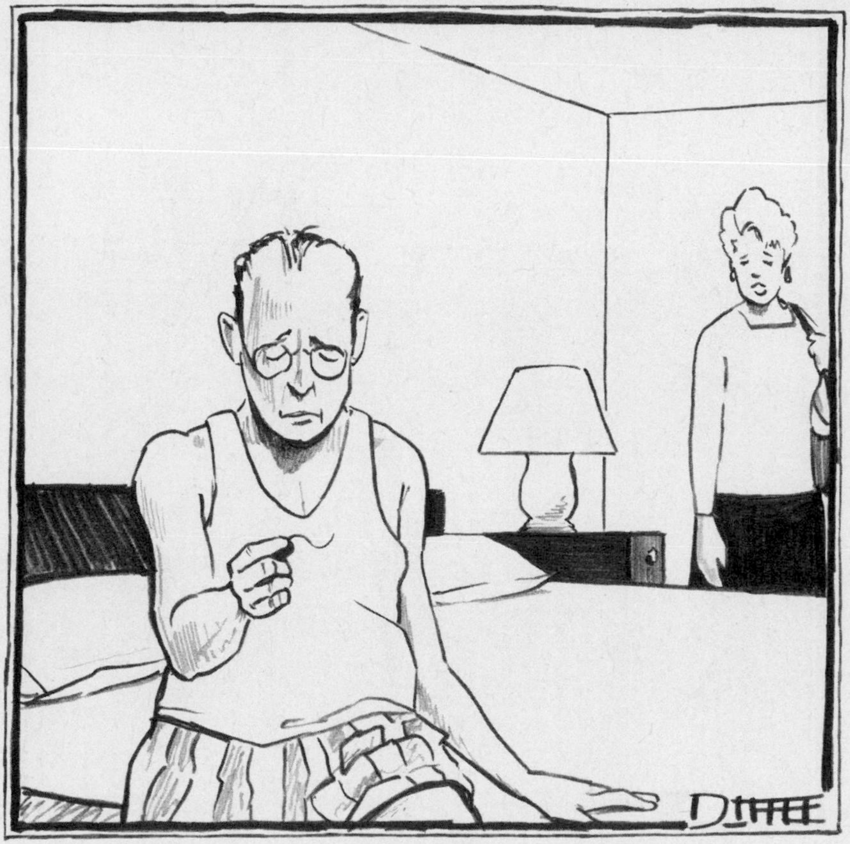
DIFFEE

"Put it under your pillow, and maybe you'll get a visit from the hair fairy."

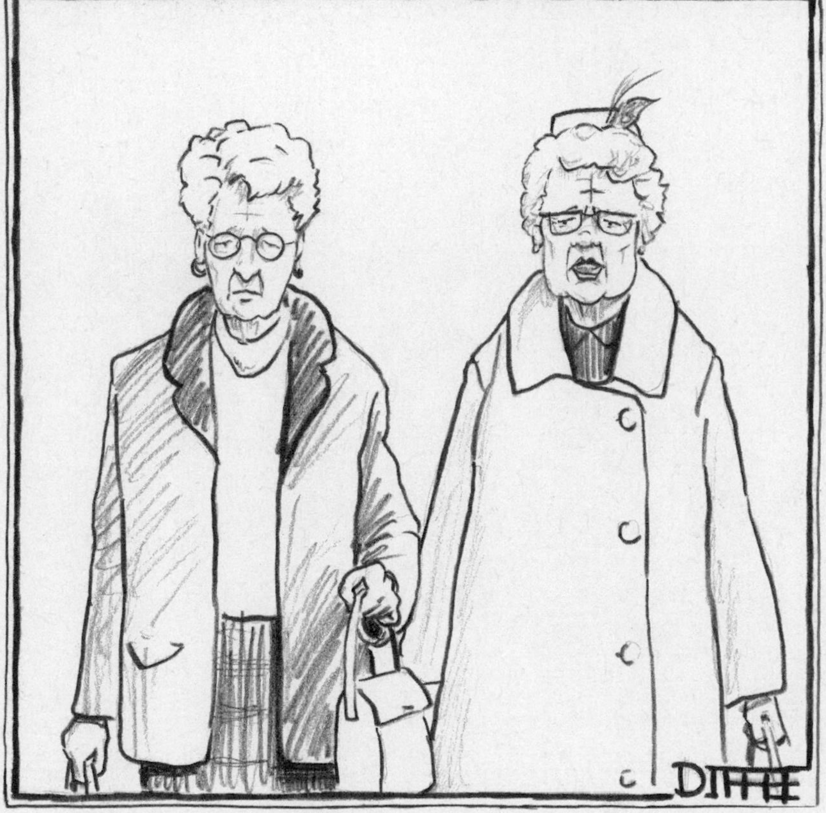
DIFFEE

"I don't know about you, Ethel, but I just can't get used to this thong."

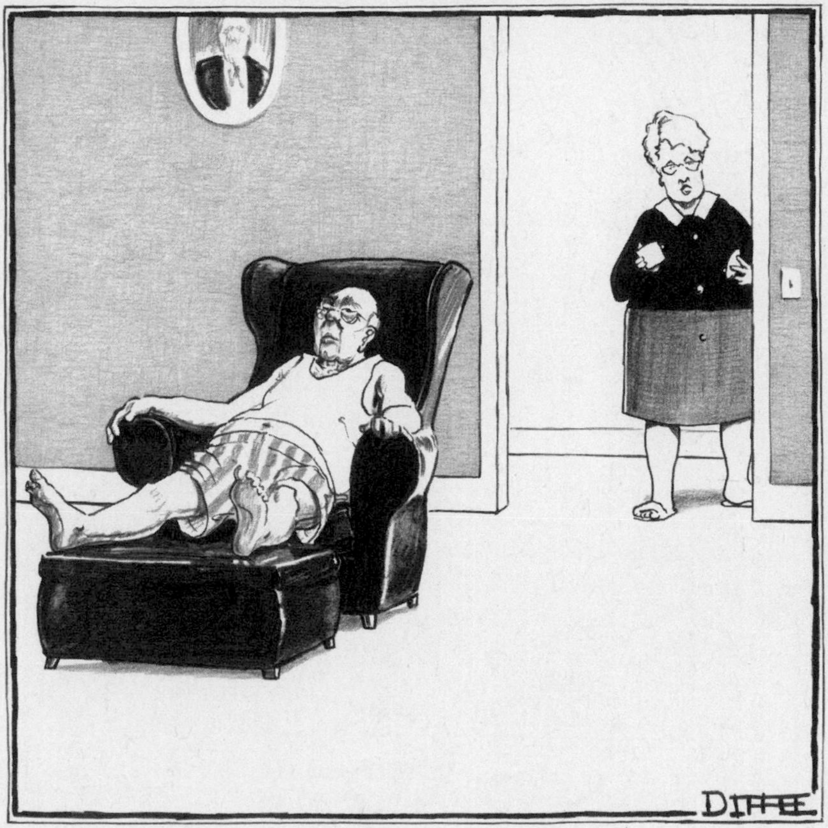
DIFFEE

"Wilfred, did you leave the lid off the body glitter?"

When I was a young man, I used to do odd jobs for an older gentleman who lived nearby. He'd give me life advice. With age comes wisdom, up to a point. Then senility sneaks in. It can be hard sometimes, to know where to draw the line.

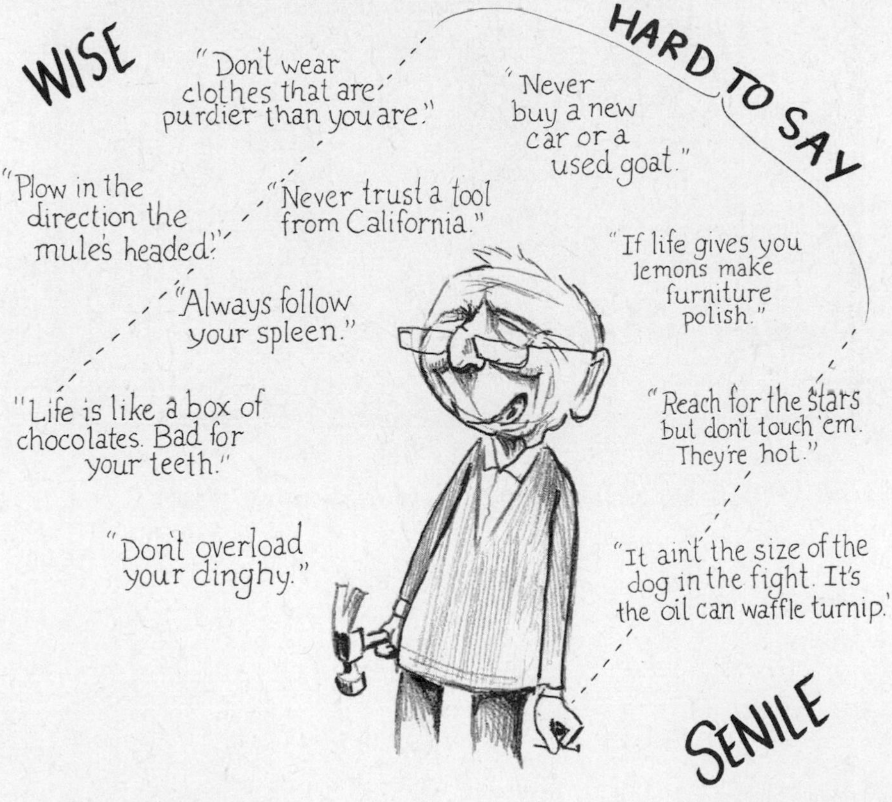

WISE
HARD TO SAY
SENILE
"Don't wear clothes that are purdier than you are."
"Never buy a new car or a used goat."
"Plow in the direction the mule's headed."
"Never trust a tool from California."
"If life gives you lemons make furniture polish."
"Always follow your spleen."
"Life is like a box of chocolates. Bad for your teeth."
"Reach for the stars but don't touch 'em. They're hot."
"Don't overload your dinghy."
"It ain't the size of the dog in the fight. It's the oil can waffle turnip."

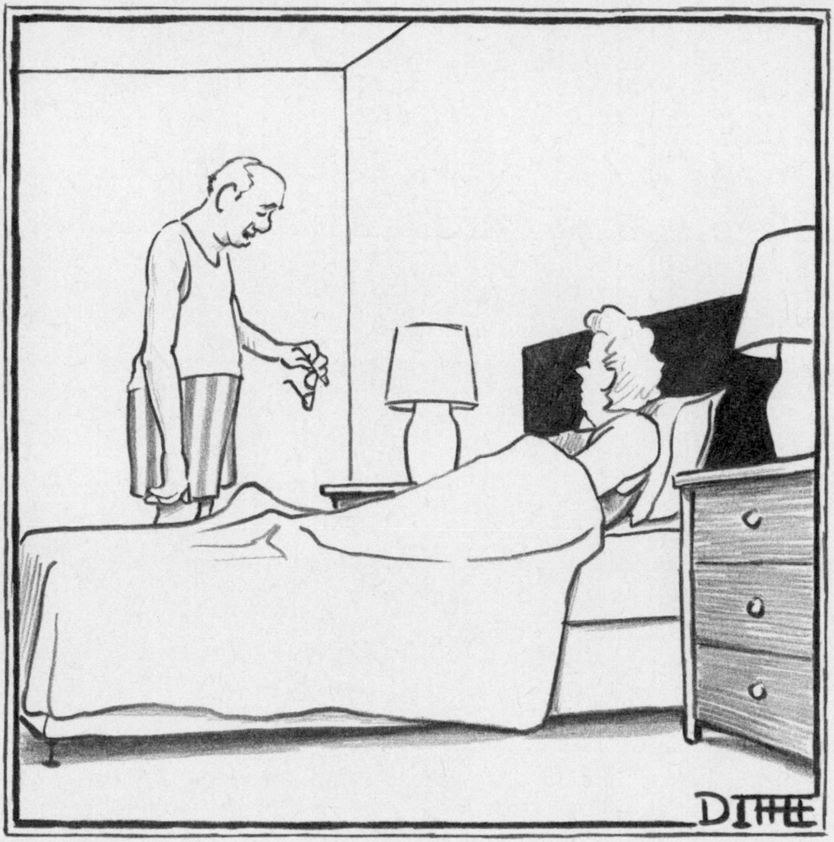
DIFFEE

"These are my reading glasses. I need my sex glasses."

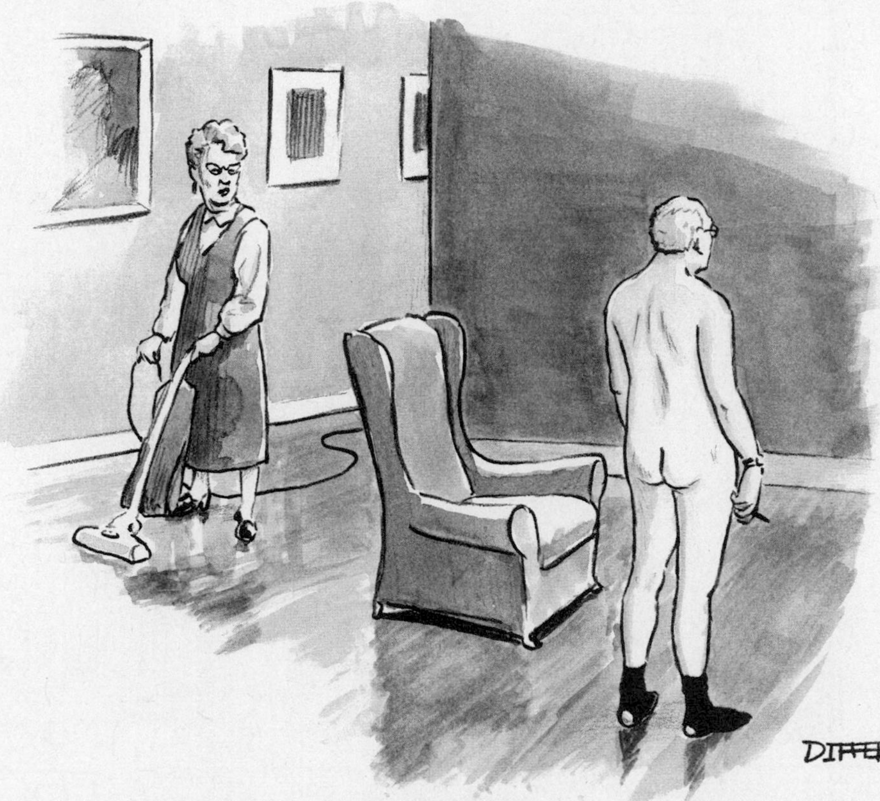
DIFFEE

"We've got company coming over, Melvin. Put on your good socks."

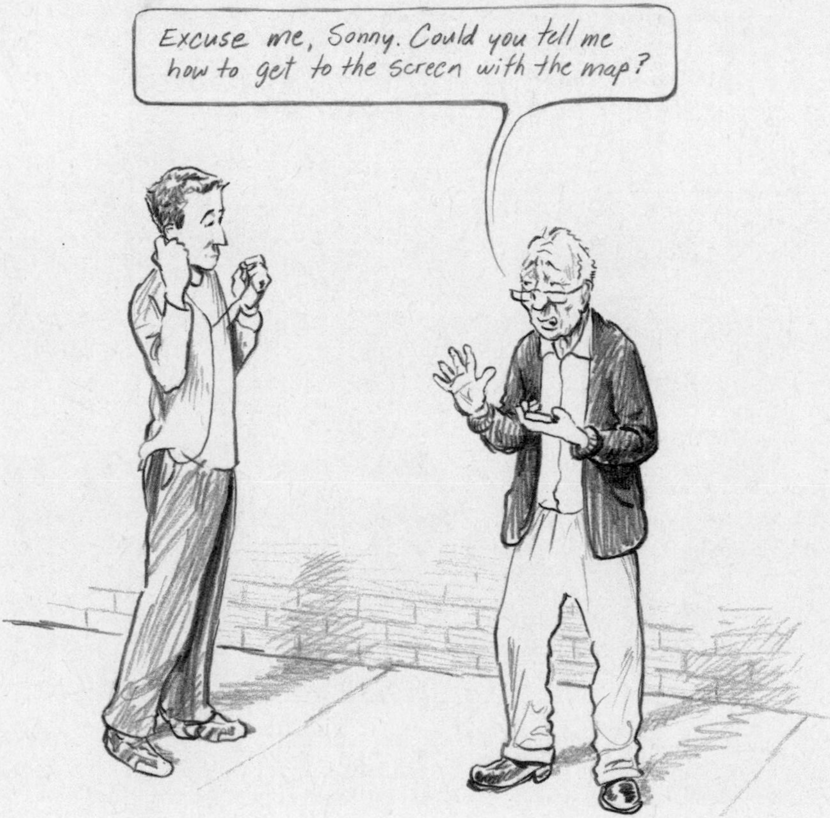
Excuse me, Sonny. Could you tell me how to get to the screen with the map?

THE THREE AGES OF MAN

Not worried about
ear hair

Worried about
ear hair

Not worried about
ear hair

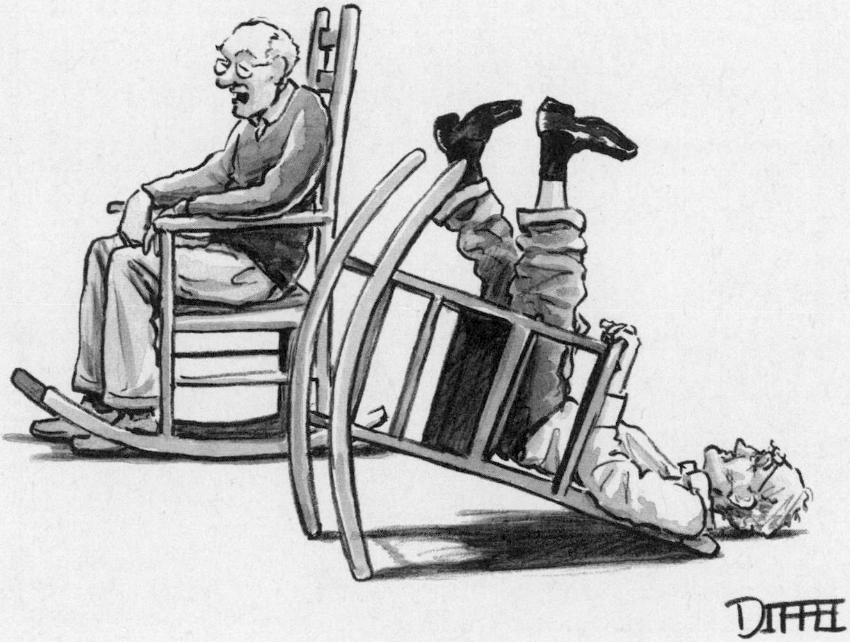
DIFFEE

"Gesundheit."

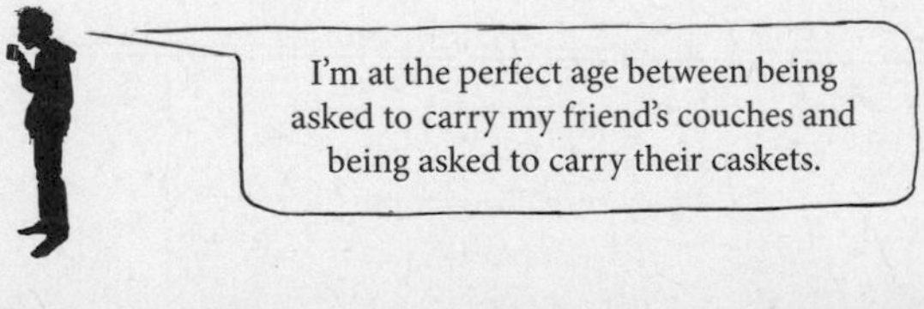
I'm at the perfect age between being asked to carry my friend's couches and being asked to carry their caskets.

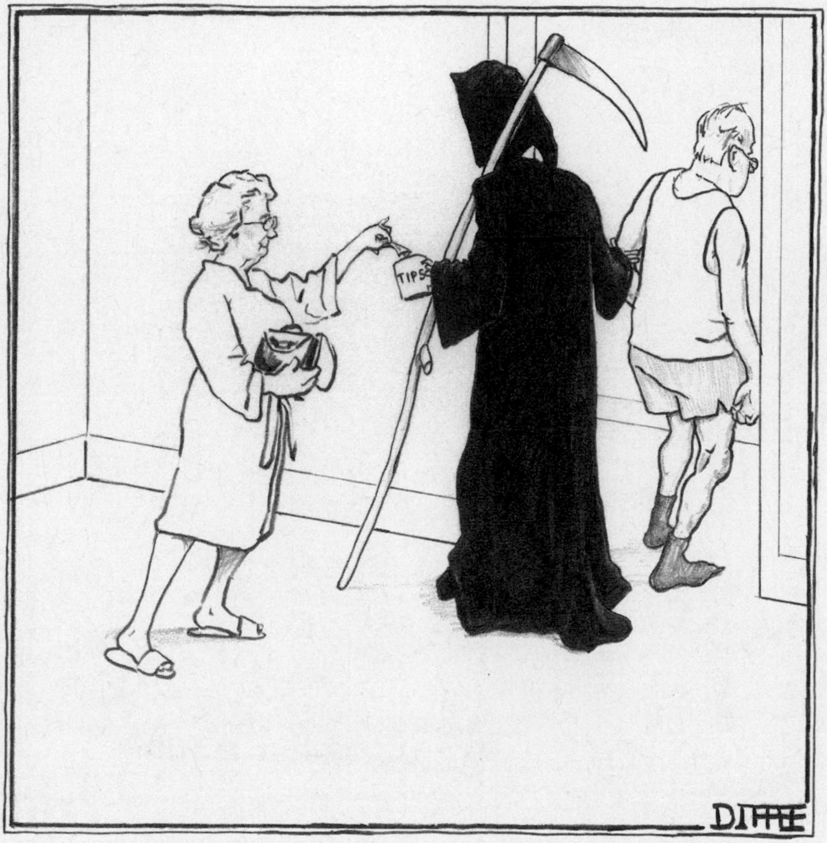
TIPS
DIFFEE

"No thanks, I'm trying to drop a casket size."

CHAPTER SIX

FOR SMART ATTRACTIVE PEOPLE WHO USE UTENSILS

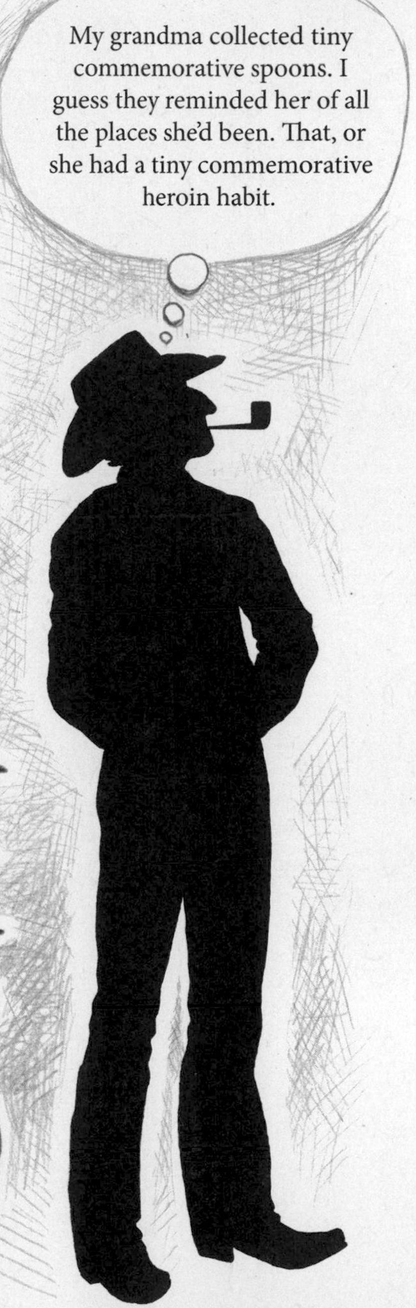
My grandma collected tiny commemorative spoons. I guess they reminded her of all the places she'd been. That, or she had a tiny commemorative heroin habit.

I'M ALL FOR UTENSILS. IT'S THE USE OF UTENSILS THAT SEPARATES US FROM CANADIANS. BUT WHAT IS A UTENSIL? WELL, IT'S BASICALLY A HAND TOOL THAT'S USED IN THE MAKING OR EATING OF FOOD. SOMETIMES IT'S HARD TO KNOW IF A THING IS A TOOL OR A UTENSIL, ESPECIALLY IF YOU'RE LIKE ME AND YOU EAT YOUR CHEETOS WITH NEEDLE-NOSE PLIERS TO AVOID MAKING CHEESE DOODLES (THINK ABOUT IT.) I GUESS THE GENERAL RULE IS THIS: IF IT'S IN THE KITCHEN, IT'S PROBABLY A UTENSIL. IF IT'S IN A P.T. CRUISER IN NEW JERSEY, IT'S PROBABLY A TOOL.

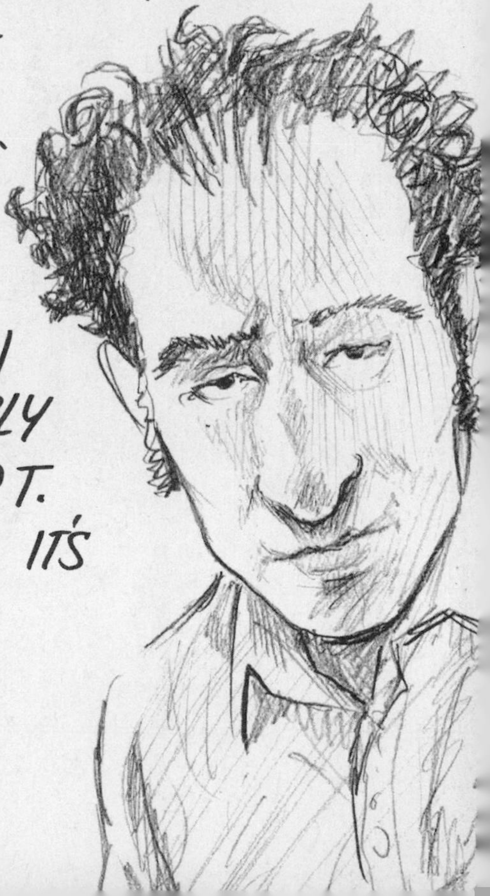

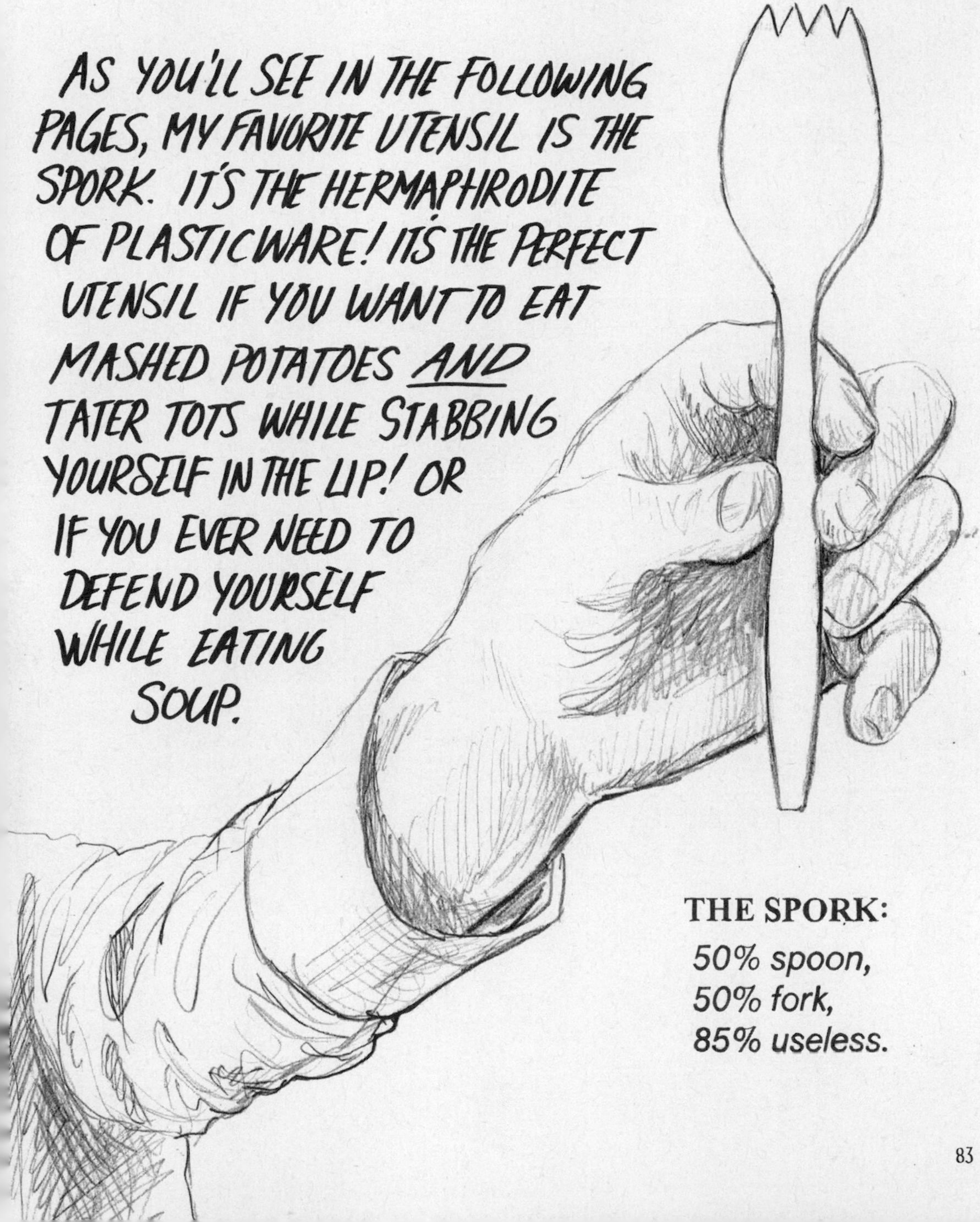
AS YOU'LL SEE IN THE FOLLOWING PAGES, MY FAVORITE UTENSIL IS THE SPORK. IT'S THE HERMAPHRODITE OF PLASTICWARE! IT'S THE PERFECT UTENSIL IF YOU WANT TO EAT MASHED POTATOES AND TATER TOTS WHILE STABBING YOURSELF IN THE LIP! OR IF YOU EVER NEED TO DEFEND YOURSELF WHILE EATING SOUP.

THE SPORK:

50% spoon,
50% fork,
85% useless.

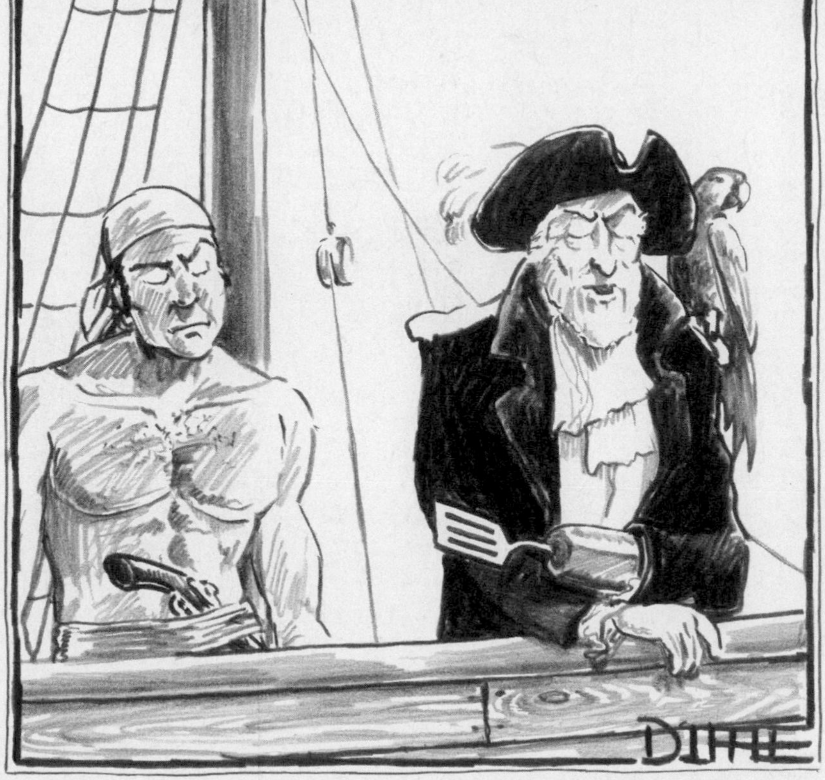
DITTE

"I was in a different place then."

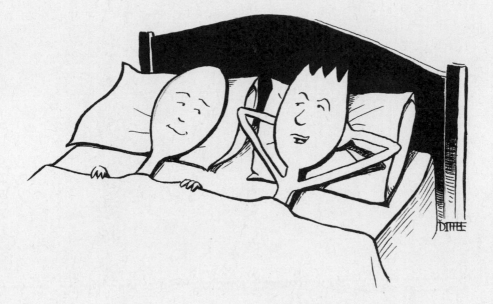

"You wanna spoon or you wanna fork?"

MASHED
POTATOES
MASHED
POTATOES
POTATO
WEDGES
POTATO
WEDGES
DIFFEE

"Looks like we're gonna need a sporklift."

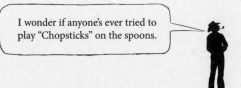

I wonder if anyone's ever tried to
play "Chopsticks" on the spoons.

Sure, the dish ran away with me but then she left me for a melon baller.

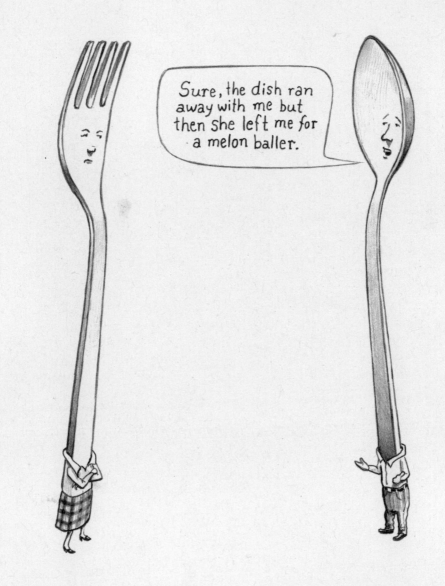

Beyond the Spork

The spork is great but why stop there? Here are some new ideas for mash-up utensils, or as I like to call them. "Newtensils"!

Sporkscrew

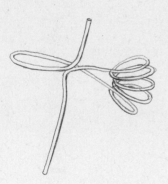

Crazy Strawhisk

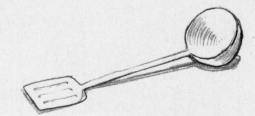

Spatuladle

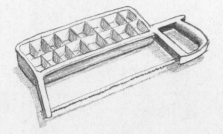

Ice Cube Track Saw

Pointing Trowelobster Fork

Pasta Clawffle Iron

Ball Peen Hammeat Tendurice
Cream Scooponkey Wrench

"Is this the spatula or the whisk?"

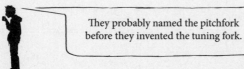

They probably named the pitchfork
before they invented the tuning fork.

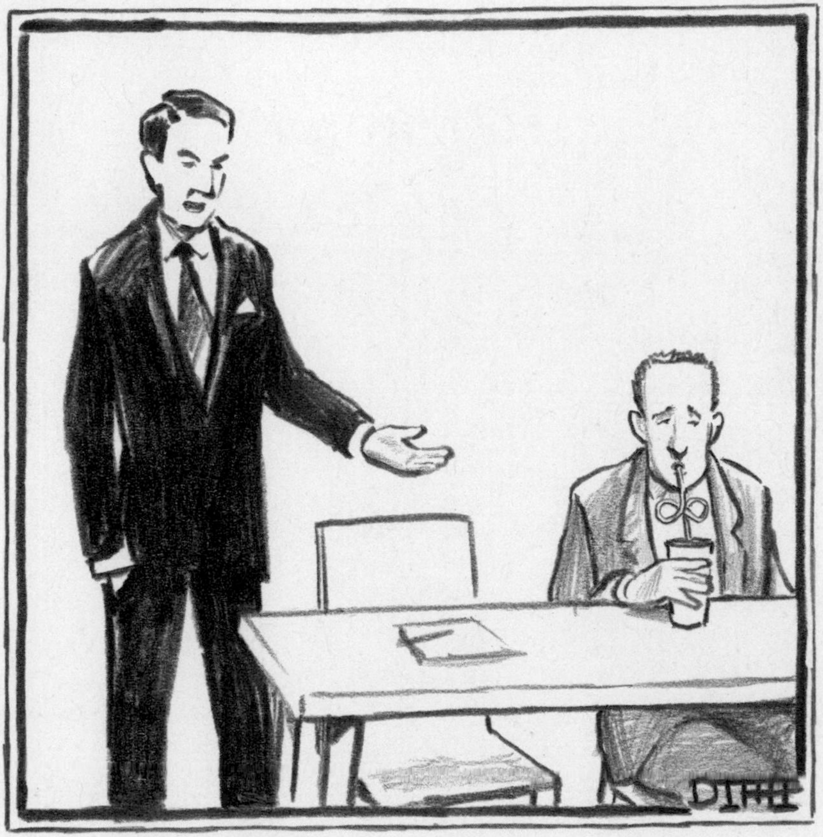
DIFFEE

"Ladies and gentlemen of the jury, I ask you, is this the straw of a sane man?"

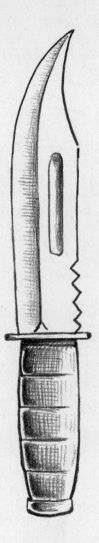

REALLY CRAZY STRAW

CHAPTER SEVEN

FOR SMART ATTRACTIVE PEOPLE with REAL JOBS

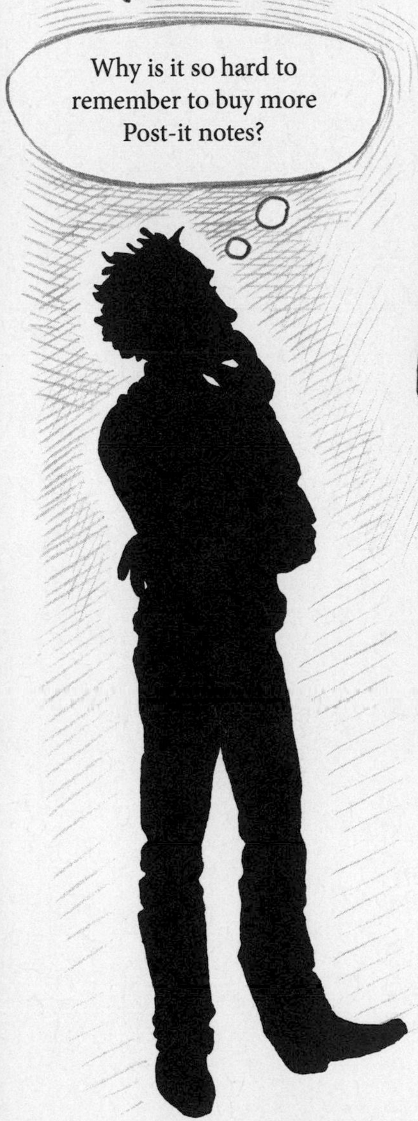
Why is it so hard to remember to buy more Post-it notes?

CARTOONING ISN'T A REAL JOB. NOT REALLY. A REAL JOB IS WHEN YOU HAVE TO WORK IN A FACTORY OR IN A CUBICLE OR IN PANTS. I GUESS I'M LUCKY THAT WAY. I'VE BEEN SELF-EMPLOYED FOR THE LAST FIFTEEN YEARS AS A FREELANCE CARTOONIST. NOT TO BRAG, BUT IN THAT TIME I'VE BEEN NAMED EMPLOYEE OF THE MONTH TWICE! HERE'S MY RÉSUMÉ.

Matthew Diffee
matt@matthewdiffee.com

OBJECTIVE   1998–present
A position utilizing my writing and drawing skills in an innovative, pantsless environment.

WORK EXPERIENCE
Freelance Cartoonist

—Responsible for all noodling and doodling.
—Instrumental in creation of all workplace playlists including "Coffee Sippin' Songs," "Tooning Tunes," and "Staring into Space Jams."
—Maintained a rigorous schedule of televised research.
—Consistently met personal goals of rising before or slightly after noon, but definitely before twoish.
—Excelled at the design, construction, and administration of all nachos.
—Initiated a company-wide Health and Wellness program involving mandatory naps and afternoon movie-going excursions which proved incredibly popular with both staff and management, increasing morale and quite possibly output.

YEP, CARTOONING AIN'T A BAD WAY TO MAKE A BUCK. NOT SO GOOD IF YOU WANNA MAKE TWO OR MORE, BUT THEN I WAS NEVER IN IT FOR THE MONEY. FOR ME IT WAS ALWAYS ABOUT THE MARKER FUMES. THERE WERE YEARS, OF COURSE, THE DARK YEARS WHEN I HAD TO DO REAL WORK.

I LOADED FREIGHT, WORKED ON ROAD CREWS, DID CONSTRUCTION, I EVEN WAITED TABLES AT APPLEBEE'S UNTIL I GOT FIRED FOR CRYING.

I GUESS MY FAVORITE REAL JOB I EVER HAD WAS WHEN I WORKED FOR A SHORT WHILE AS A SIGN PAINTER. THAT'S A SKILL YOU CAN ALWAYS USE, NO MATTER HOW BAD THINGS GET.

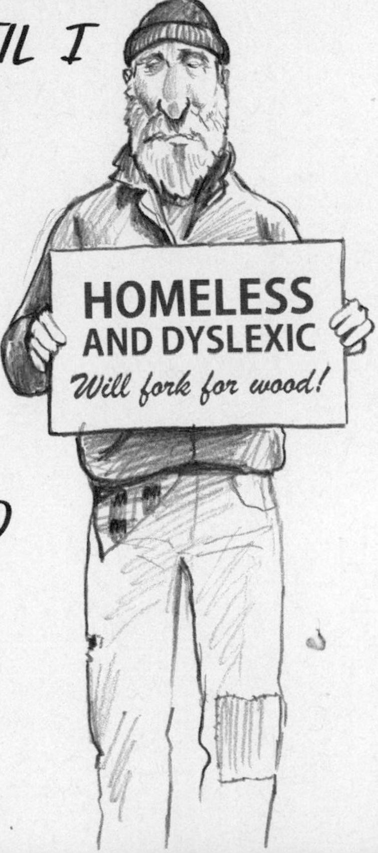
HOMELESS
AND DYSLEXIC
Will fork for wood!

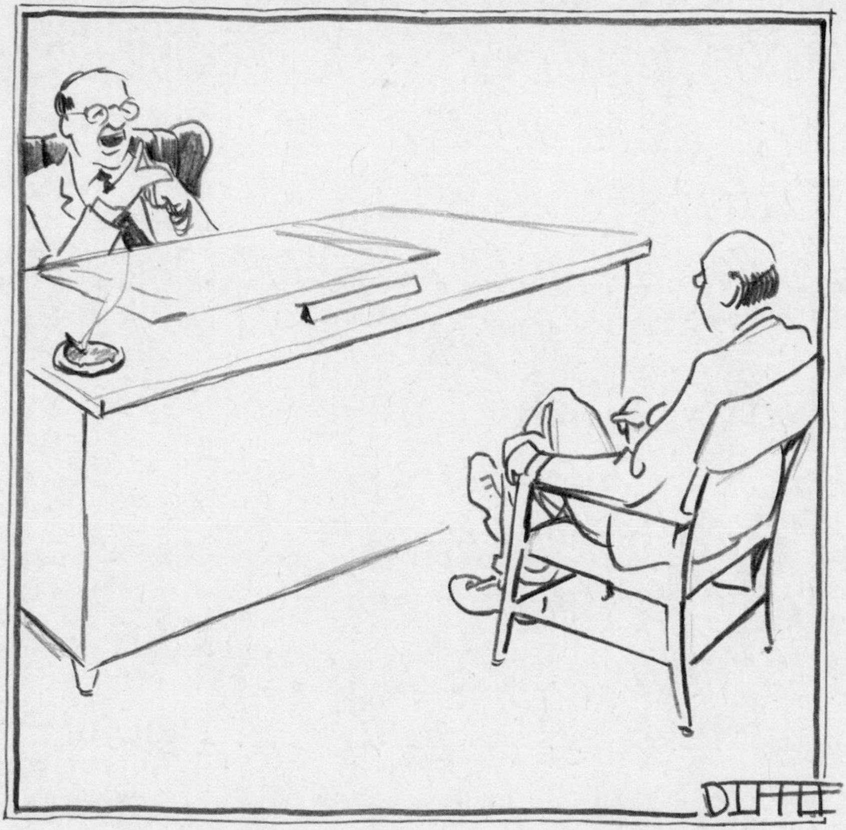
DIFFEE

"So, Jim, where do you see yourself in ten minutes?"

"Oh, sorry, wrong cubicle."

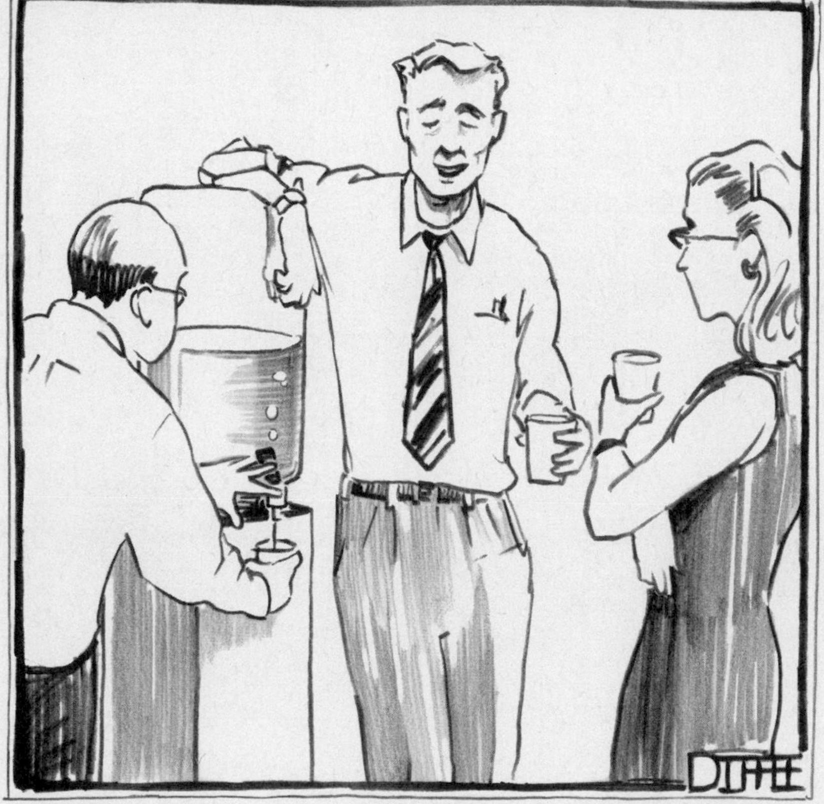
DIFFEE

"You always get the good gossip out here around the vodka cooler."

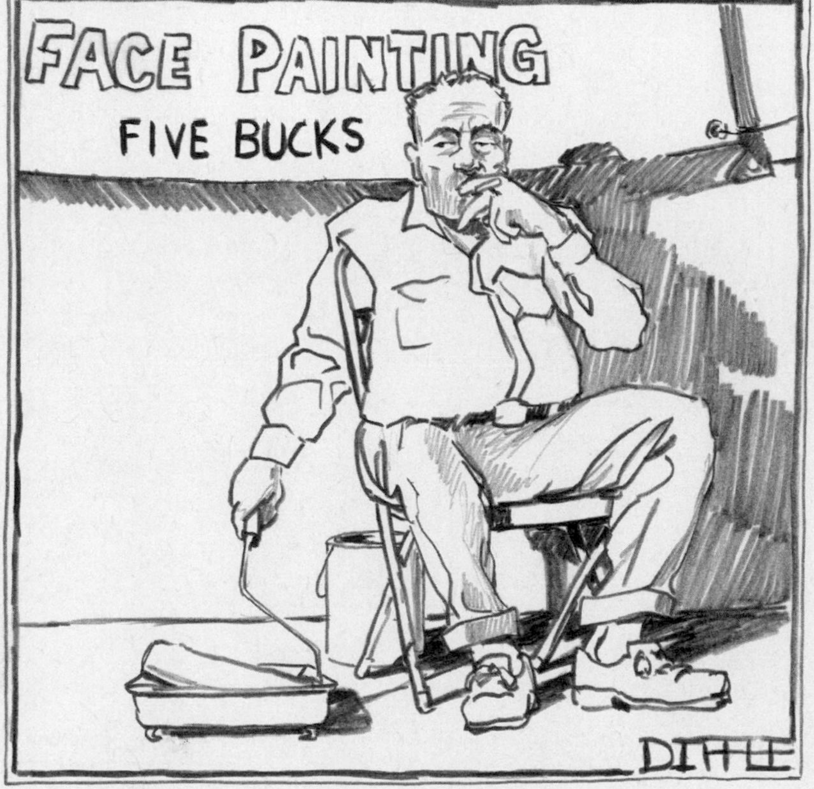
FACE PAINTING
FIVE BUCKS

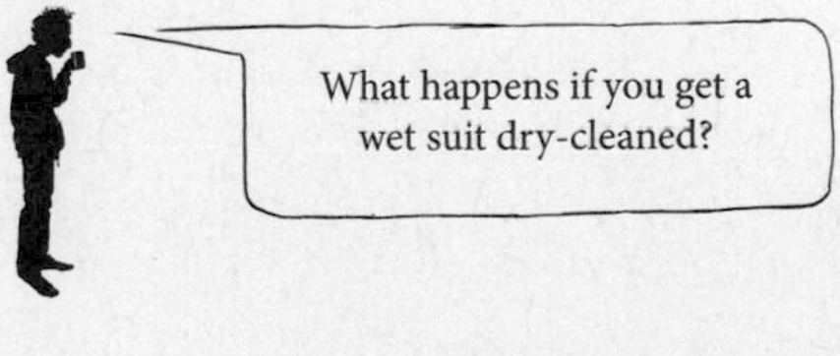
What happens if you get a wet suit dry-cleaned?

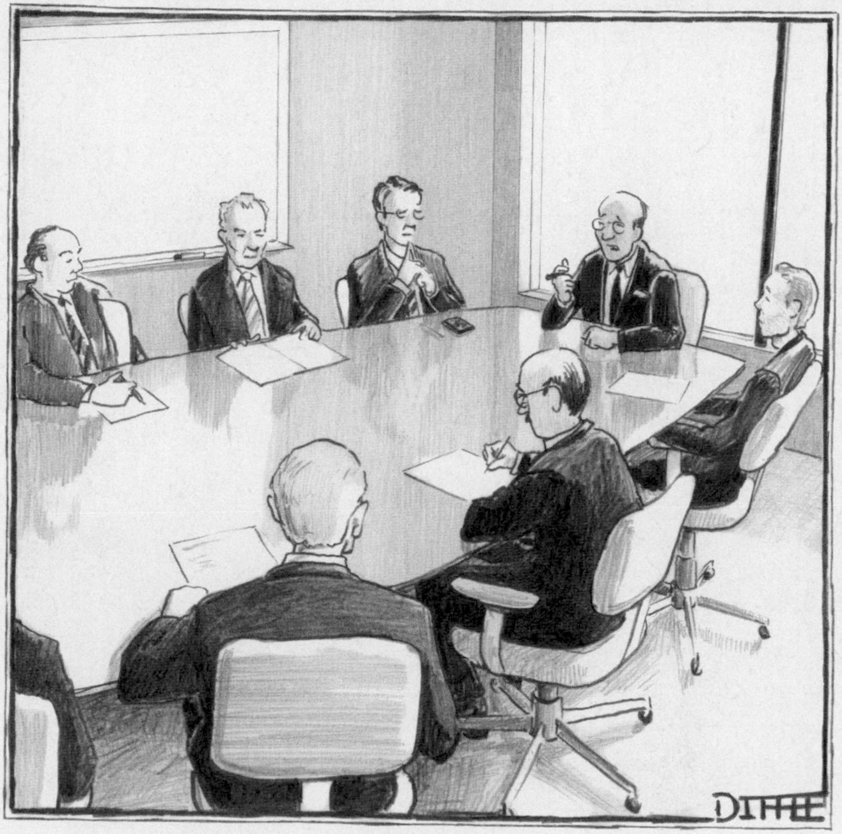
DIFFEE

"Sounds good. We'll just have to run it by the Hawaiian Shirts."

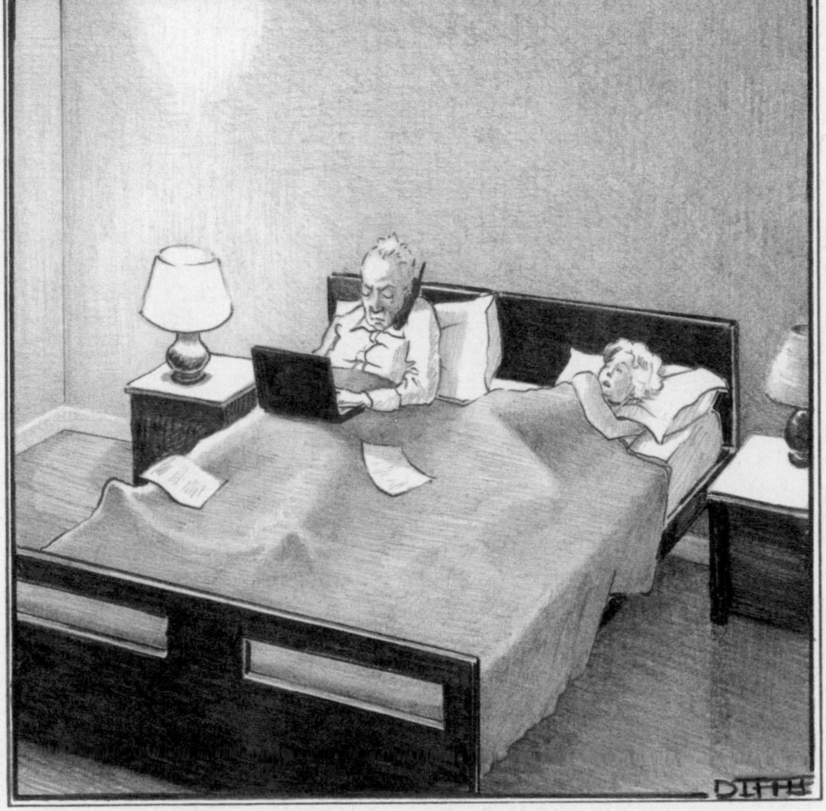
DIFFEE

"Honey, you're sleepworking again."

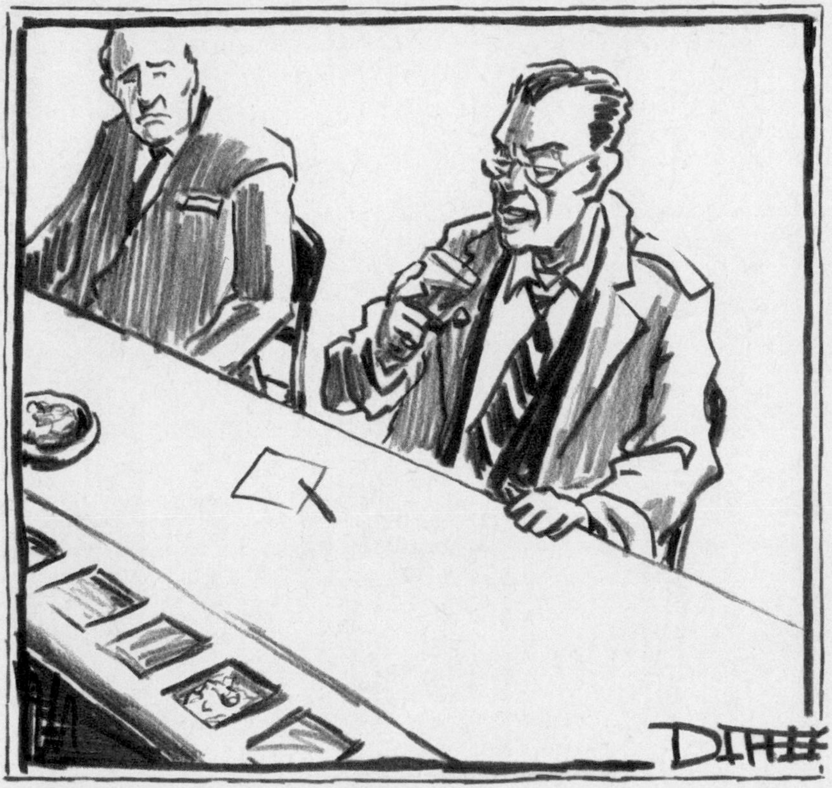
DIFFEE

"I'm a stay-at-work dad."

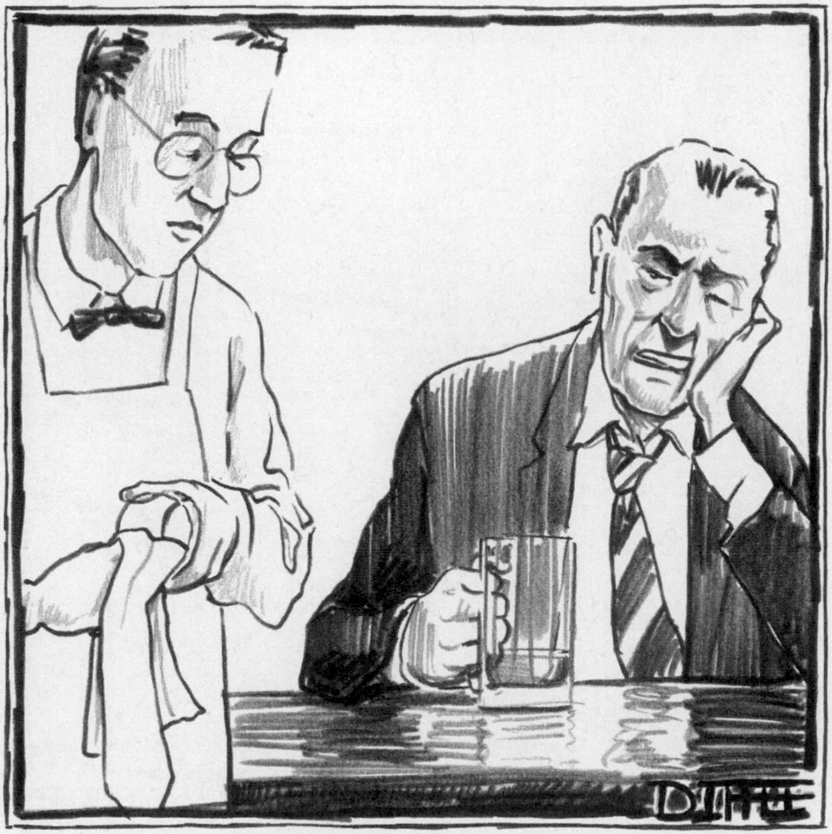
DIFFEE

"I feel like a man trapped in a woman's salary."

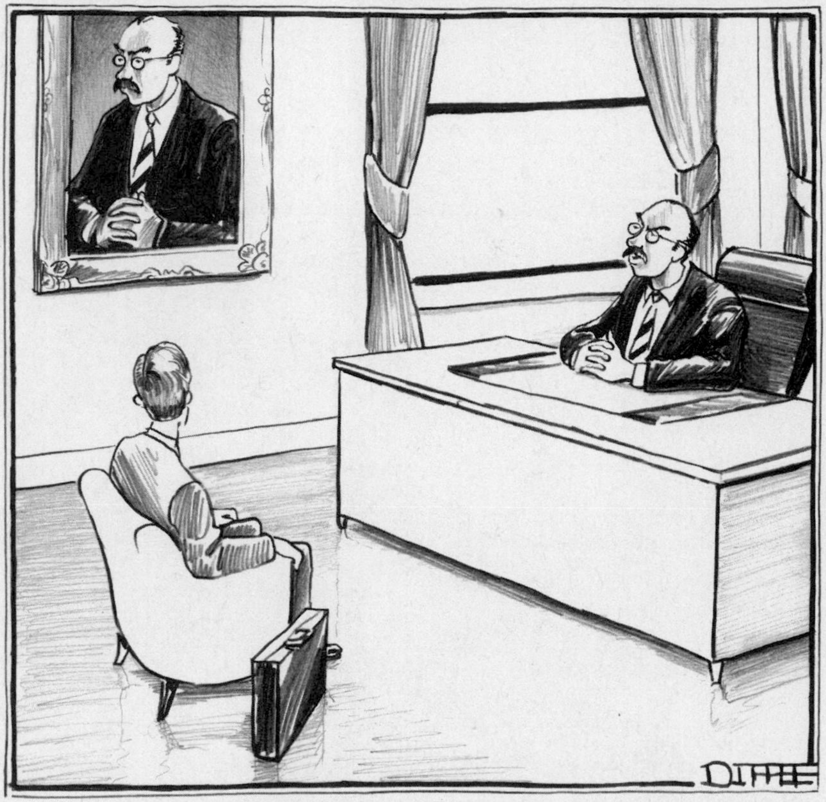
DIFFEE

"It helps me stay focused on what matters most."

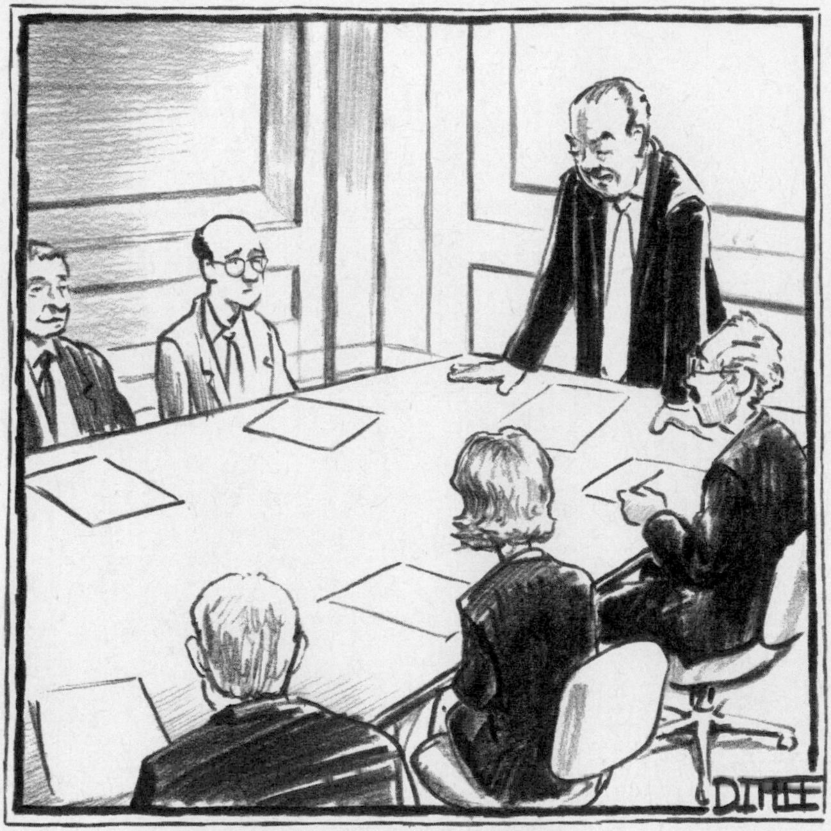
DIFFEE

"We realize it's a win-win, Jenkins—we're trying to figure out a way to make it win-lose."

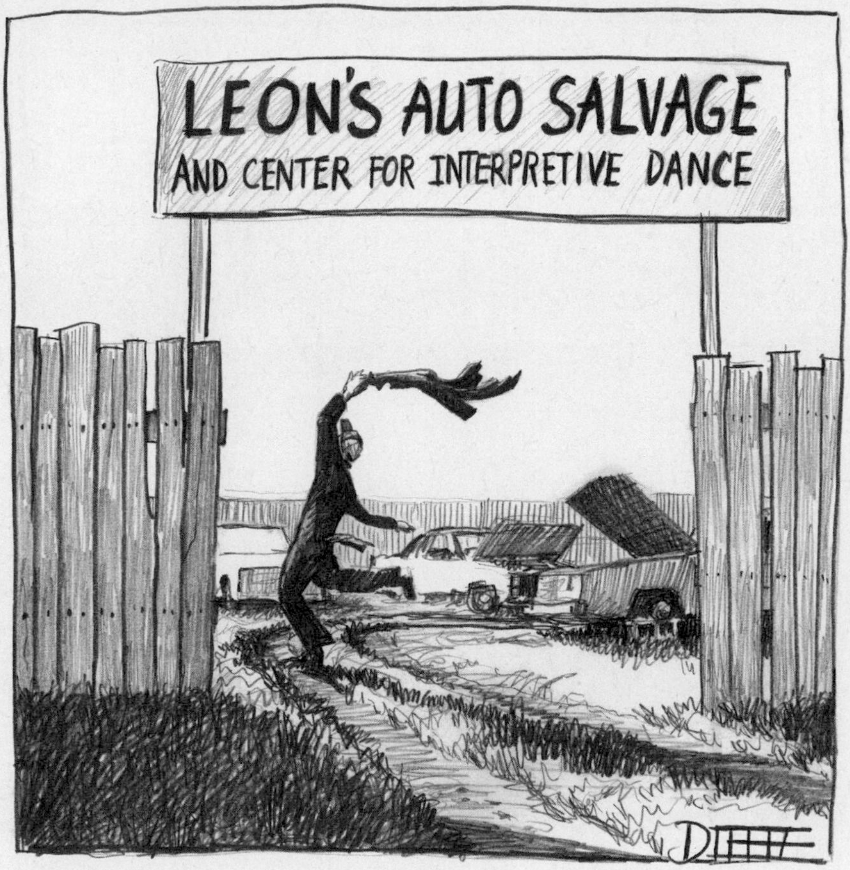
LEON'S AUTO SALVAGE
AND CENTER FOR INTERPRETIVE DANCE

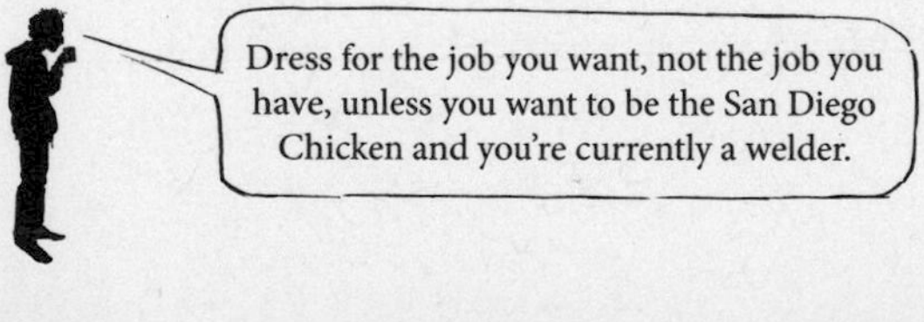
Dress for the job you want, not the job you have, unless you want to be the San Diego Chicken and you're currently a welder.

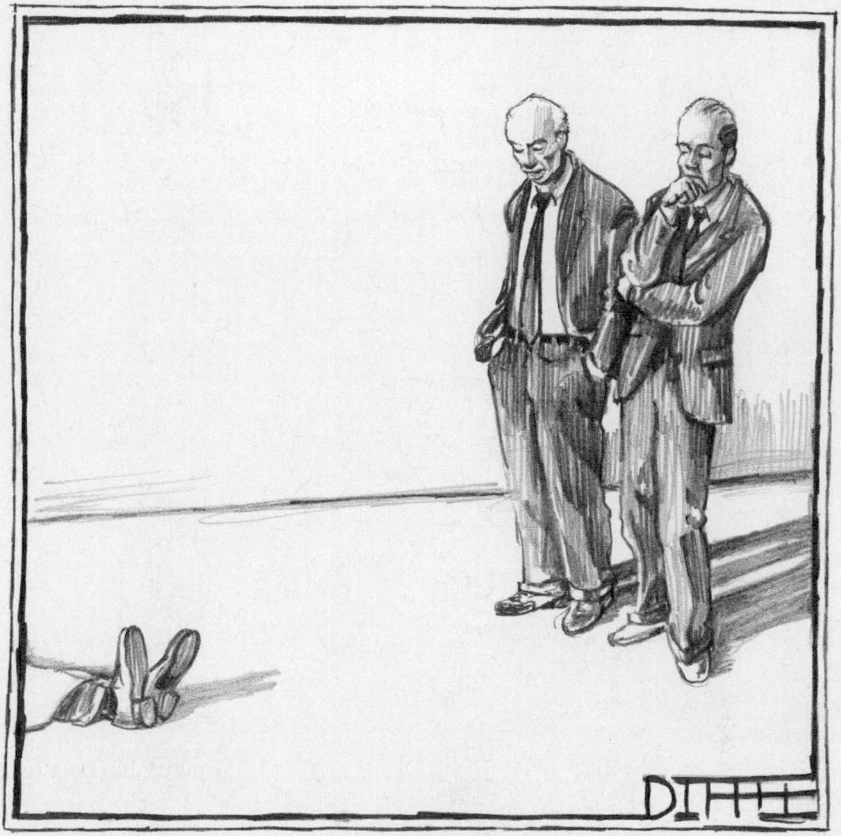
DIFFEE

"By the violent nature of the multiple stab wounds, I'd say the victim was probably a consultant."

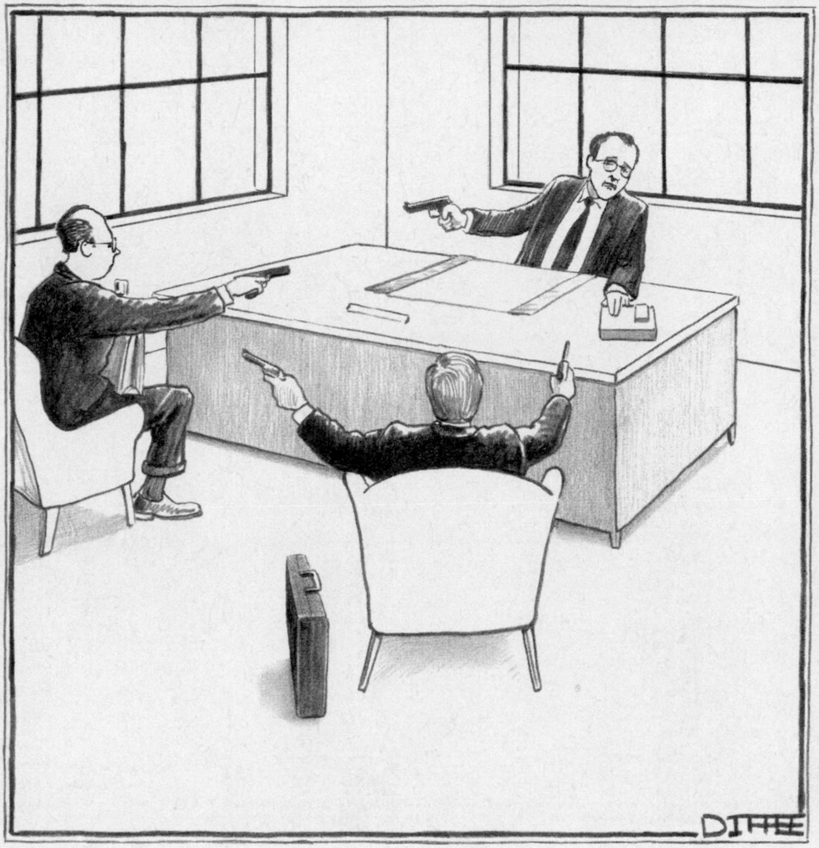
DIFFEE

"Uh, Trudy, how's that coffee coming?"

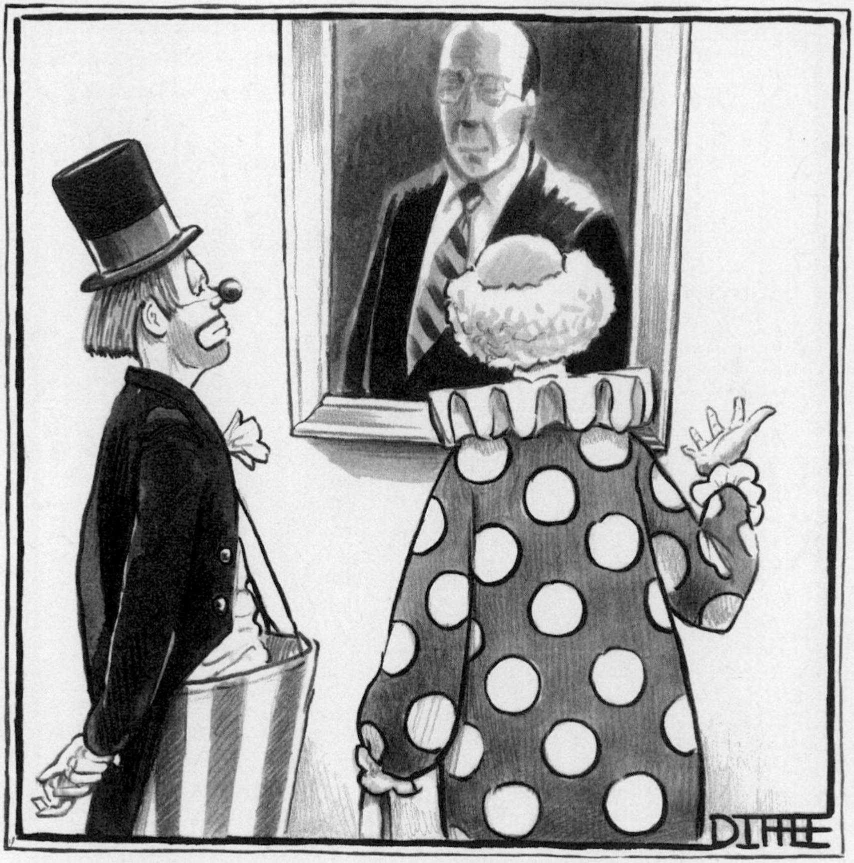
DIFFEE

"I always find paintings like this a little creepy."

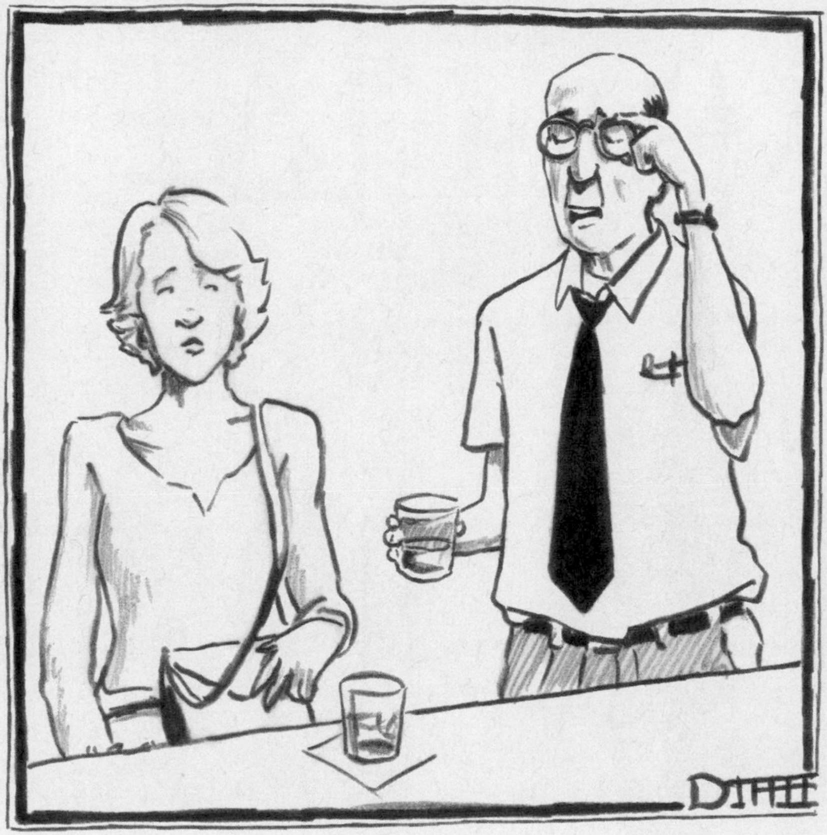
DIFFEE

"To be honest—I'm not sure that accounting can be taught."

CHAPTER EIGHT

FOR SMART ATTRACTIVE INDIANS AND ESKIMOS

Whenever I'm around more than one Native American and they're smoking, I worry that they might secretly be talking about me.

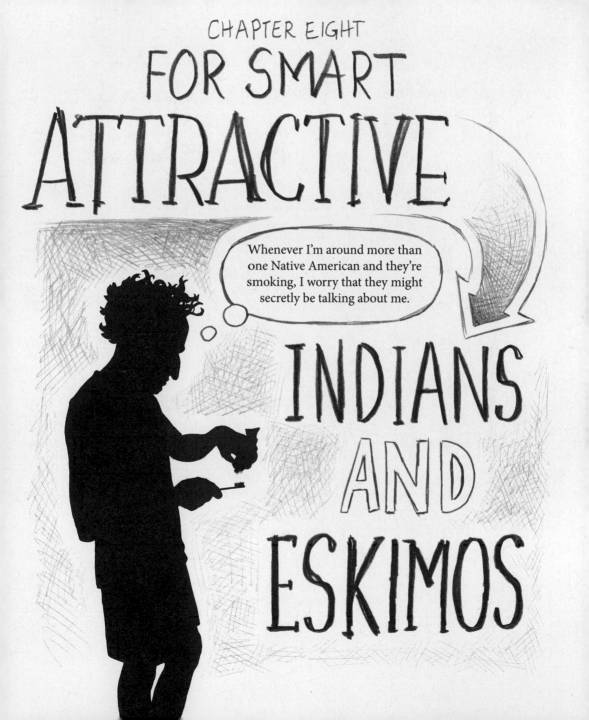

One of the coolest and funniest things about Indians is their names. When I was a kid I was in a father-and-son program called Indian Guides. We all had to come up with our own Indian names. My brother was "Bear Claw." Cool name. My dad was "Falling Rock." Pretty funny. Me? I was "Flapping Eagle."

Yes,

Flapping.

If I had to come up with an Indian name now,

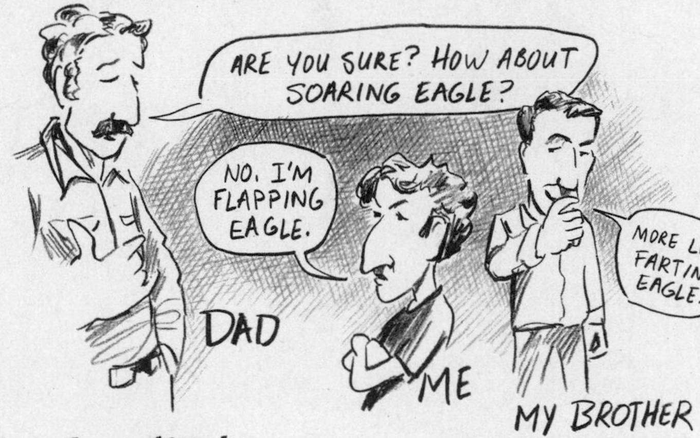
ARE YOU SURE? HOW ABOUT SOARING EAGLE?
NO. I'M FLAPPING EAGLE.
MORE LIKE FARTING EAGLE.
DAD
ME
MY BROTHER

I'd probably go with "Dances with Awkwardness." It's true. I'm no dancer. The only difference between me dancing and me putting out a grass fire

IS THE PRESENCE OF MUSIC. NOW, ESKIMO NAMES ARE DIFFERENT. ALL I KNOW IS THAT THEY'RE BASED ON THE SOUNDS MADE BY RUTTING WALRUSES.

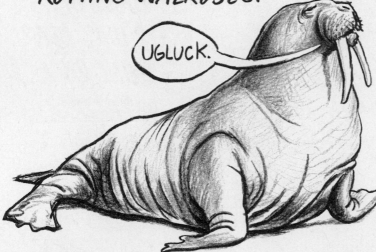

UGLUCK.

The Pacific Walrus
"Ice manatee." Closely related to the saber-toothed tiger and the banana slug. Diet consists mostly of fish. Males often migrate southward to host right-wing radio shows.

THE TRUTH IS I DON'T REALLY KNOW MUCH ABOUT ESKIMOS OR INUITS EXCEPT THIS: IT'S EXTREMELY RARE TO FIND ONE WHO'S ANTI-FUR.

TUNDRA TIMES
ANOTHER FROZEN PROTESTER FOUND

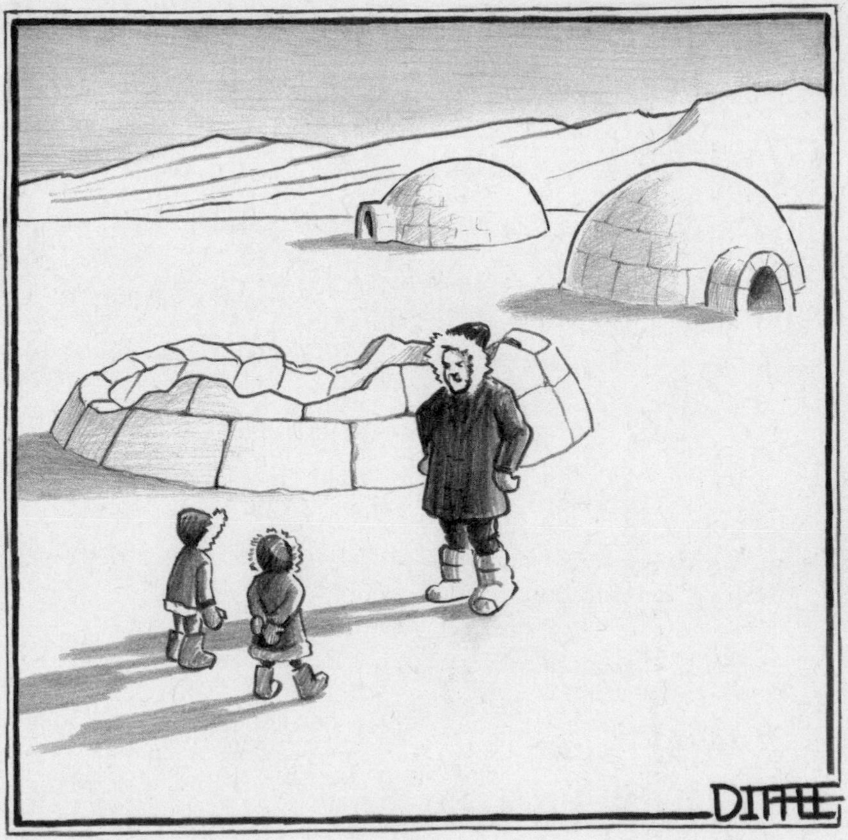
DIFFEE

"All right, which one of you fiddled with the thermostat?"

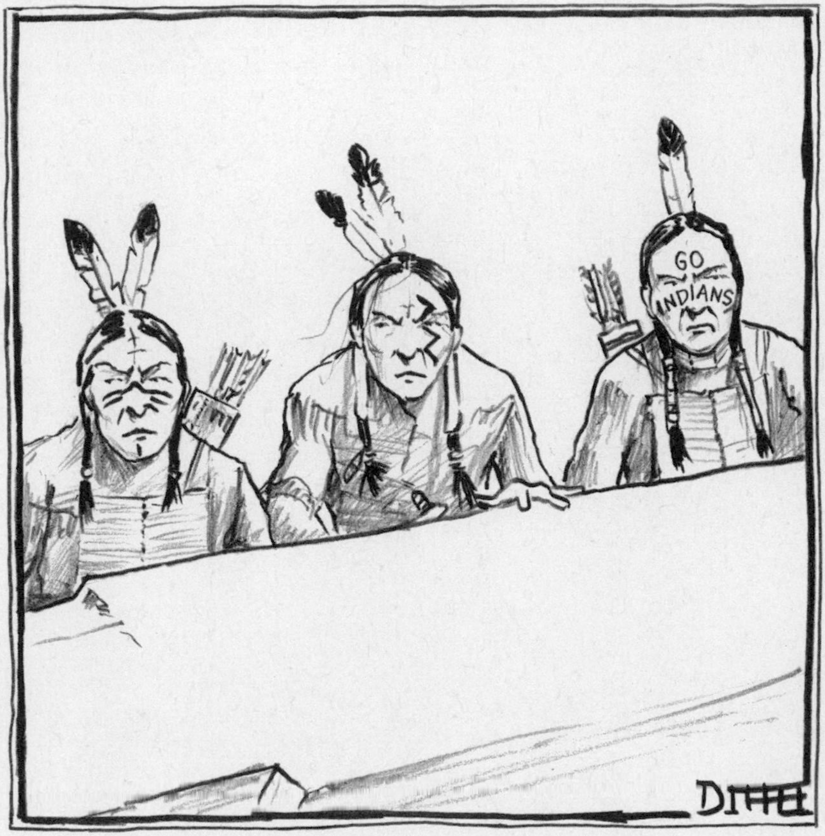
GO INDIANS
DIFFEE

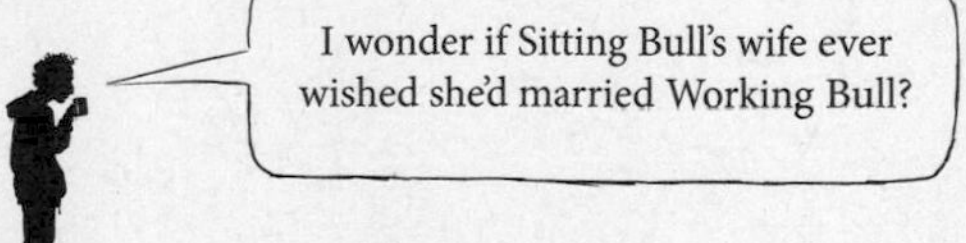
I wonder if Sitting Bull's wife ever wished she'd married Working Bull?

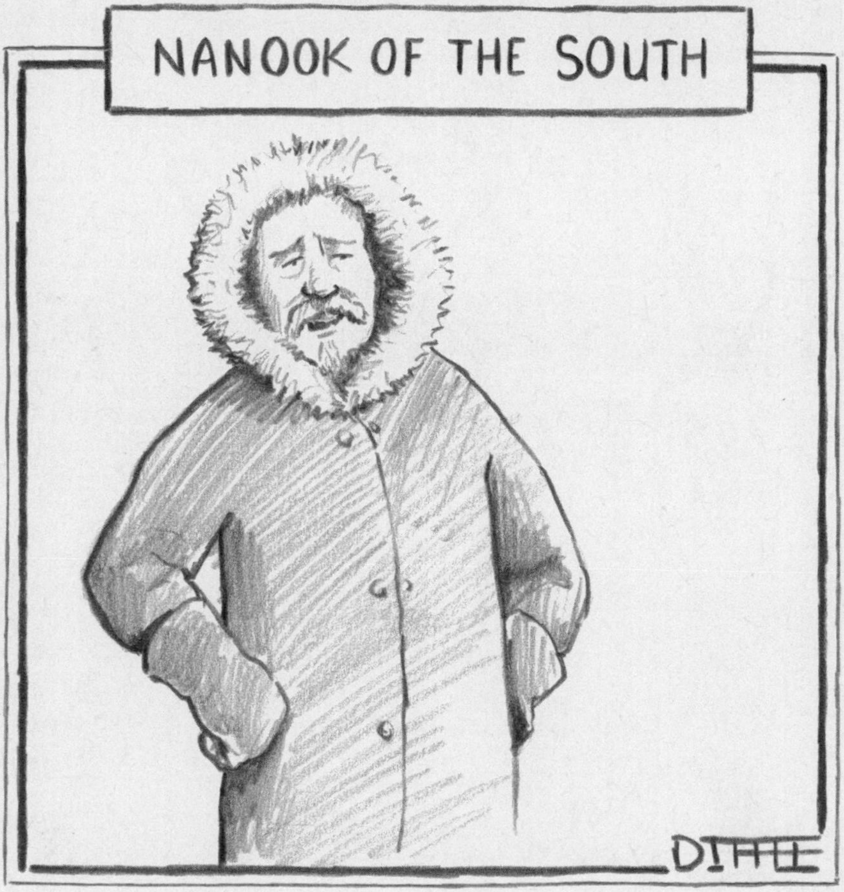
NANOOK OF THE SOUTH
DIFFEE

"I have over a hundred words for black people."

SLED DOGS

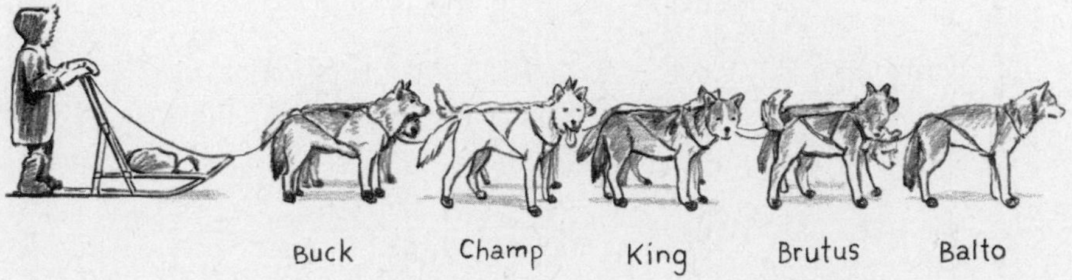
Buck
Champ
King
Brutus
Balto

SLED PUGS

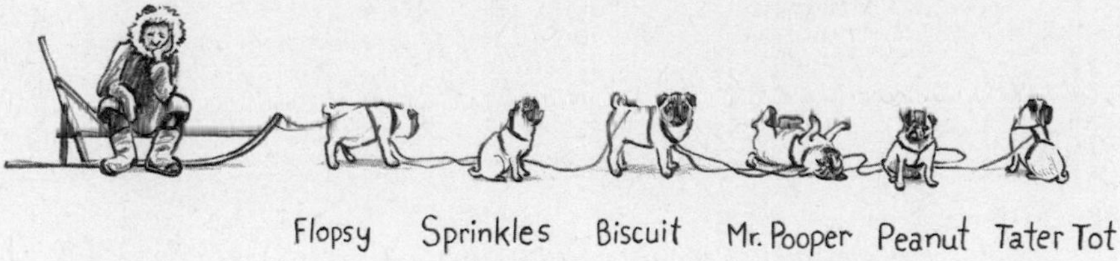
Flopsy
Sprinkles
Biscuit
Mr. Pooper
Peanut
Tater Tot

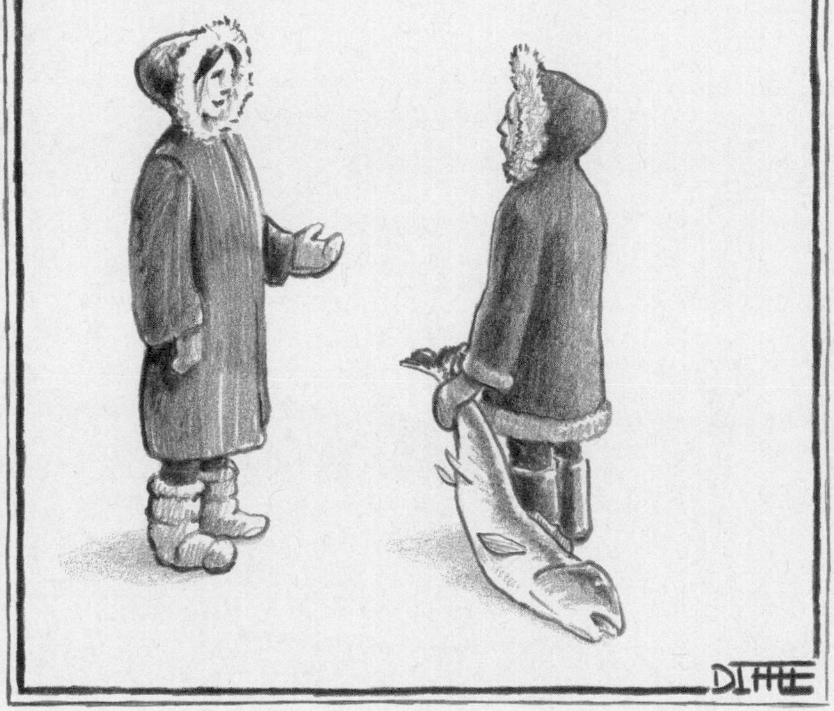
DIFFEE

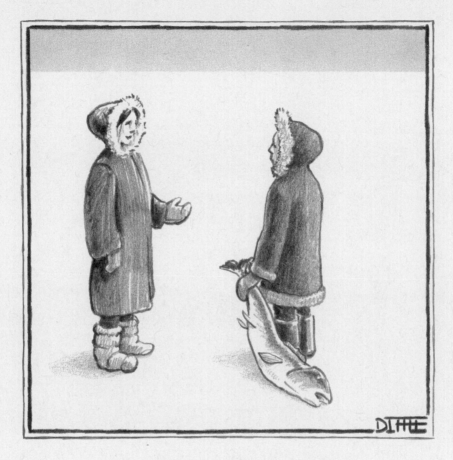

"I can still fit into my high school kayak."

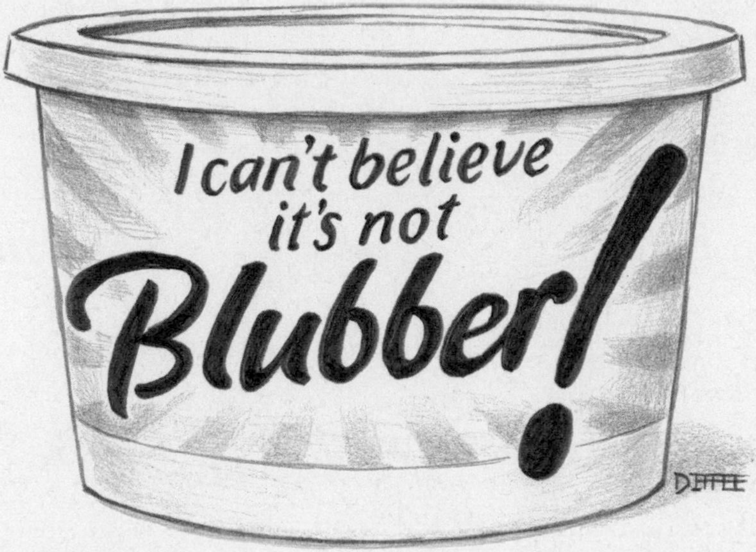
I can't believe it's not Blubber!

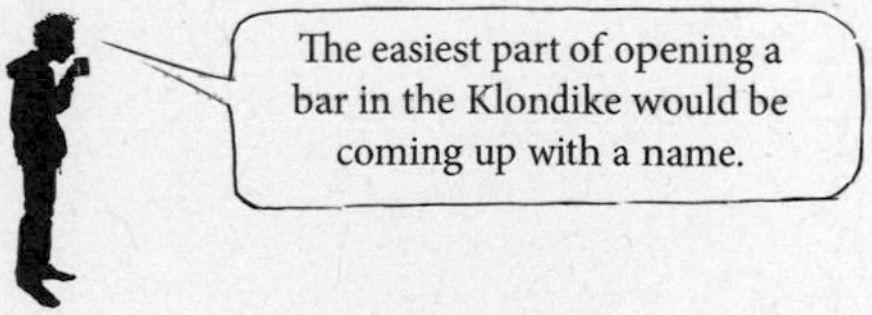
The easiest part of opening a bar in the Klondike would be coming up with a name.

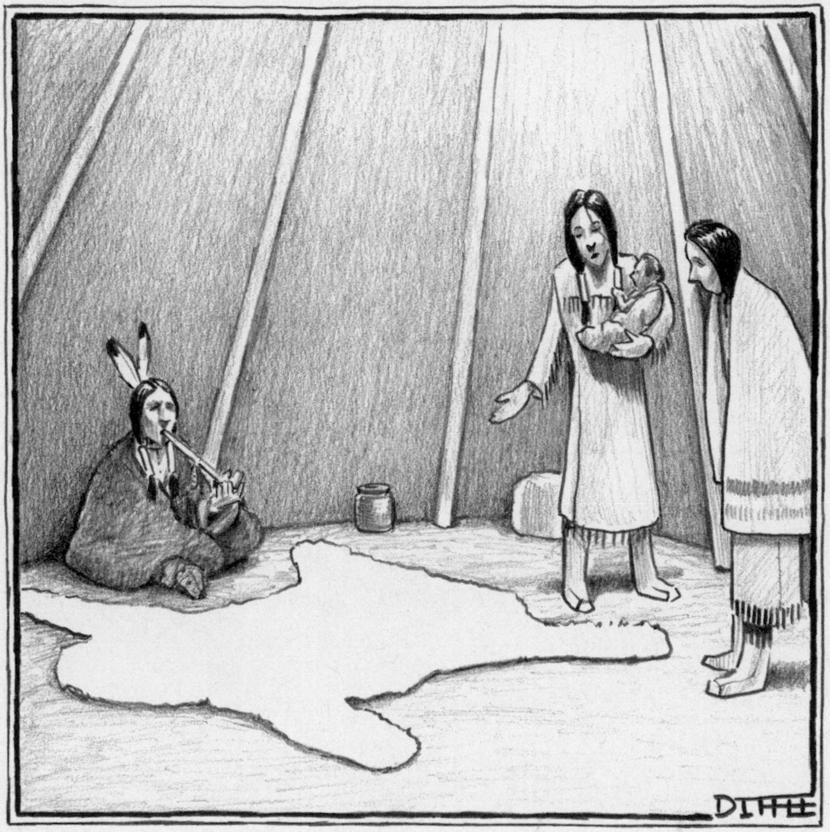
DITTLE

"The white buffalo protects us from evil spirits and brings good fortune in the harvest, but it's almost impossible to keep clean."

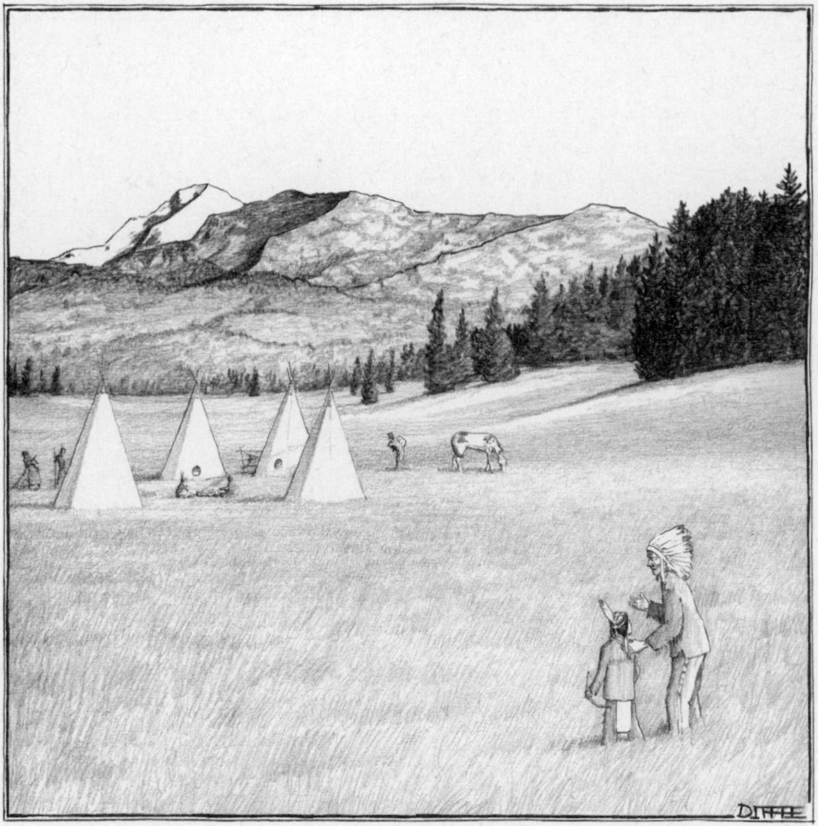
DIFFEE

"I remember when all this was completely undeveloped."

"You keep saying 'ice fishing' like there's some other kind."

"*Watch out for that one. They call her Dances With Crabs.*"

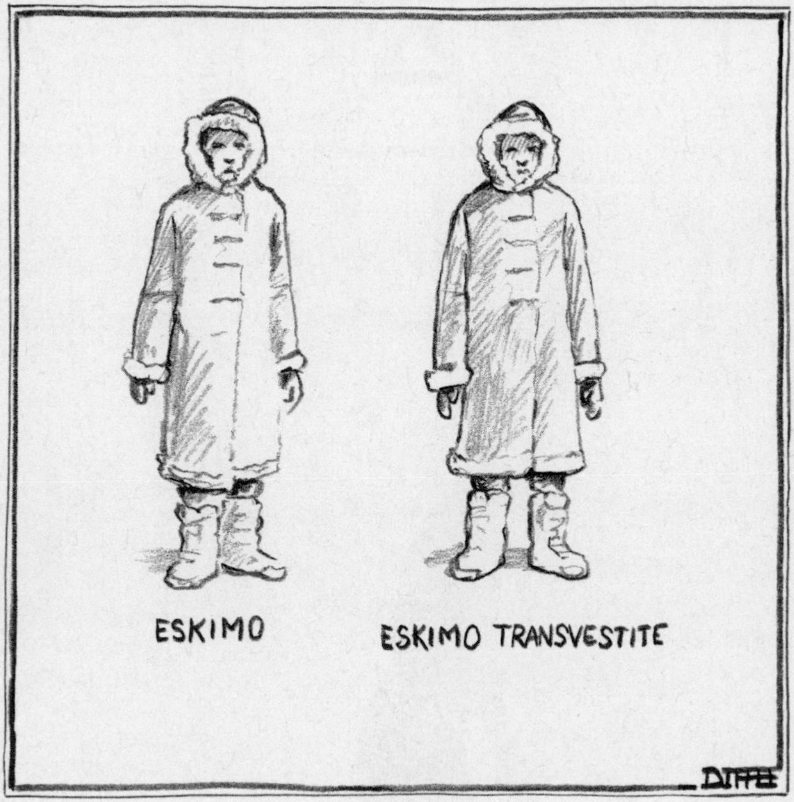
ESKIMO
ESKIMO TRANSVESTITE
DIFFEE

CHAPTER NINE: FOR SMART ATTRACTIVE PEOPLE WHO ENJOY FOOD

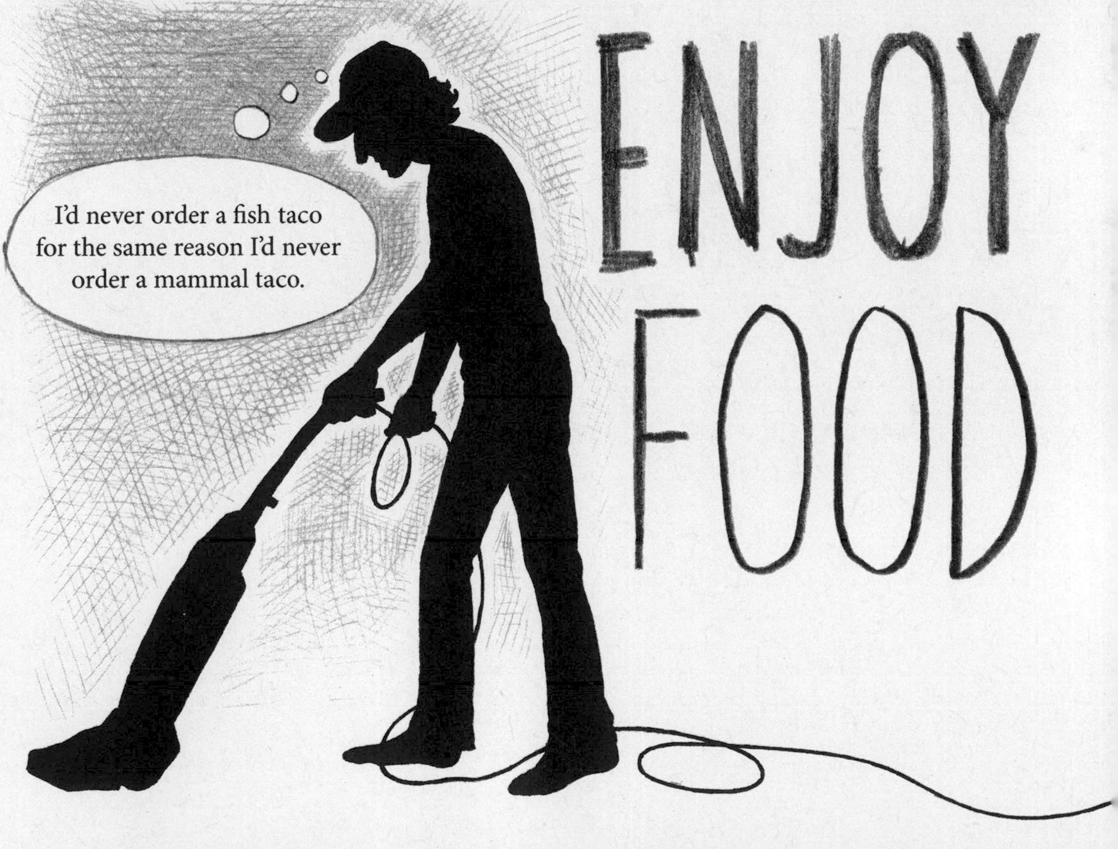
I'd never order a fish taco for the same reason I'd never order a mammal taco.

I ENJOY EATING AND ONE OF MY FAVORITE THINGS TO EAT IS FOOD BUT I DON'T CALL MYSELF A "FOODIE." IT JUST SEEMS SILLY TO USE THAT TERM WHEN YOUR FAVORITE FOODS COME ON STICKS OR IN BUCKETS. ACTUALLY, IT SEEMS SILLY ALWAYS. DO WE REALLY NEED A WORD FOR PEOPLE WHO LIKE FOOD? WHO DOESN'T? AND WHAT DO WE CALL THEM? STARVIES? AND I DON'T THINK IT'S FOOD EXACTLY THAT FOODIES LIKE ANYWAY. I THINK IT'S FOOD FADS. SO REALLY WE SHOULD CALL THEM "FOOD FADDIES."

So, Charles tells me you're a bookie. Fiction or nonfiction?

FOOD FADS THROUGH HISTORY

Gruel	Hard Tack	Figgy Pudding	Pemmican	Jell-O with stuff in it
1750		1800s	1970s	

SPEAKING OF CALLING THINGS THINGS, IS SUCCOTASH
THE BEST FOOD NAME EVER? IT'S JUST CORN AND
LIMA BEANS, BUT WHEN YOU CALL IT SUCCOTASH IT
SOUNDS PRETTY DANG EXCITING.
DEFINITELY THE BEST THING
THAT EVER HAPPENED TO
LIMA BEANS. (CLEARLY THE ART
GARFUNKEL OF THAT DUO.) I GUESS I JUST LIKE
THAT SOMEONE TOOK THE EFFORT TO GIVE IT A
GOOD NAME. UNLIKE SOME OTHER VEGGIE DISHES.
YEAH, I'M TALKING ABOUT YOU, PEAS AND CARROTS.
NOT A LOT OF CREATIVITY IN THAT NAME. IT WAS
PROBABLY THE SAME GUY WHO NAMED
THE MEATBALL.

I PUT THE
"SUCC" IN
SUCCOTASH!

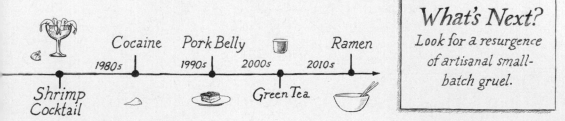

Shrimp
Cocktail   1980s   Pork Belly   2000s   2010s   Ramen
              Cocaine   1990s   Green Tea

What's Next?
Look for a resurgence
of artisanal small-
batch gruel.

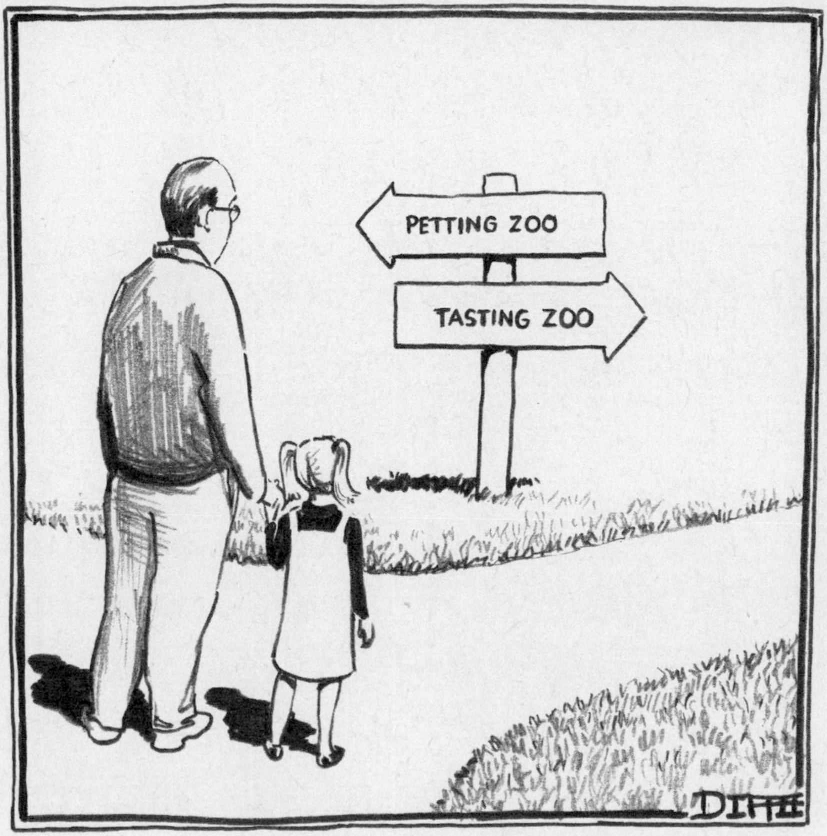
PETTING ZOO
TASTING ZOO
DIFFEE

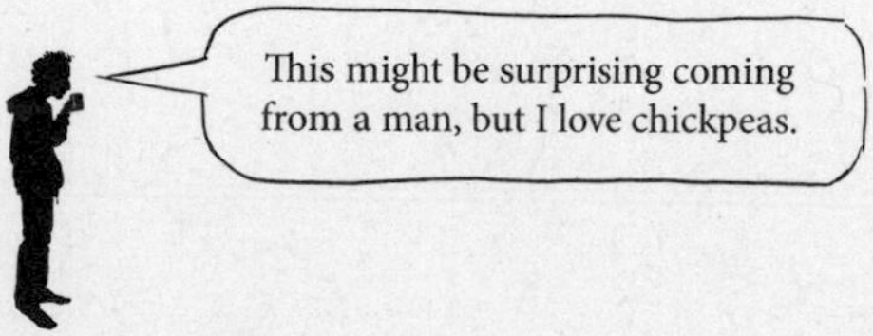
This might be surprising coming from a man, but I love chickpeas.

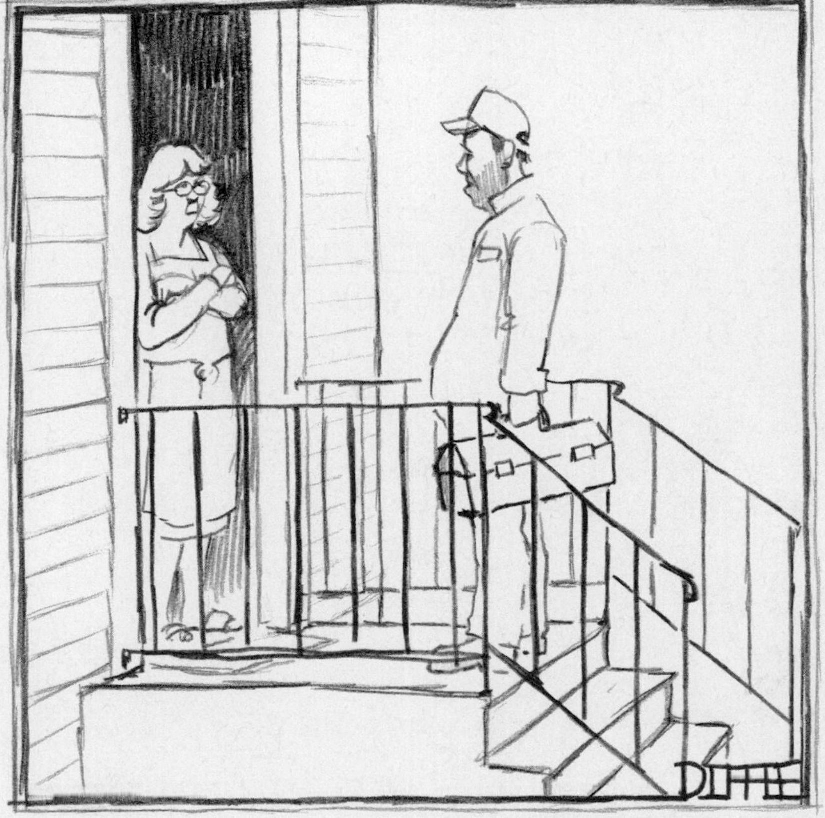
DIFFEE

"I'm here to fix the lasagna."

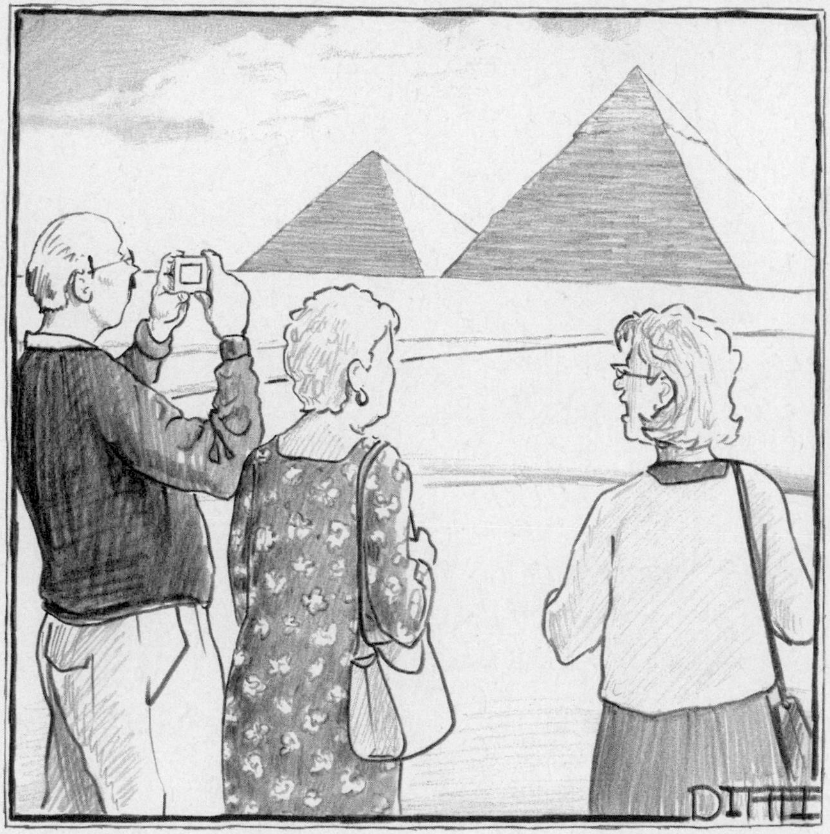
DIFFEE

"Yeah, but the one in Vegas has an endless shrimp buffet."

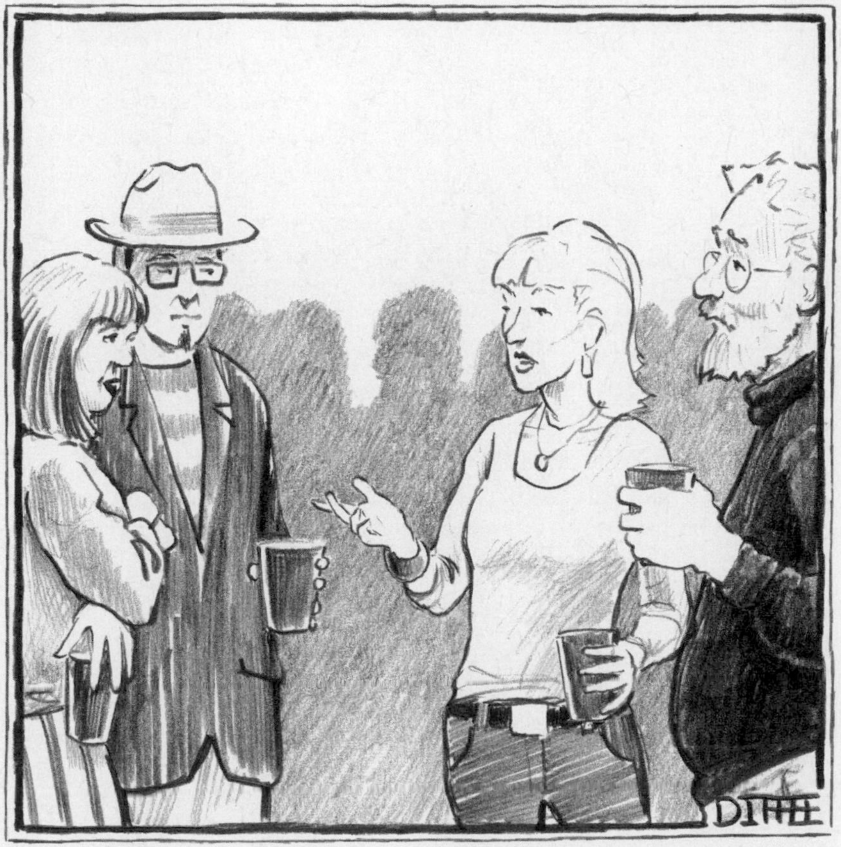
DIFFEE

"We tried a vegan Thanksgiving this year, but our family still showed up."

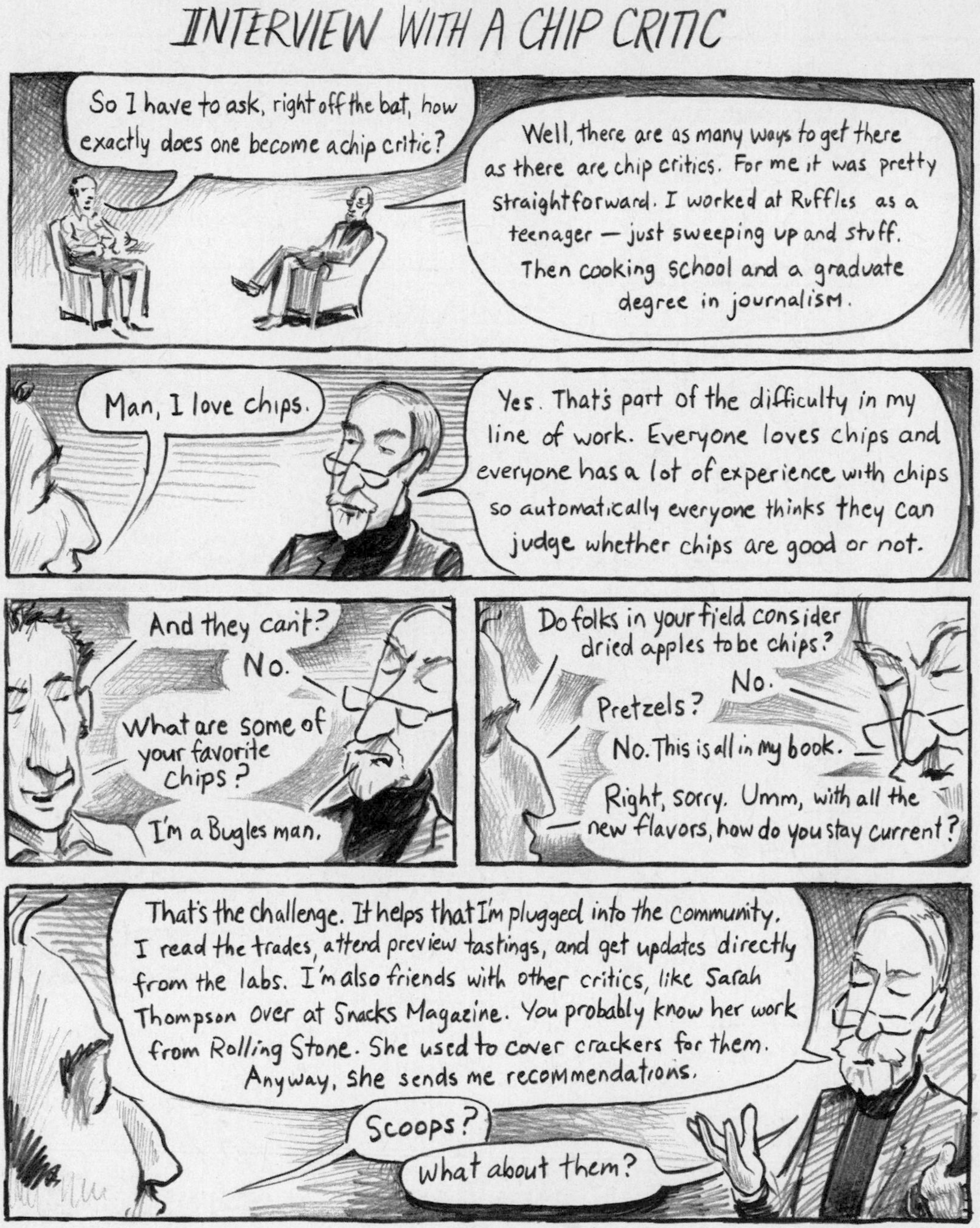
INTERVIEW WITH A CHIP CRITIC
So I have to ask, right off the bat, how exactly does one become a chip critic?
Well, there are as many ways to get there as there are chip critics. For me it was pretty straightforward. I worked at Ruffles as a teenager — just sweeping up and stuff. Then cooking school and a graduate degree in journalism.
Man, I love chips.
Yes. That's part of the difficulty in my line of work. Everyone loves chips and everyone has a lot of experience with chips so automatically everyone thinks they can judge whether chips are good or not.
And they can't?
No.
What are some of your favorite chips?
I'm a Bugles man.
Do folks in your field consider dried apples to be chips?
No.
Pretzels?
No. This is all in my book.
Right, sorry. Umm, with all the new flavors, how do you stay current?
That's the challenge. It helps that I'm plugged into the community. I read the trades, attend preview tastings, and get updates directly from the labs. I'm also friends with other critics, like Sarah Thompson over at Snacks Magazine. You probably know her work from Rolling Stone. She used to cover crackers for them. Anyway, she sends me recommendations.
Scoops?
What about them?

No, I was just... Never mind. Go on.

That's it really. I just stay plugged in and I network at the conventions. Next week I'll be at The Chiposium in Grand Rapids and then there's Snackworld Tokyo, Chipapalooza, and of course Munching Man.

What's one thing people can do to assure they're choosing good chips?

I'll say this, be wary of strong complex flavors that don't occur in nature. that's often used to mask an inferior pulp.

"Pulp" sounds kinda gross.

It is kinda.

What's the worst chip you ever had?

I once tried a potato-corn hybrid chip flavored with cinnamon. That was pretty bad. There was also a very short-lived offering from Nabisco called Flounder & Cabbage Crunchies. I wrote about that one. It was a terrible blunder and is no longer available except in some sectors of the Inuit community.

One last question: why is there always one weird green chip in every bag of potato chips?

You know what, we still don't know. And that's exactly the kind of mystery that keeps me working in the chip industry. As much as we think we know, there's always so much more to learn.

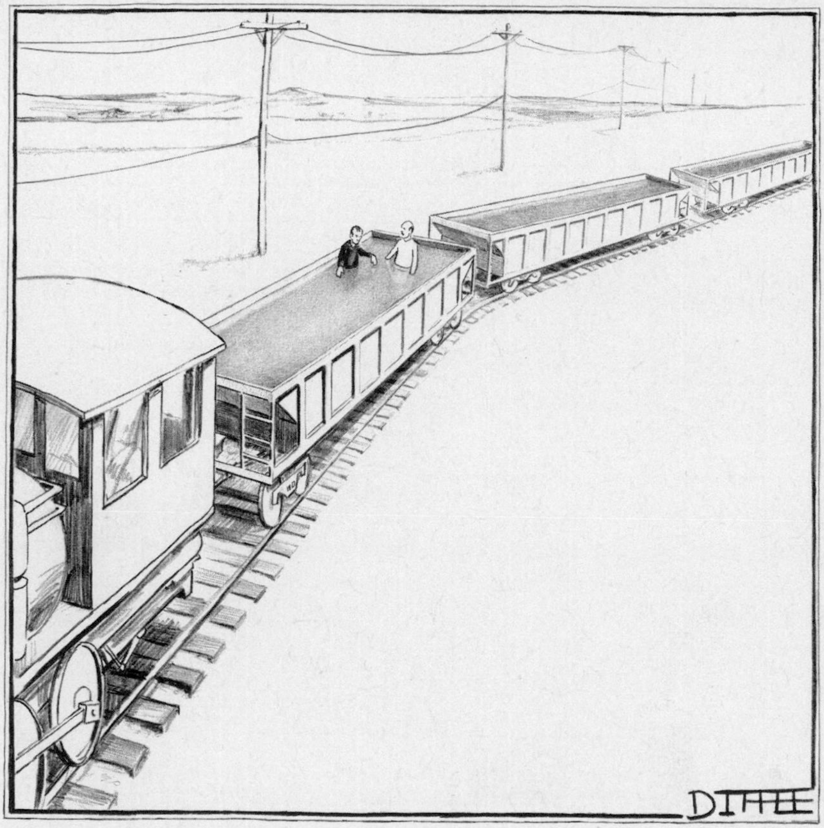
DIFFEE

"Till now I always thought of the gravy train as a good thing."

"Careful, these plates are extremely dirty."

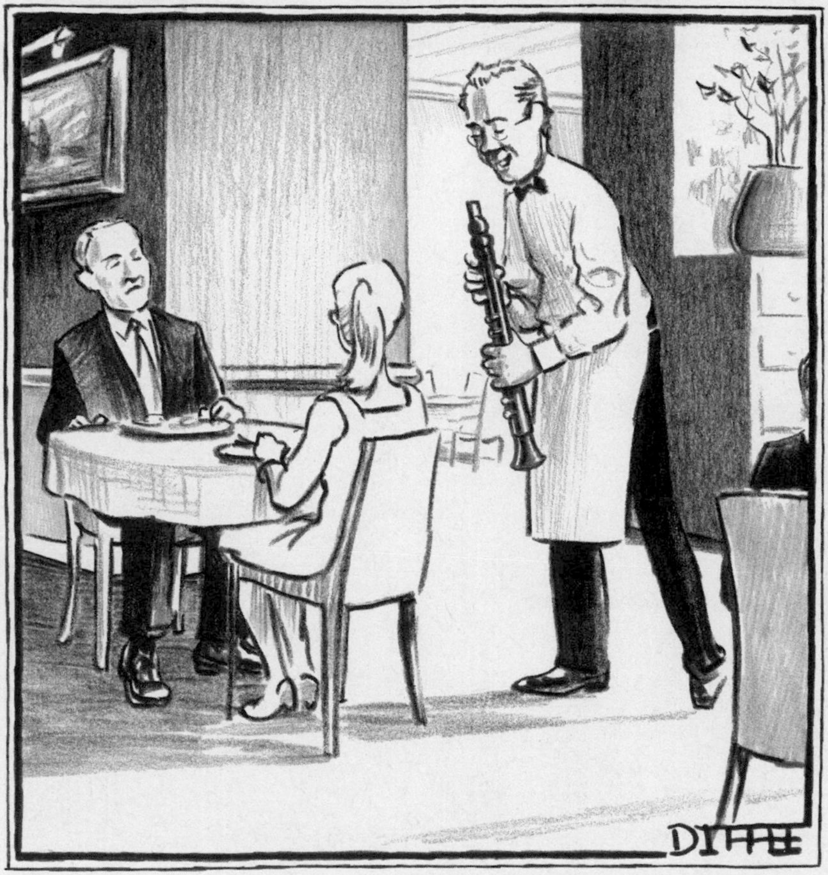
DIFFEE

"Would you care for some fresh-ground pepper and/or a clarinet solo?"

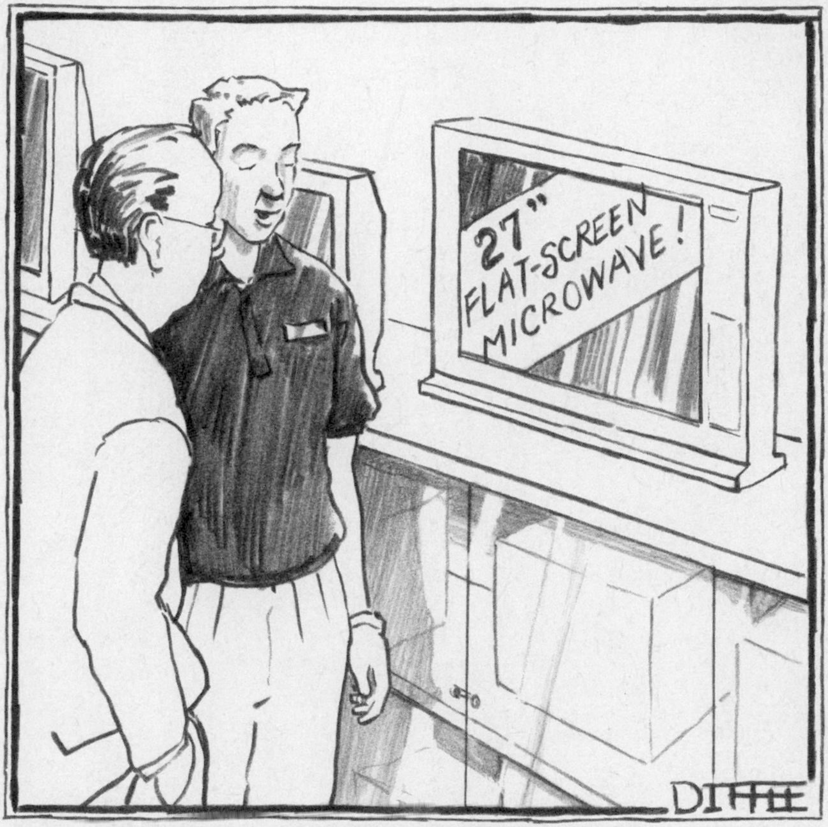
27"
FLAT-SCREEN
MICROWAVE!
DIFFEE

"It's great for quesadillas."

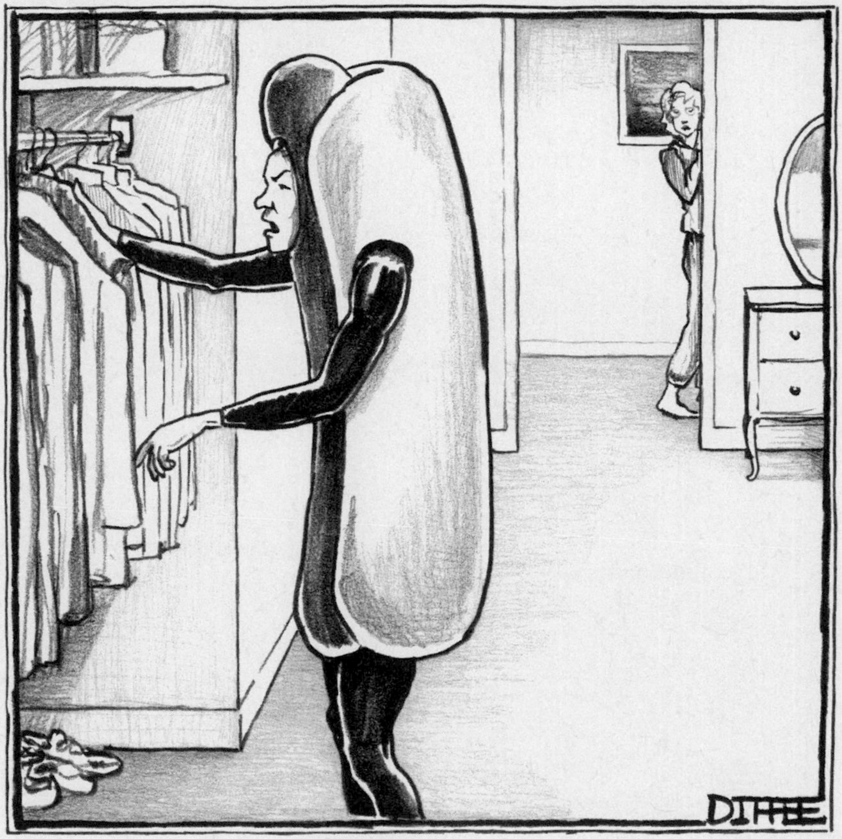
DIFFEE

"Honey, have you seen my onions?"

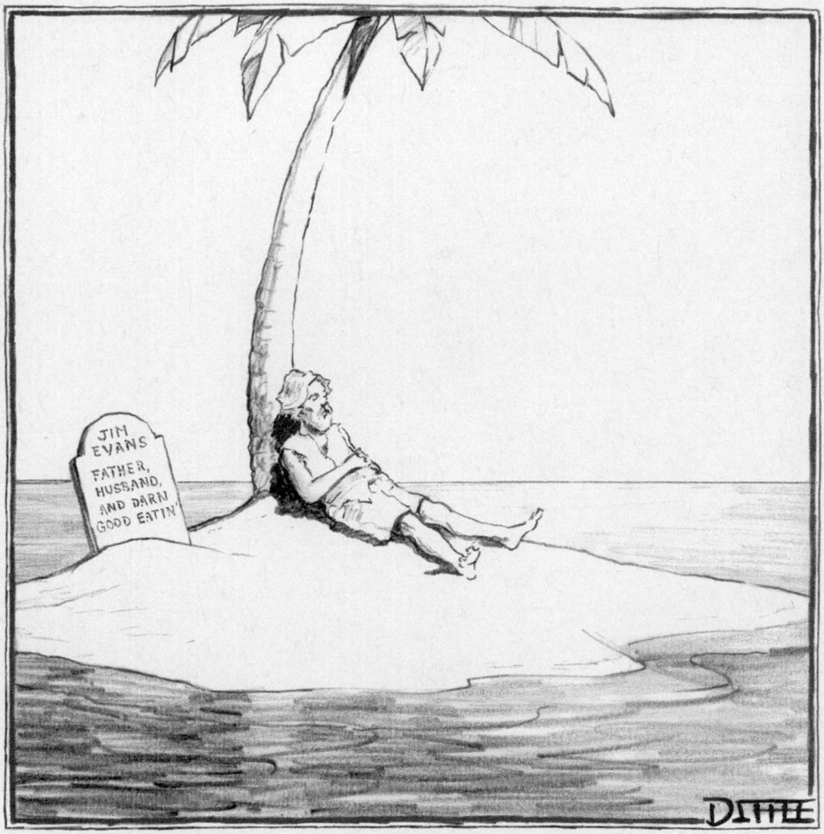
JIM EVANS
FATHER, HUSBAND, AND DARN GOOD EATIN'

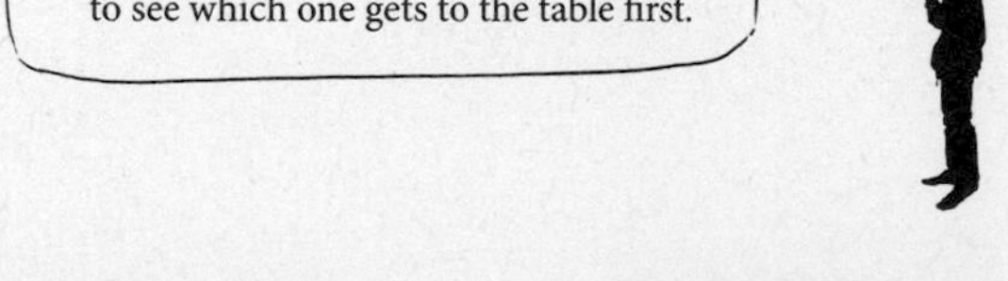
Sometimes at restaurants, I like to order the rabbit stew *and* the turtle soup just to see which one gets to the table first.

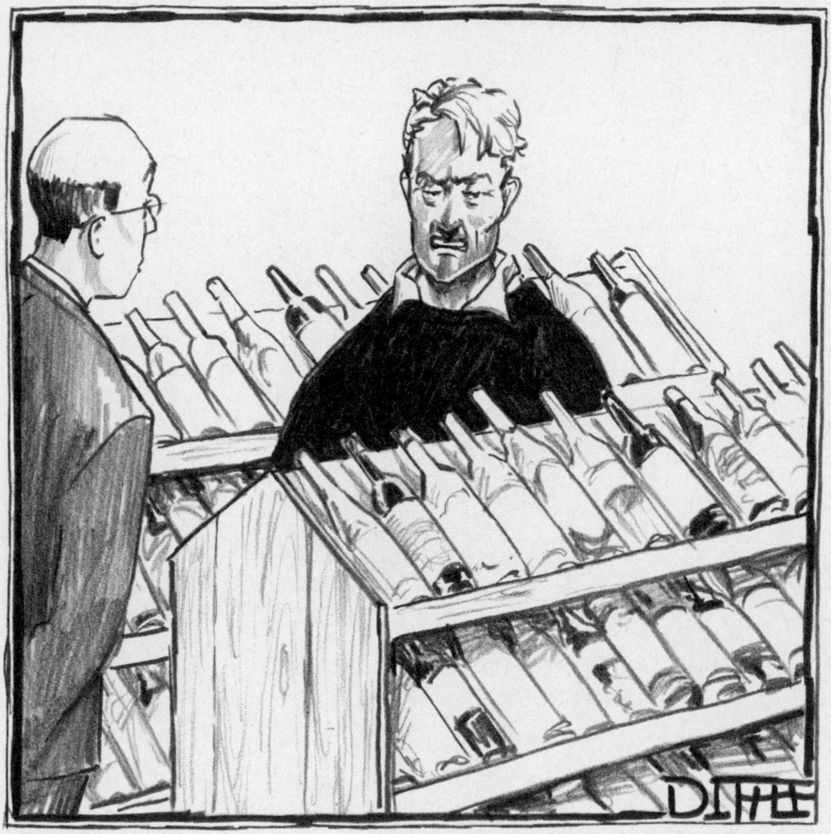
DITTE

"What wine goes best with vodka?"

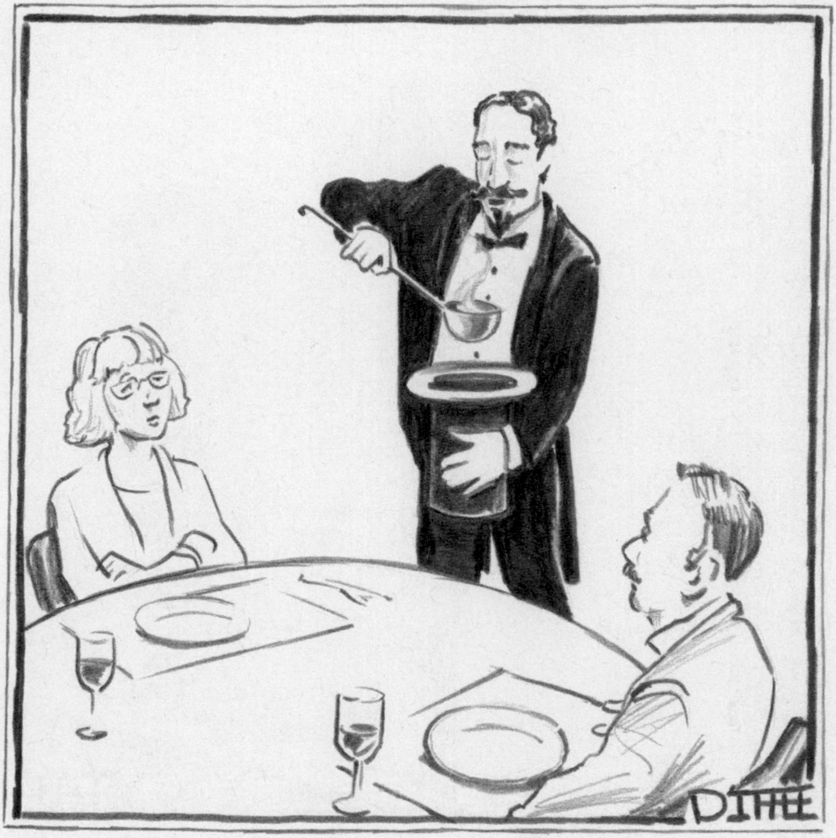
DIFFEE

"And PRESTO, rabbit stew!"

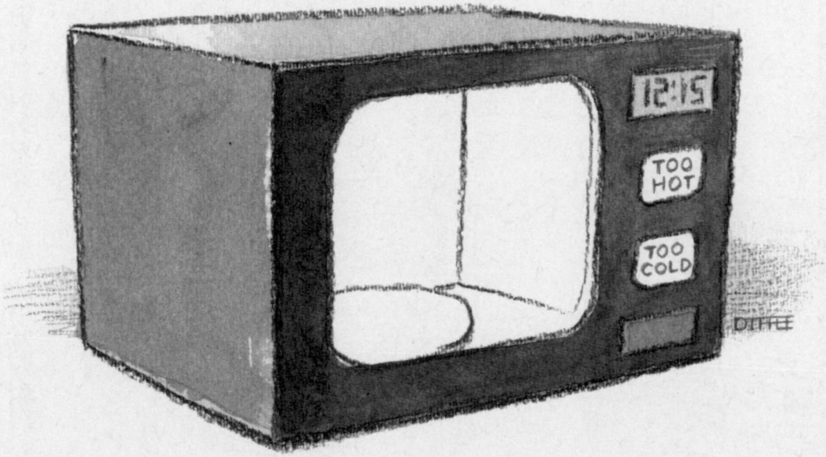
12:15
TOO HOT
TOO COLD

MY MICROWAVE

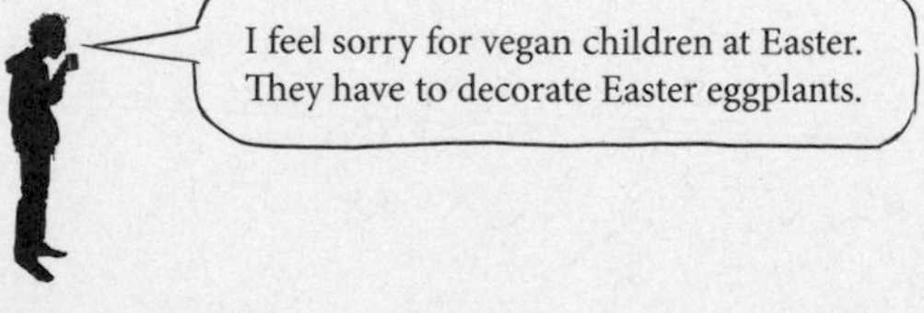
I feel sorry for vegan children at Easter. They have to decorate Easter eggplants.

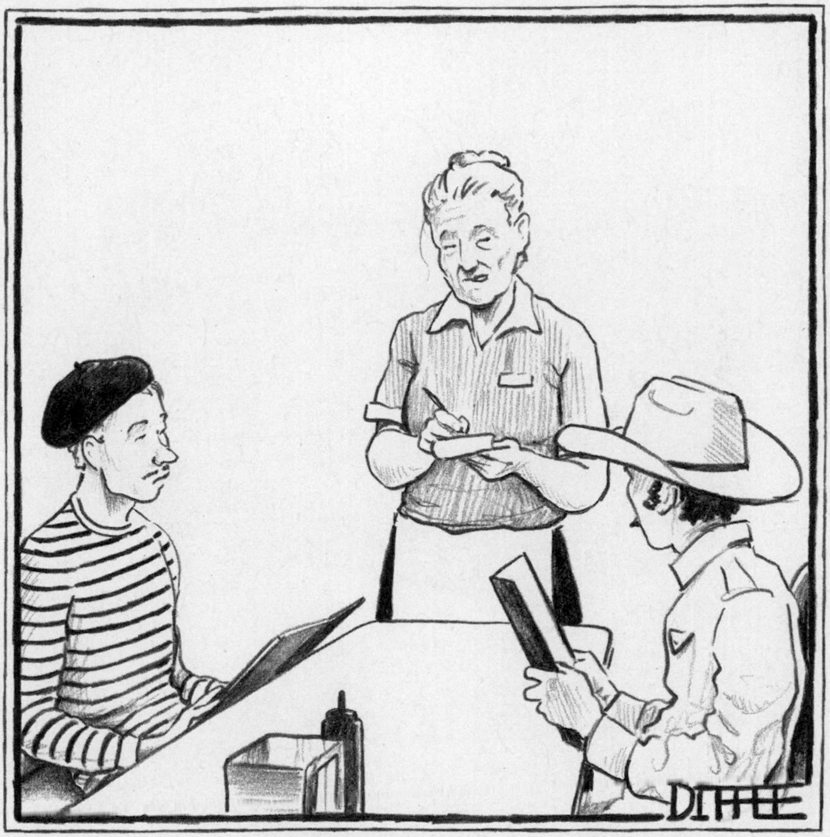
DIFFEE

"Let me guess . . . You want French and you want Ranch."

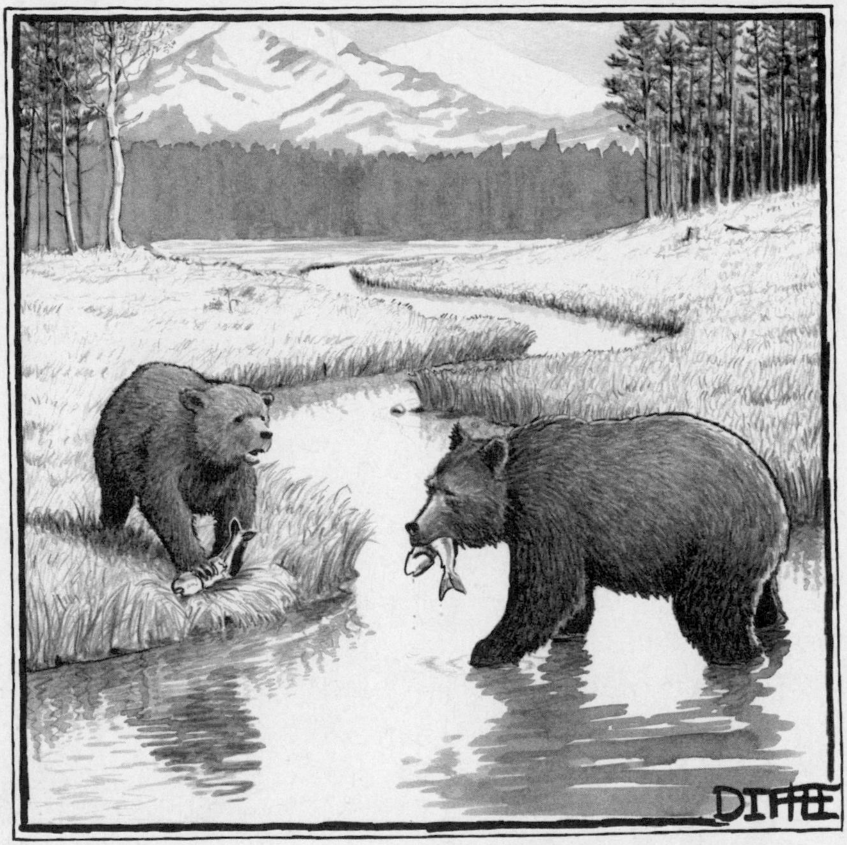
DIFFEE

"It could use some wasabi."

CHAPTER TEN

FOR SMART ATTRACTIVE Sexy PEOPLE

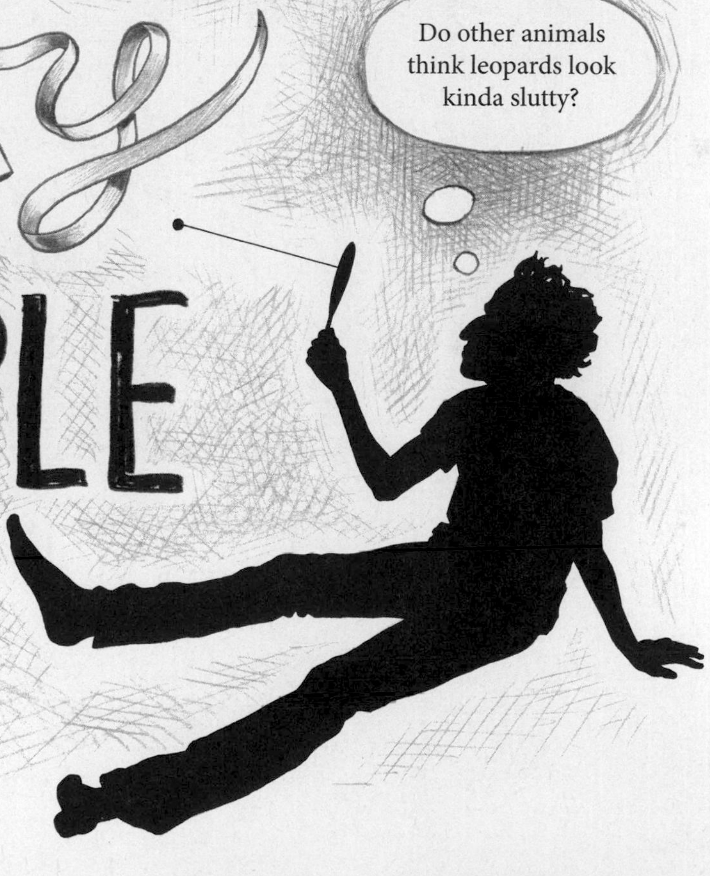
Do other animals think leopards look kinda slutty?

SINCE WHEN DID STRIP CLUBS BECOME ALL ABOUT SEX? IT'S GOTTEN SO YOU CAN'T EVEN TAKE YOUR KIDS ANYMORE, AND WHEN YOU DO, YOU FEEL LIKE SOME KIND OF SEX EDUCATION TEACHER.

Okay, kids, a stripper is a person who takes their clothes off for drug money.
What's a burlesque dancer?
That's a stripper who went to art school.

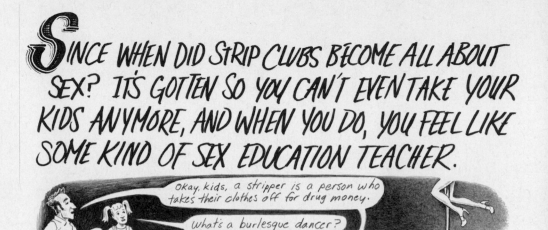

WHEN I WAS A KID I WASN'T SEX EDUCATED AT ALL. I LEARNED THINGS THE OLD-FASHIONED WAY BY RIDING THE BUS TO ELEMENTARY SCHOOL. FUNNY THING IS I COULD PROBABLY STILL LEARN SOME THINGS THAT WAY. THESE KIDS THESE DAYS WITH THEIR HOOKUPS AND THEIR SEXTING. WHEN I WAS A KID, WE WERE ALL EQUALLY UNINFORMED. THERE WAS A BOY NAMED TERRY WHO TOLD US,

BABIES HAPPEN WHEN A LADY HAS TOO MANY HEADACHES.

HOW WRONG CAN YOU BE, RIGHT? THE TRUTH IS BABIES COME FROM WHEN YOU <u>DON'T</u> HAVE ENOUGH HEADACHES AND HEADACHES COME FROM WHEN YOU HAVE TOO MANY BABIES. AM I RIGHT, MOMS? WAIT, IS MY MOM GONNA READ THIS?

FORGET WHAT I SAID EARLIER ABOUT STRIP CLUBS. I MEANT STRIP MALLS.

THE THING ABOUT SEXY IS IT'S NOT AN EXACT SCIENCE. WHAT ONE PERSON SEES AS SEXY ANOTHER MIGHT SEE AS GROSS OR TRESPASSING. TAKE FISHNET STOCKINGS. PRETTY SEXY, BUT MAYBE NOT IF YOU'RE A FISHERMAN. IT MIGHT JUST REMIND YOU OF WORK. OR TAKE NAKEDNESS. YOU'D THINK THAT NAKEDNESS WOULD ALWAYS BE SEXY, RIGHT? BUT IT DEPENDS. IMAGINE MICHAEL MOORE NAKED OR A PERSON WITH LEPROSY. THINK ABOUT MICHAEL MOORE WITH LEPROSY NAKED. I SHOULD DRAW THAT. OH, GOOD, I'M OUT OF ROOM!

"And will he know what this is regarding?"

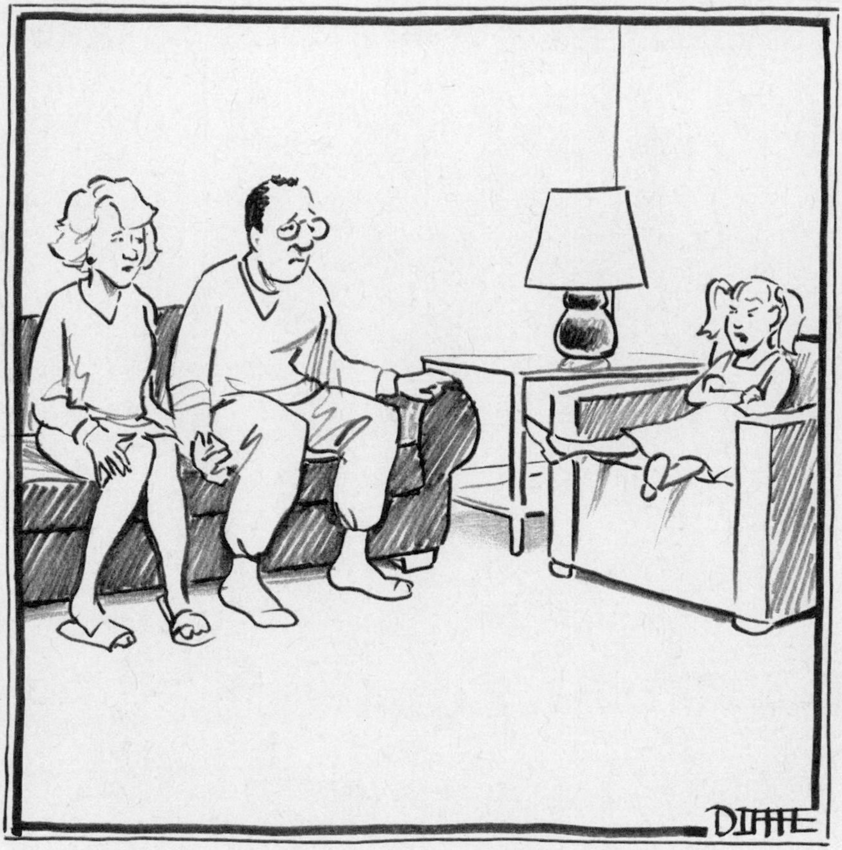
DIFFEE

"You said we were gonna talk about birds and bees.
Why all this sex talk?"

A WHIMSICAL EXCHANGE AMONGST GENTLEMEN

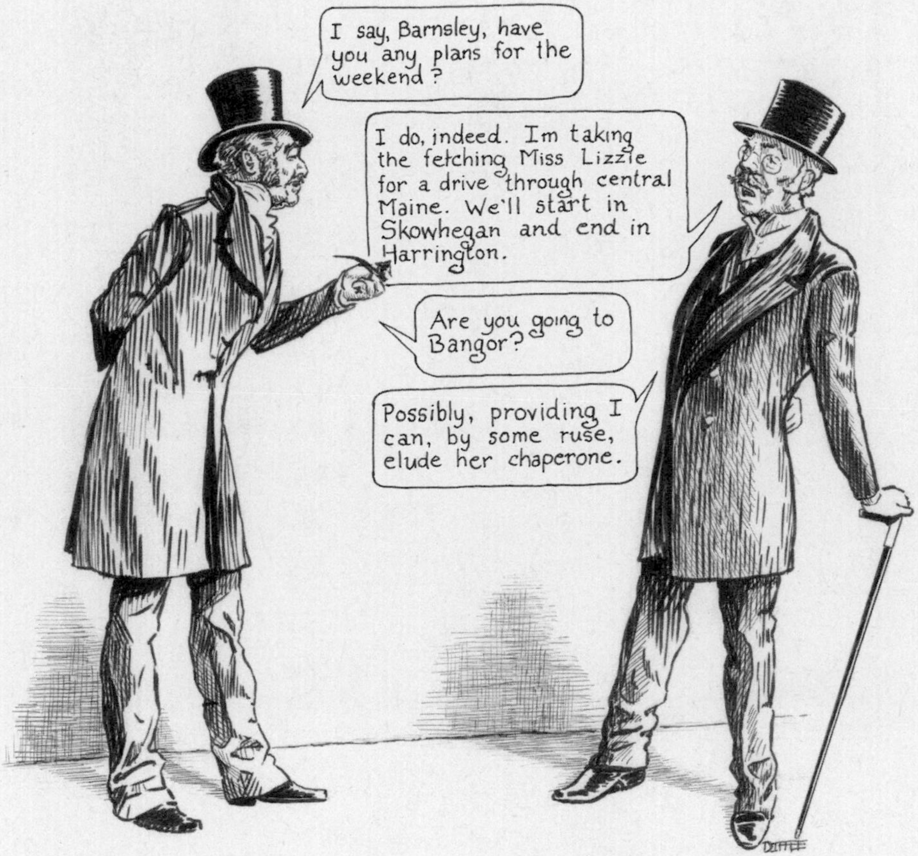
I say, Barnsley, have you any plans for the weekend?
I do, indeed. Im taking the fetching Miss Lizzie for a drive through central Maine. We'll start in Skowhegan and end in Harrington.
Are you going to Bangor?
Possibly, providing I can, by some ruse, elude her chaperone.

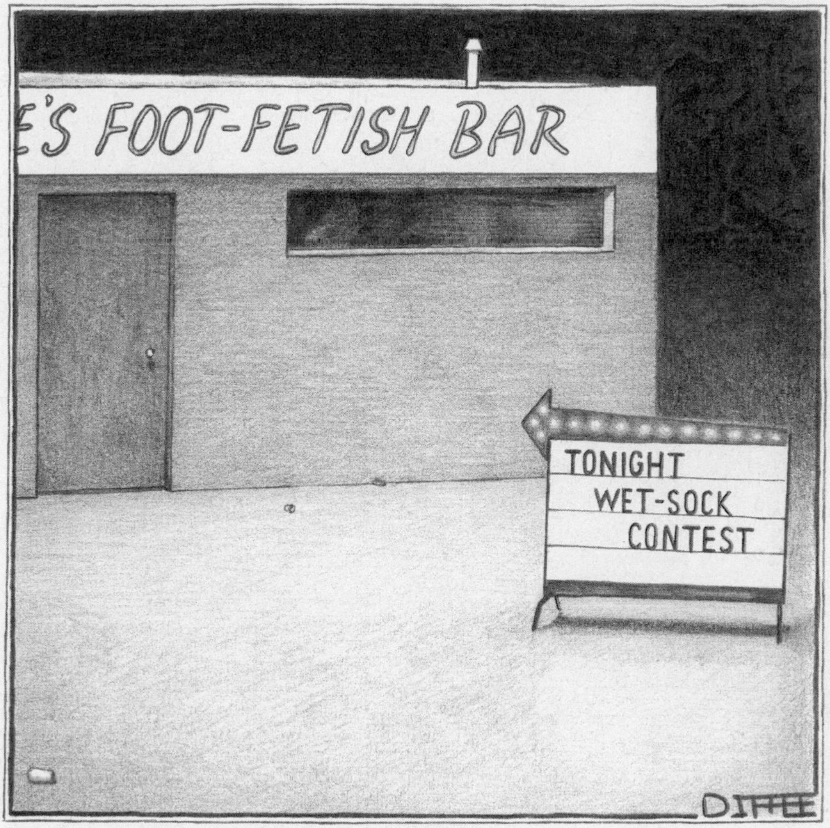
E'S FOOT-FETISH BAR
TONIGHT
WET-SOCK
CONTEST
DIFFEE

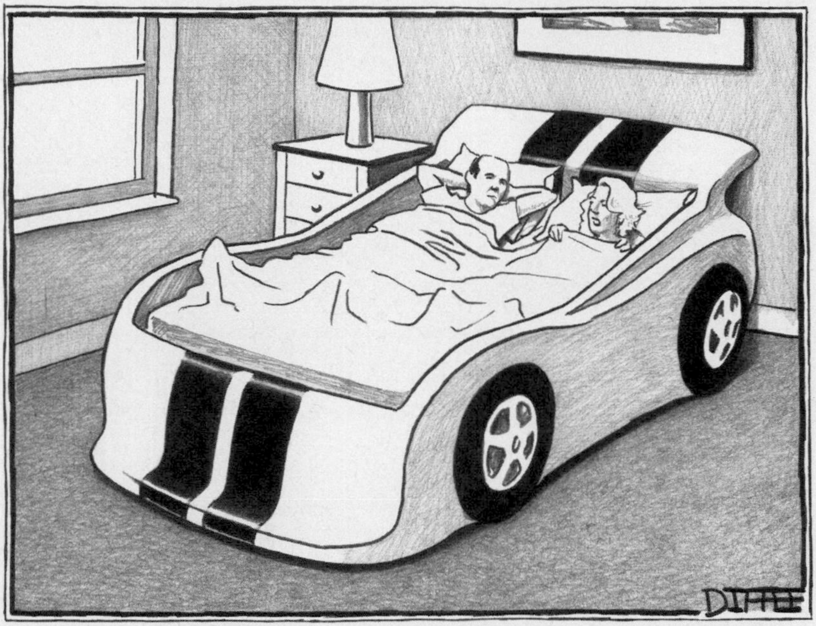
DIFFEE

"Would it kill you to ask for directions?"

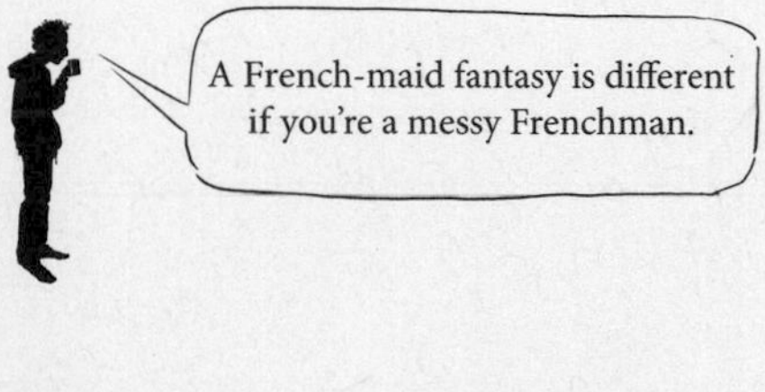
A French-maid fantasy is different
if you're a messy Frenchman.

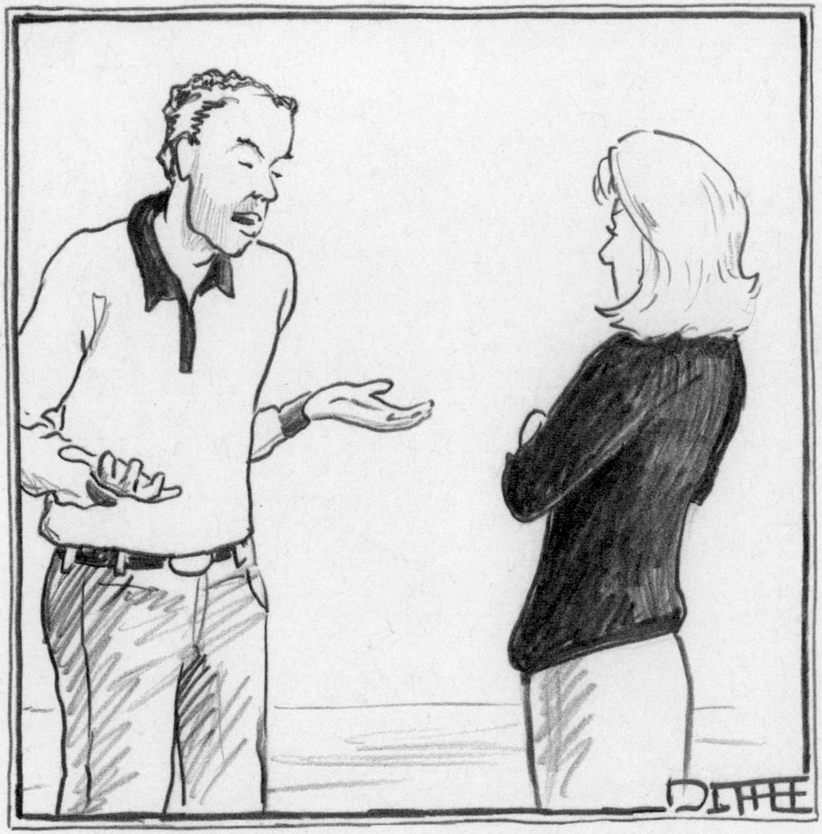
DIFFEE

"You say sex pervert. I say horse enthusiast."

ALTERNATIVES TO
SEX, DRUGS, and ROCK'N'ROLL

THE IDEA OF SEX, SHERRY, AND ATONAL JAZZ

PROCREATION, MILK, AND HYMNS

NOTHINGNESS, NOTHINGNESS, AND TIBETAN THROAT SINGING

ANIMAL HUSBANDRY, CORN LIQUOR, AND BLUEGRASS

HOPELESS NECROMANTIC

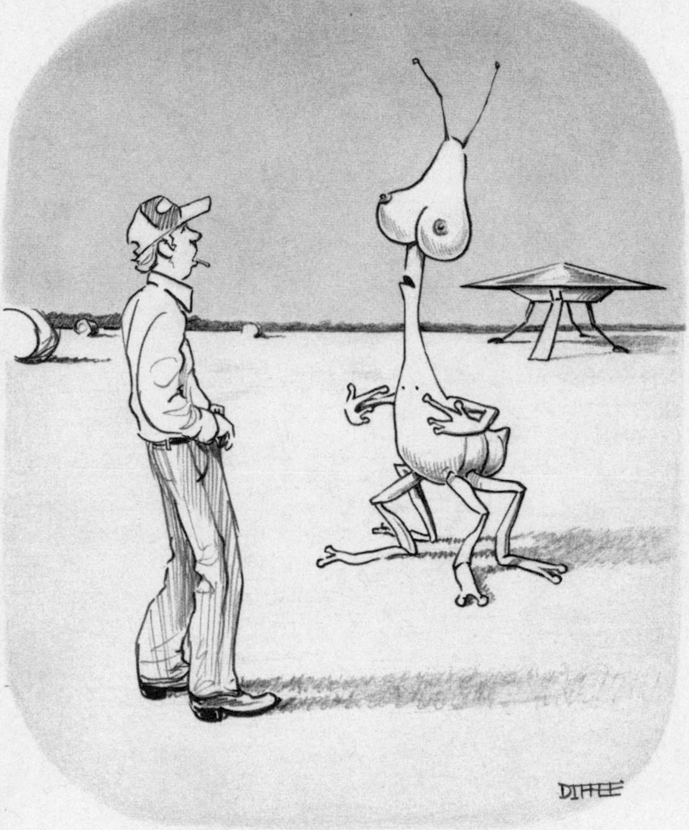
DIFFEE

"Hey, Buddy, my eyes are down here."

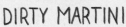

MARTINI   DIRTY MARTINI   REALLY DIRTY
MARTINI

"CHASTITY BELT"

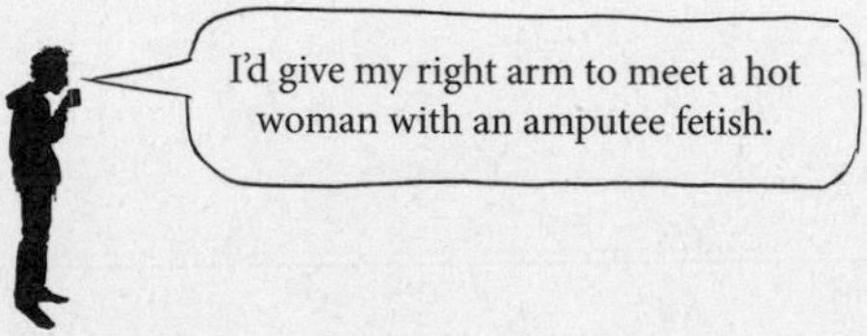

I'd give my right arm to meet a hot woman with an amputee fetish.

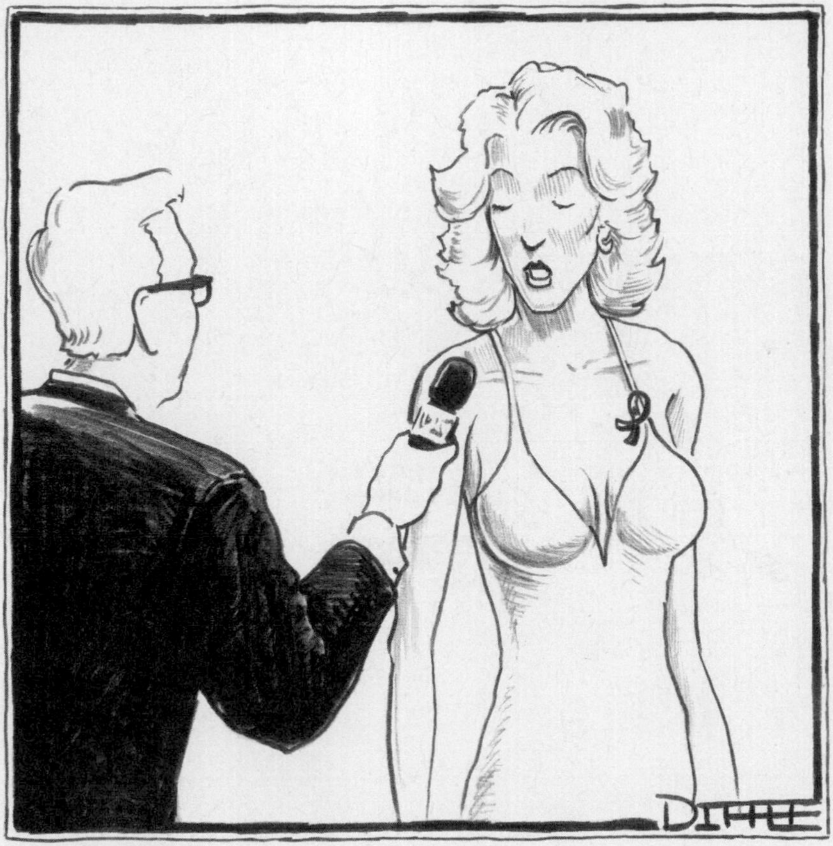
DIFFEE

"I'm wearing this ribbon to raise awareness of my breasts."

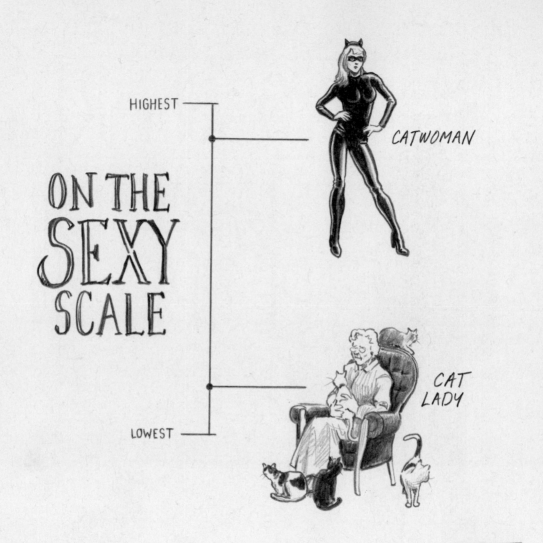

ON THE SEXY SCALE

HIGHEST

CATWOMAN

LOWEST

CAT LADY

DIFFEE

CHAPTER ELEVEN

FOR SMART ATTRACTIVE PEOPLE IN PRISON

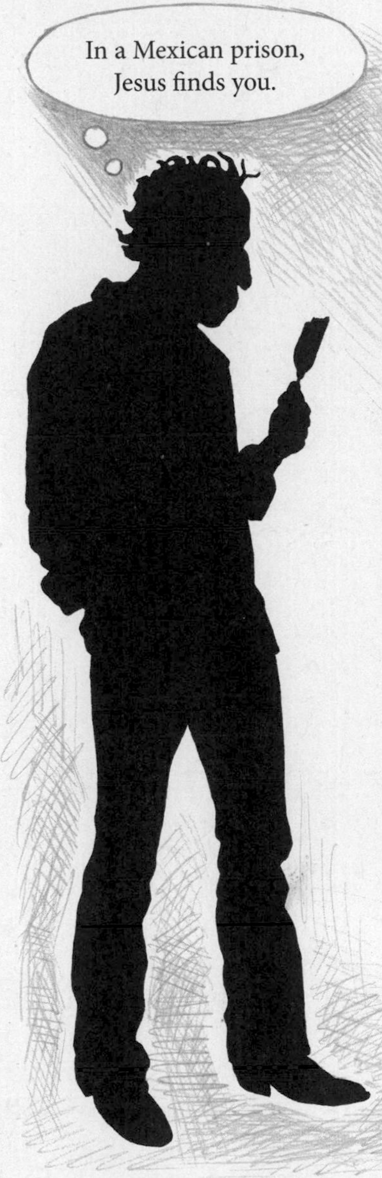
In a Mexican prison,
Jesus finds you.

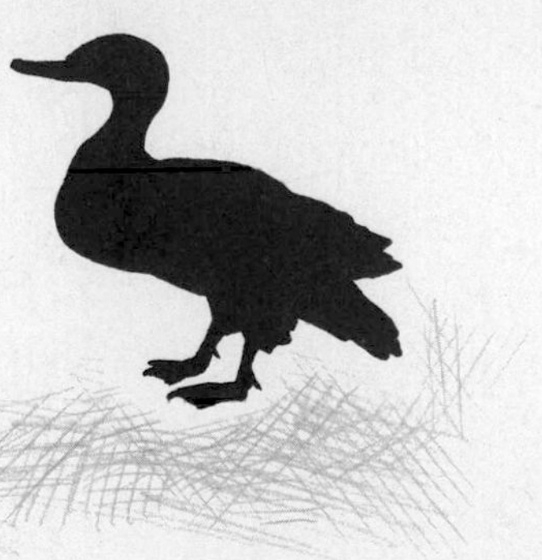

I'VE NEVER BEEN TO PRISON BUT I'VE BEEN ON A CRUISE SHIP. I KNOW THEY'RE NOT EXACTLY THE SAME, PRISON HAS LESS SHRIMP AND PROBABLY MORE SHOWER SHIVVINGS, BUT IT'S PRETTY CLOSE. YOU SPEND MOST OF YOUR TIME IN A TINY WINDOWLESS ROOM AND THE REST TRYING TO AVOID INTERACTION WITH MEMBERS OF THE ARYAN NATION.

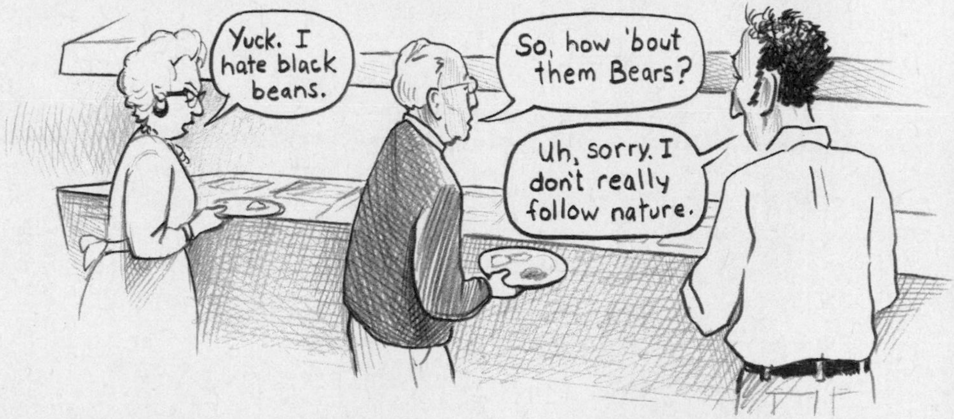
Yuck. I hate black beans.
So, how 'bout them Bears?
Uh, sorry. I don't really follow nature.

BUT PRISON IS BETTER THAN A CRUISE SHIP FOR ONE MAIN REASON:

FREE JUMPSUITS!

NO MORE TOUGH FASHION CHOICES. →

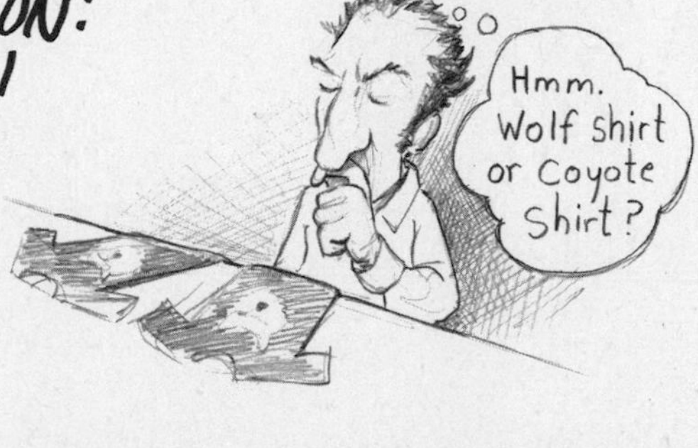
Hmm. Wolf shirt or Coyote Shirt?

UNFORTUNATELY, PRISON IS HARD TO BREAK INTO. THE BEST WAY IS TO DO SOME SORT OF CRIME.

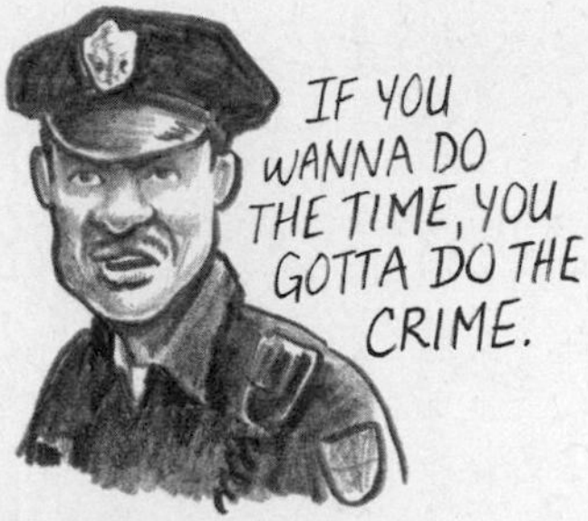
IF YOU WANNA DO THE TIME, YOU GOTTA DO THE CRIME.

I'M JUST NOT SURE WHAT KIND OF CRIME I SHOULD DO. SOMETHING I'M GOOD AT. MAYBE LOITERING. I CAN DO THAT ALL DAY. I JUST DON'T KNOW HOW MUCH PRISON TIME YOU GET AND IF IT WOULD BE MAXIMUM SECURITY OR NOT. I DEFINITELY WANT TO BE MAXIMUMLY SECURE. I GUESS I'LL JUST HAVE TO DO SOMETHING VIOLENT. THAT'S FINE I GUESS. I'M NOT ONE OF THOSE PEOPLE WHO THINK VIOLENCE IS NEVER THE ANSWER. SOMETIMES IT'S THE ONLY ANSWER, LIKE WHEN SOMEONE ASKS YOU, "HEY, WHAT'S NEVER THE ANSWER?"

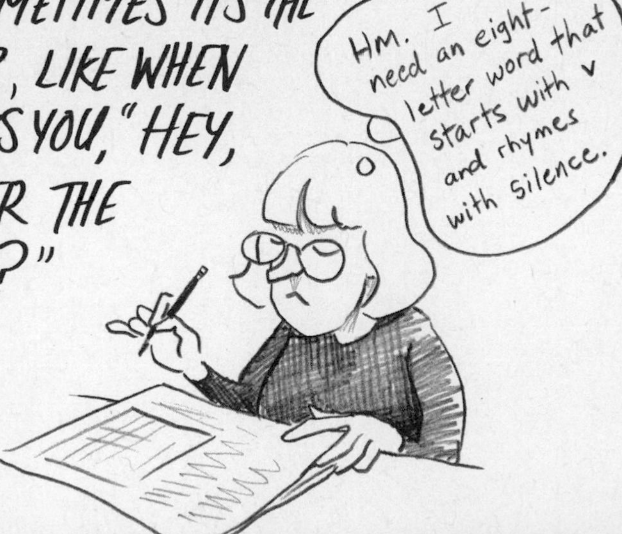
Hm. I need an eight-letter word that starts with v and rhymes with silence.

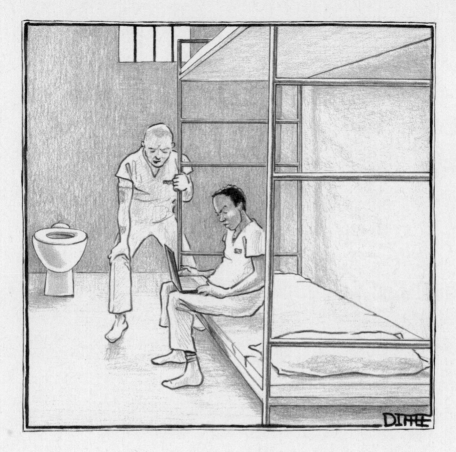

"What happens if you hit escape?"

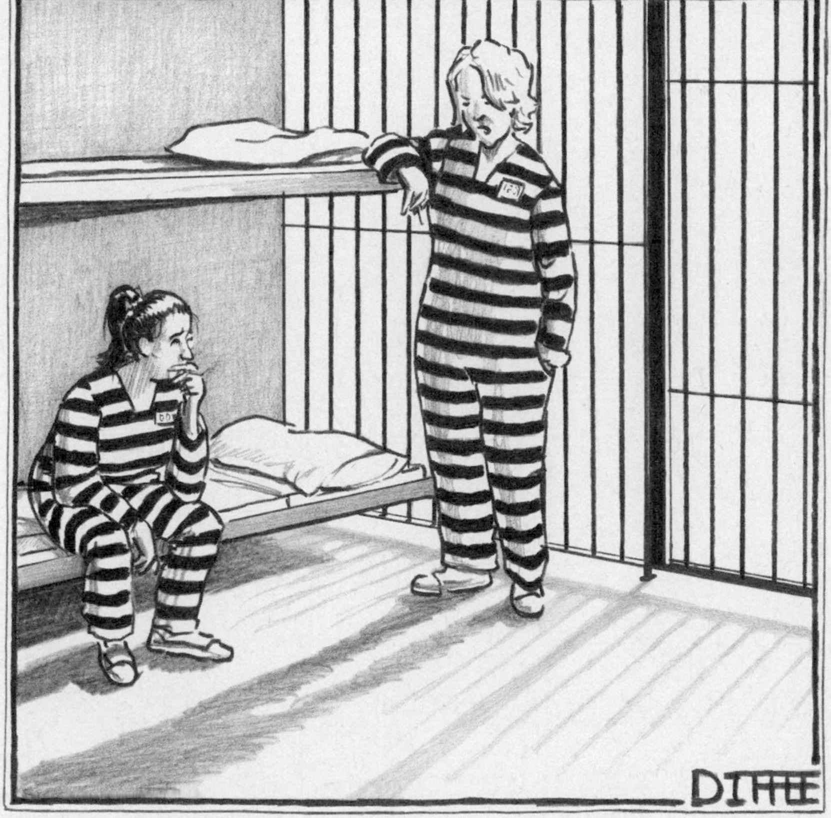
DIFFEE

"The worst part is the horizontal stripes."

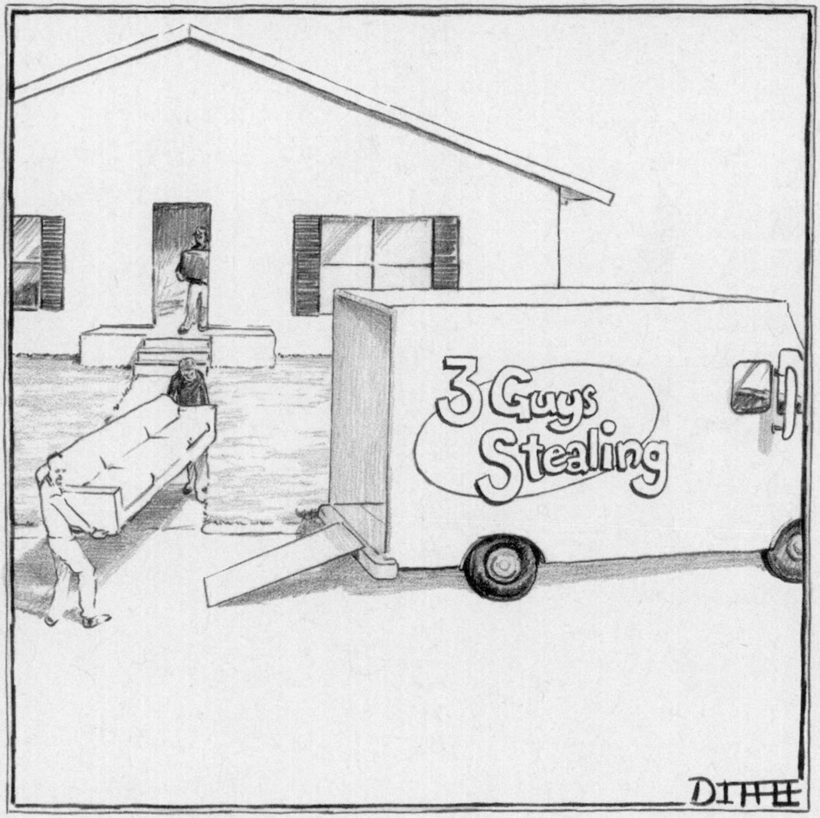
3 Guys Stealing
DIFFEE

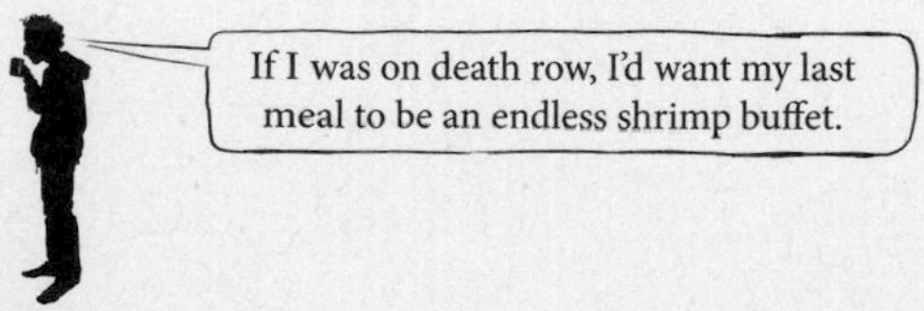
If I was on death row, I'd want my last meal to be an endless shrimp buffet.

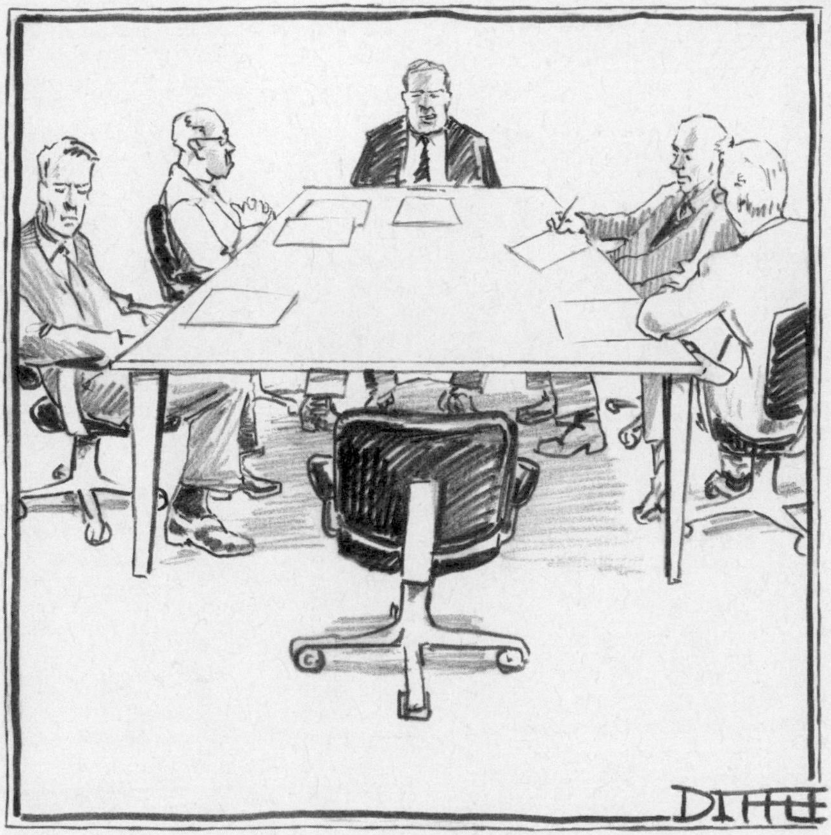
DIFFEE

"It's just us today, Campbell called in ethical."

*"Don't worry. I haven't been here that long. I'm just
a huge ZZ Top fan."*

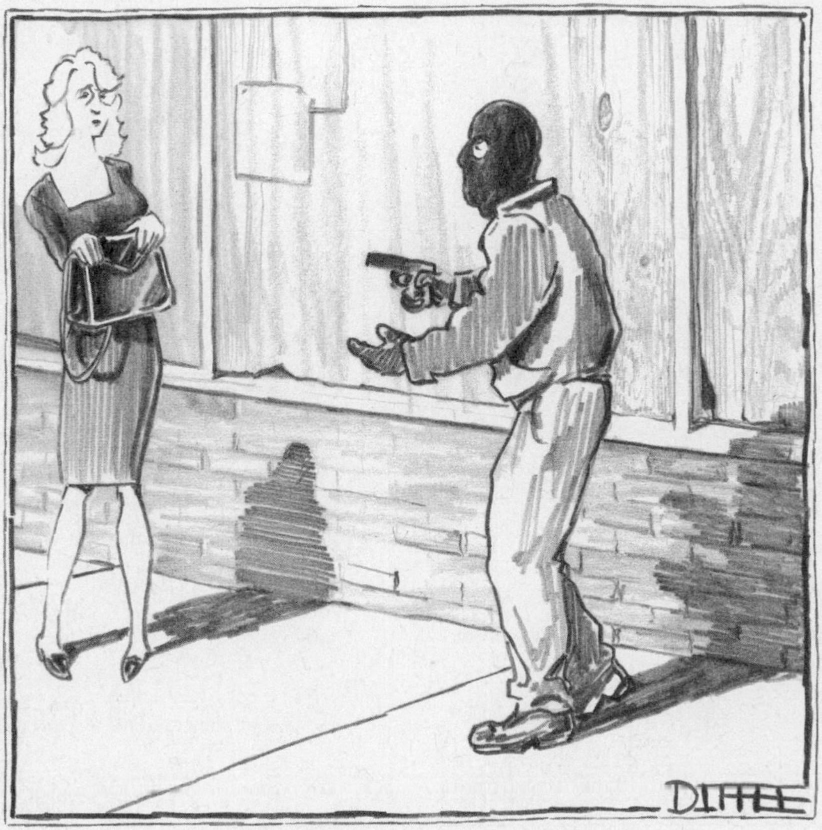
DIFFEE

"Gimme the purse and the matching pumps."

"In the interest of increasing revenue this quarter, Evan, here,
will be leading an initiative to rip off liquor stores."

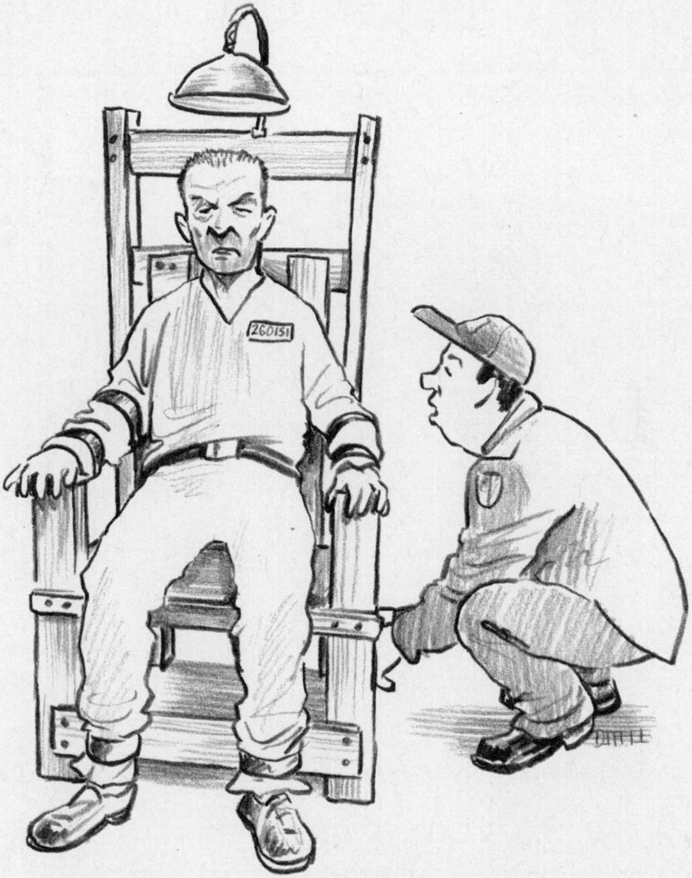
260151

"How's the lumbar support?"

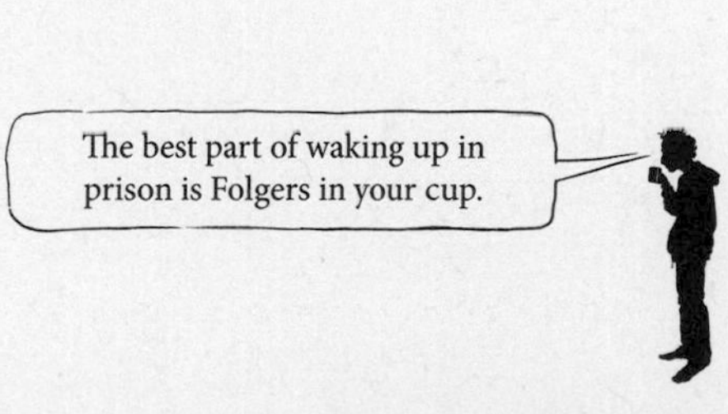
The best part of waking up in
prison is Folgers in your cup.

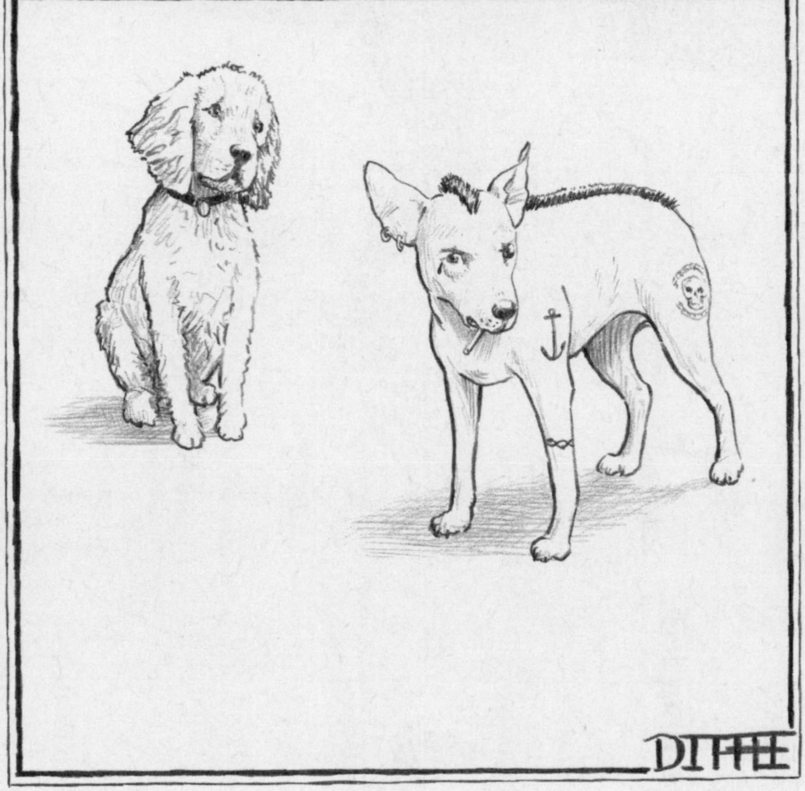
DIFFEE

"Kennel changes a dog, Muffin."

CHAPTER TWELVE

I wonder what primitive man thought when they saw their first rainbow. Probably that God was gay.

FOR SMART ATTRACTIVE RELIGIOUS PEOPLE

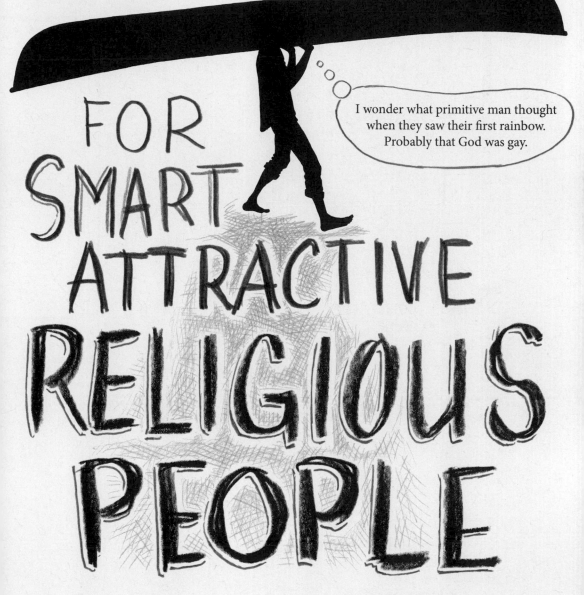

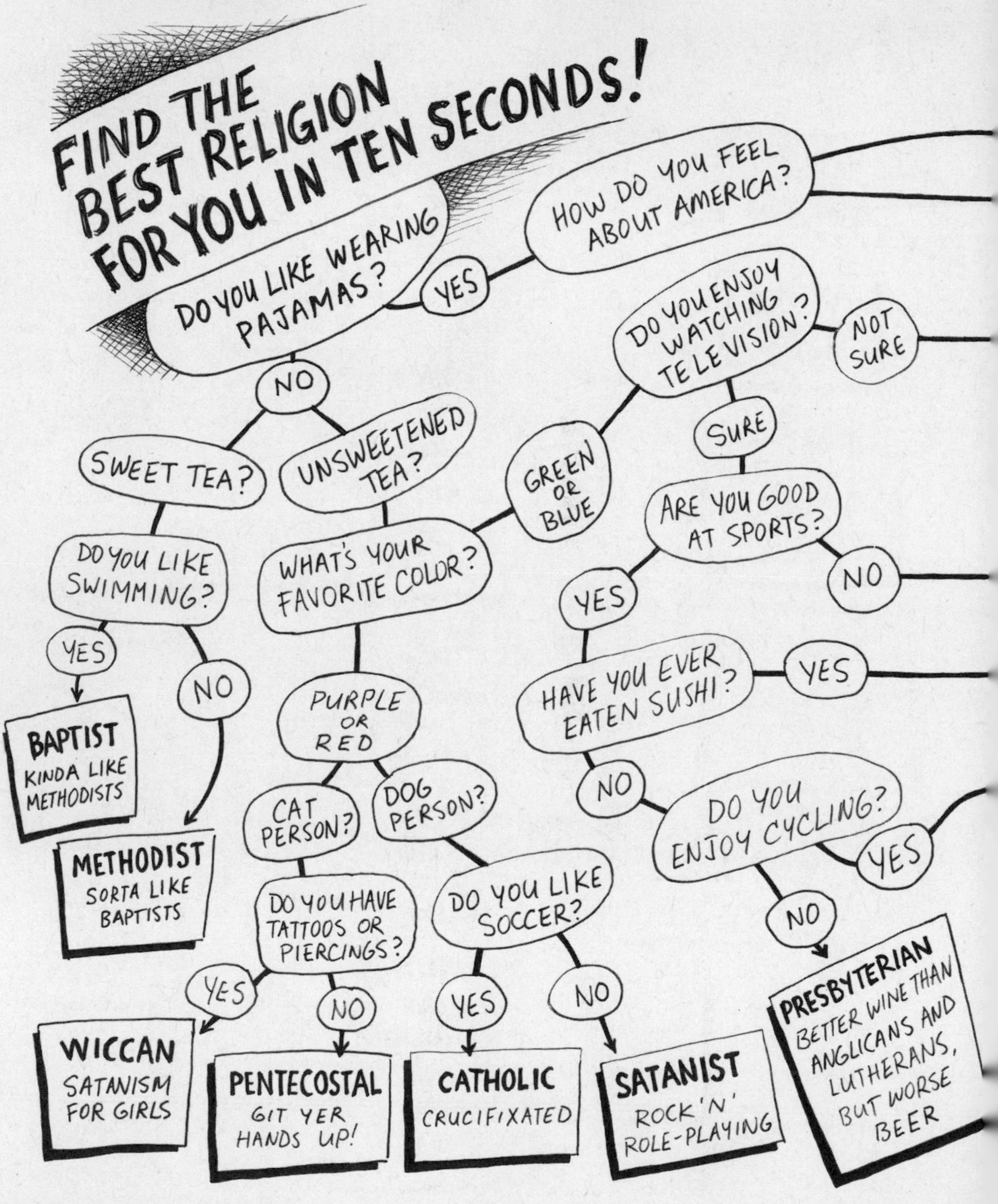

FIND THE BEST RELIGION FOR YOU IN TEN SECONDS!
DO YOU LIKE WEARING PAJAMAS?
YES
HOW DO YOU FEEL ABOUT AMERICA?
NO
SWEET TEA?
UNSWEETENED TEA?
DO YOU LIKE SWIMMING?
YES
NO
BAPTIST
KINDA LIKE METHODISTS
METHODIST
SORTA LIKE BAPTISTS
WHAT'S YOUR FAVORITE COLOR?
GREEN OR BLUE
PURPLE OR RED
CAT PERSON?
DOG PERSON?
DO YOU HAVE TATTOOS OR PIERCINGS?
YES
NO
WICCAN
SATANISM FOR GIRLS
PENTECOSTAL
GIT YER HANDS UP!
DO YOU LIKE SOCCER?
YES
NO
CATHOLIC
CRUCIFIXATED
SATANIST
ROCK 'N' ROLE-PLAYING
DO YOU ENJOY WATCHING TELEVISION?
NOT SURE
SURE
ARE YOU GOOD AT SPORTS?
YES
NO
HAVE YOU EVER EATEN SUSHI?
YES
NO
DO YOU ENJOY CYCLING?
YES
NO
PRESBYTERIAN
BETTER WINE THAN ANGLICANS AND LUTHERANS, BUT WORSE BEER

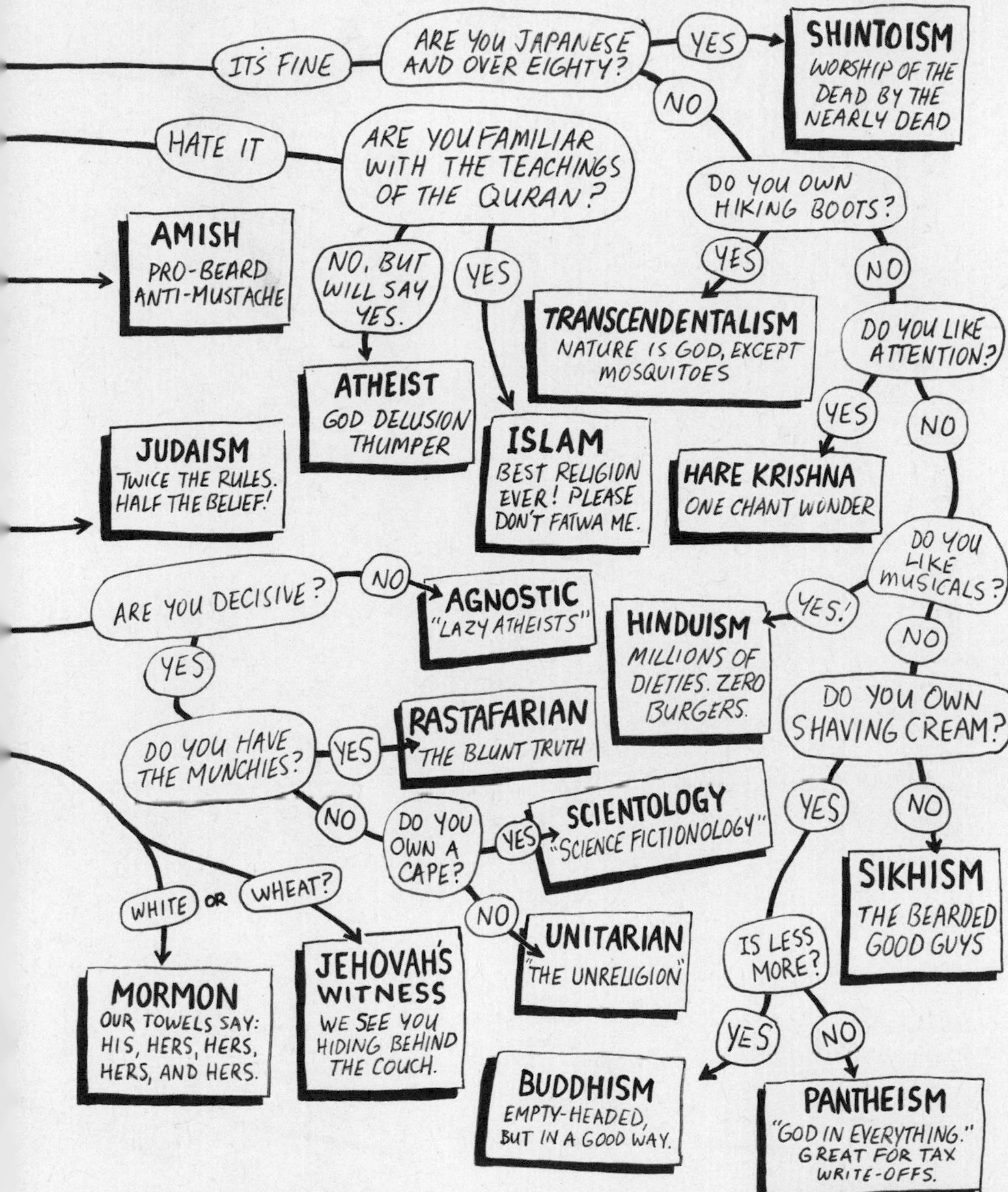
IT'S FINE
ARE YOU JAPANESE AND OVER EIGHTY?
YES
SHINTOISM
WORSHIP OF THE DEAD BY THE NEARLY DEAD
NO
HATE IT
ARE YOU FAMILIAR WITH THE TEACHINGS OF THE QURAN?
DO YOU OWN HIKING BOOTS?
AMISH
PRO-BEARD ANTI-MUSTACHE
NO, BUT WILL SAY YES.
YES
YES
NO
TRANSCENDENTALISM
NATURE IS GOD, EXCEPT MOSQUITOES
DO YOU LIKE ATTENTION?
ATHEIST
GOD DELUSION THUMPER
YES
NO
JUDAISM
TWICE THE RULES. HALF THE BELIEF!
ISLAM
BEST RELIGION EVER! PLEASE DON'T FATWA ME.
HARE KRISHNA
ONE CHANT WONDER
DO YOU LIKE MUSICALS?
ARE YOU DECISIVE?
NO
AGNOSTIC
"LAZY ATHEISTS"
YES!
HINDUISM
MILLIONS OF DIETIES. ZERO BURGERS.
NO
YES
DO YOU OWN SHAVING CREAM?
RASTAFARIAN
THE BLUNT TRUTH
DO YOU HAVE THE MUNCHIES?
YES
YES
NO
NO
DO YOU OWN A CAPE?
YES
SCIENTOLOGY
"SCIENCE FICTIONOLOGY"
SIKHISM
THE BEARDED GOOD GUYS
WHITE OR WHEAT?
NO
UNITARIAN
"THE UNRELIGION"
IS LESS MORE?
MORMON
OUR TOWELS SAY: HIS, HERS, HERS, HERS, AND HERS.
JEHOVAH'S WITNESS
WE SEE YOU HIDING BEHIND THE COUCH.
YES
NO
BUDDHISM
EMPTY-HEADED, BUT IN A GOOD WAY.
PANTHEISM
"GOD IN EVERYTHING." GREAT FOR TAX WRITE-OFFS.

ANOTHER WAY TO KEEP AN EMPTY SEAT BESIDE YOU ON THE TRAIN.

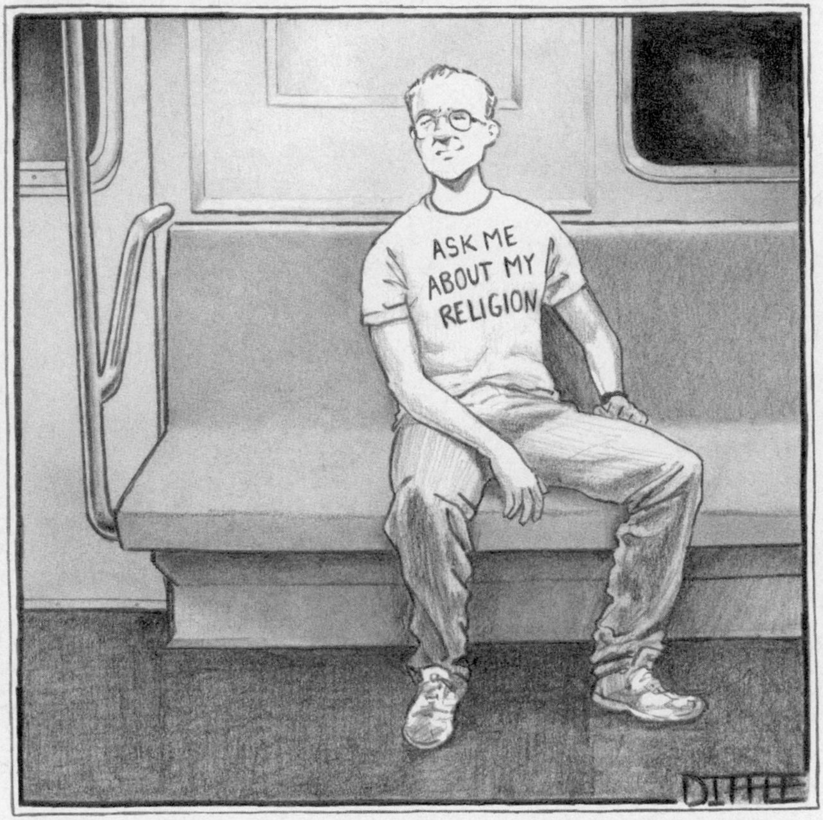
ASK ME ABOUT MY RELIGION
DIFFEE

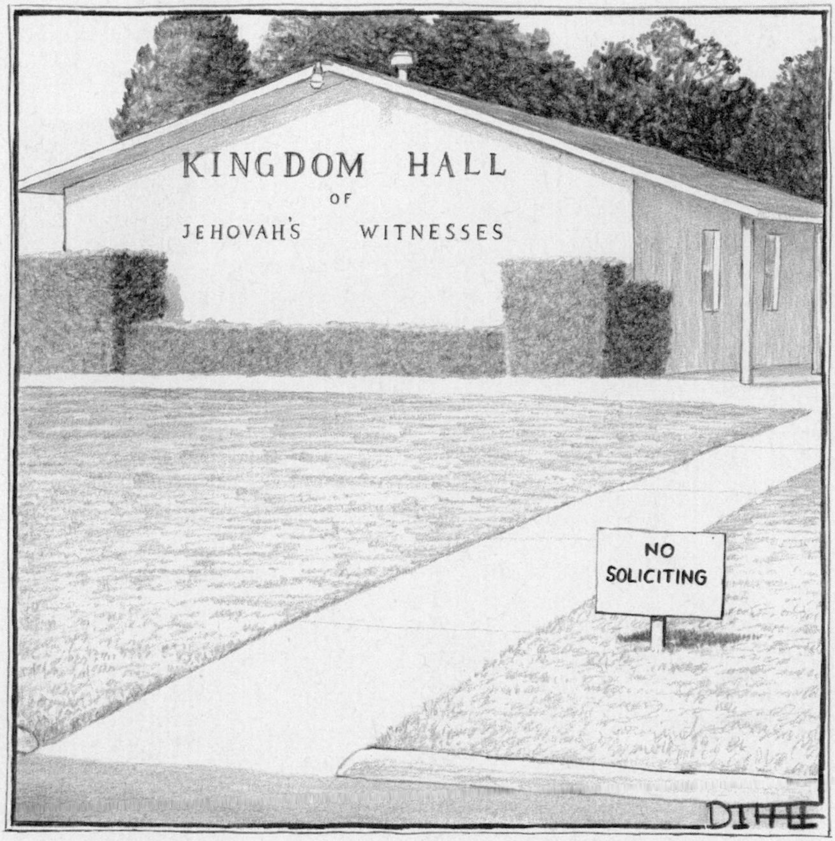
KINGDOM HALL
OF
JEHOVAH'S WITNESSES
NO SOLICITING
DIFFEE

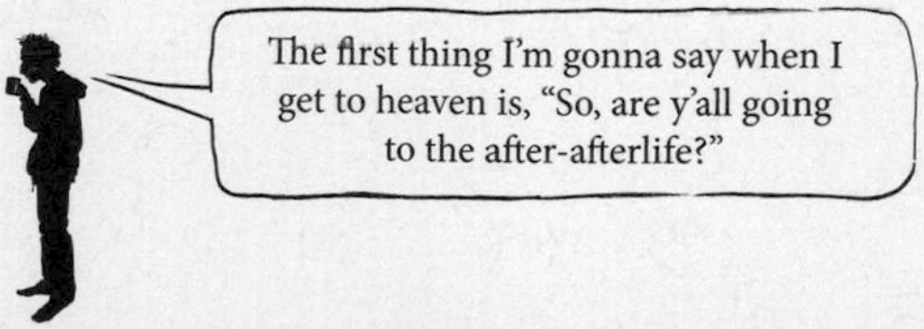
The first thing I'm gonna say when I get to heaven is, "So, are y'all going to the after-afterlife?"

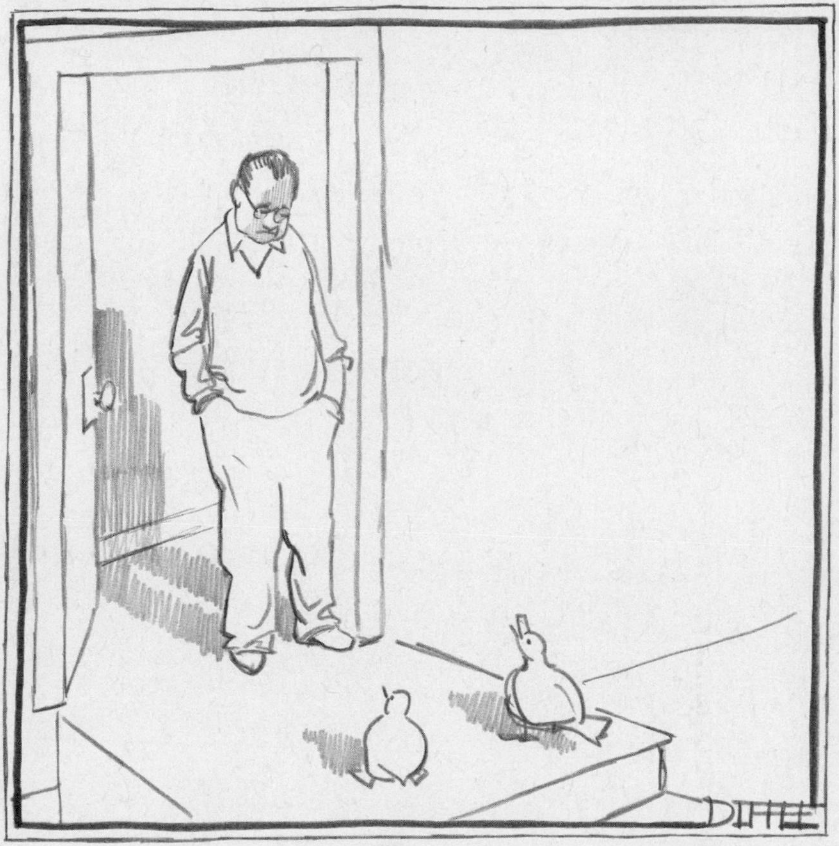
DIFFEE

"Have you ever thought about becoming a duck?"

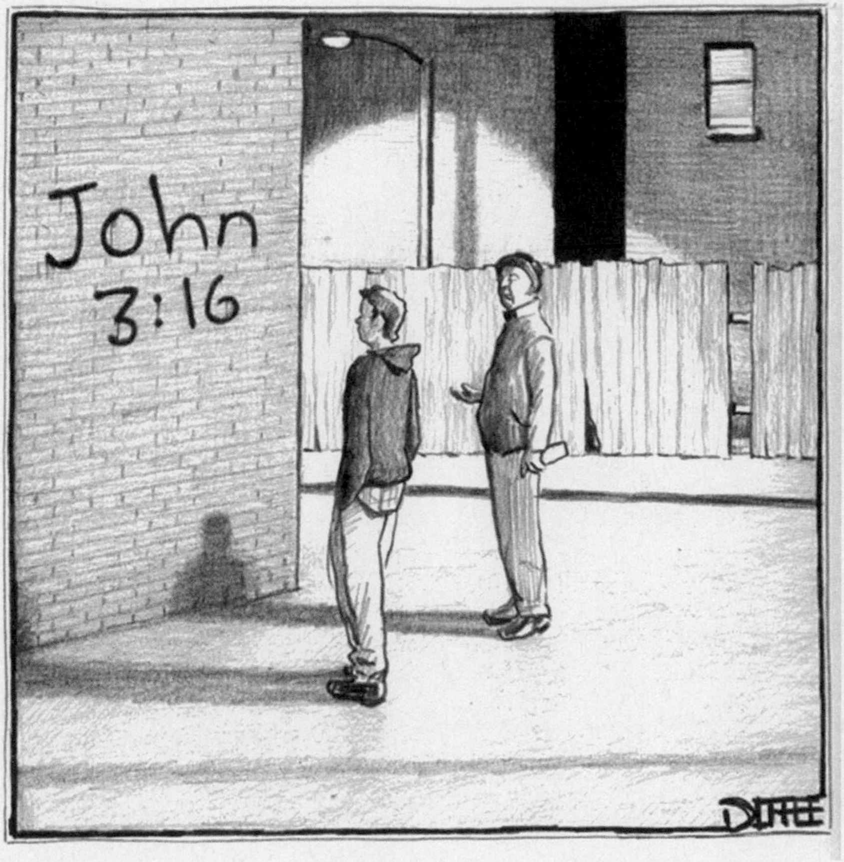
John
3:16
DUFFEE

"I just ask myself, 'What would Jesus spray-paint?' "

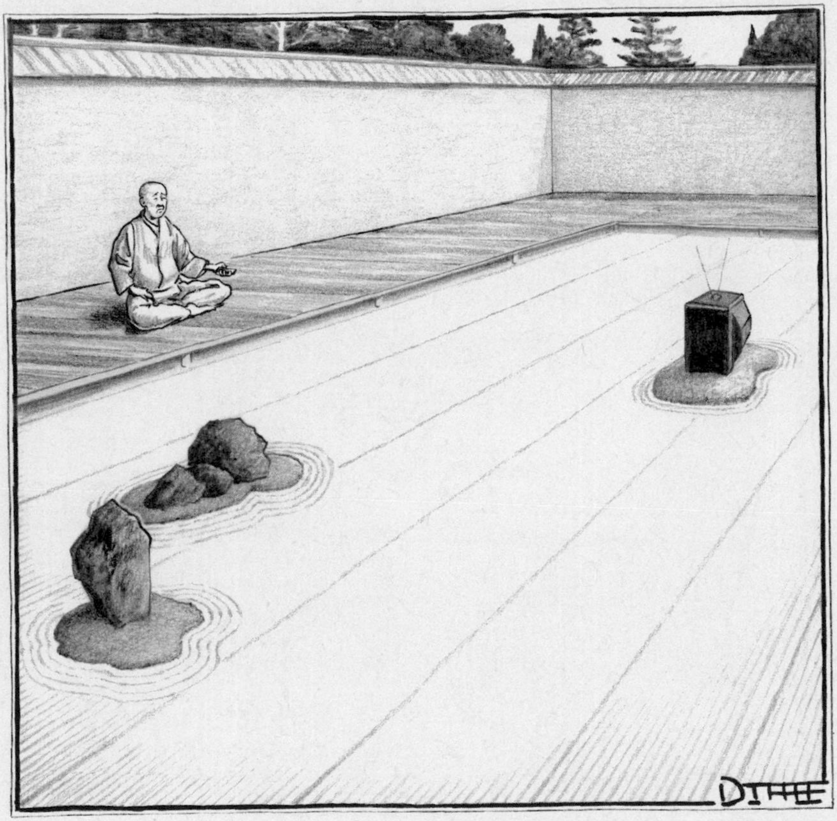
DIFFEE

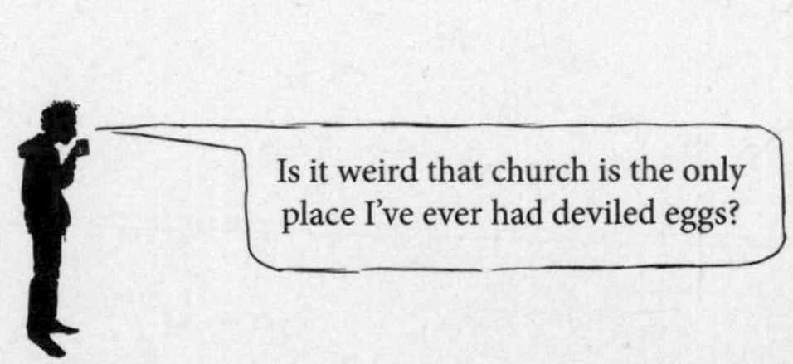
Is it weird that church is the only place I've ever had deviled eggs?

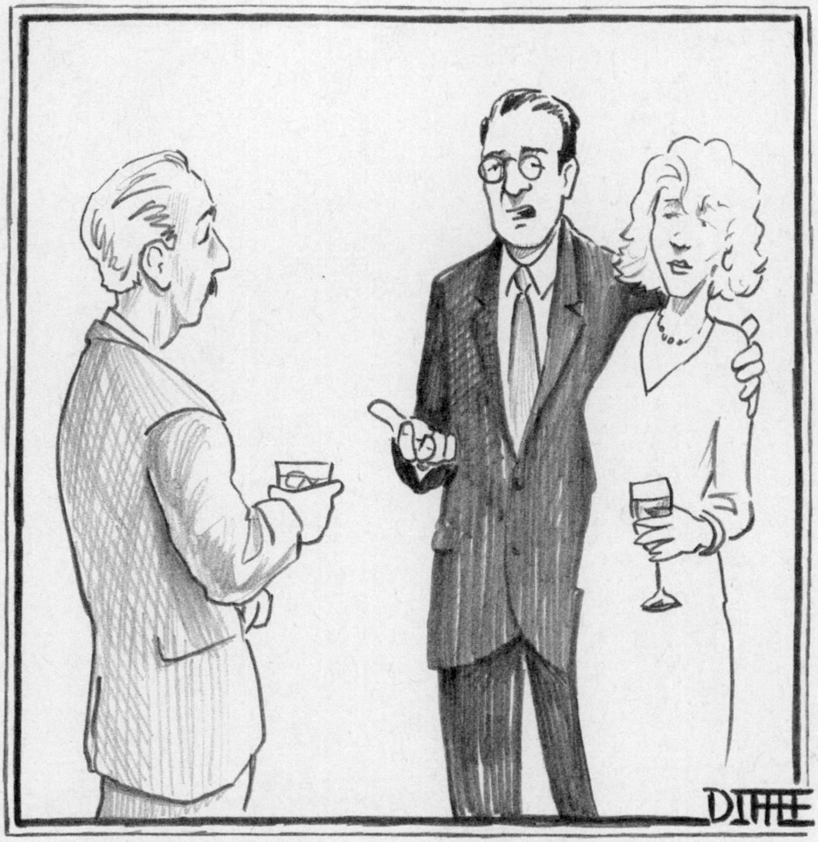
DIFFEE

"I'm a Moonie and Carol's a Wiccan, so we're raising our kids as nut jobs."

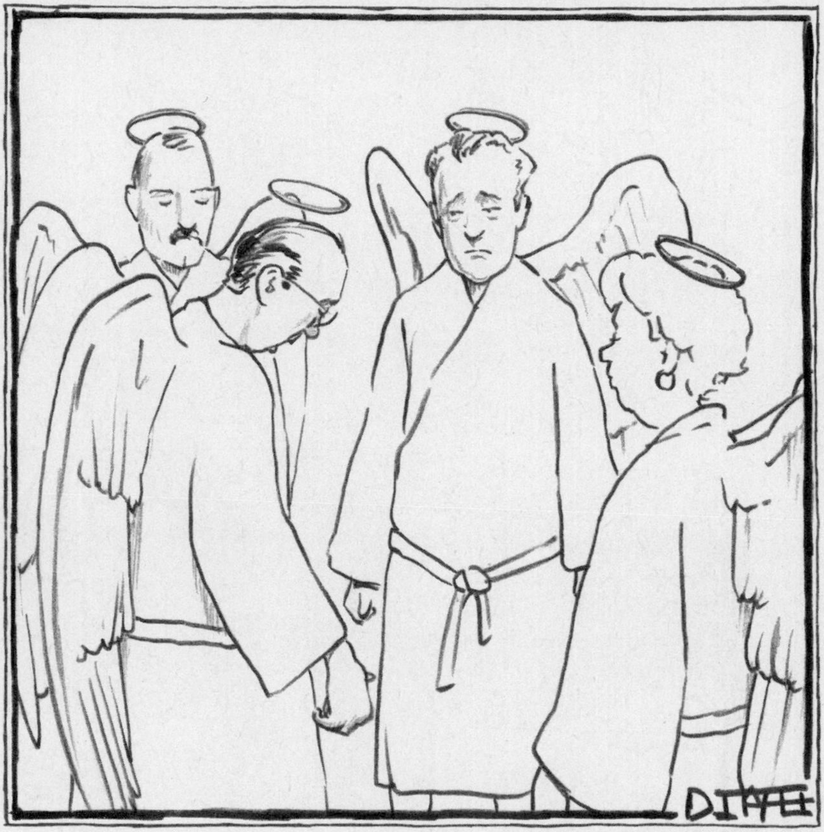
DIFFEE

"Does anyone else's robe say 'Hyatt'?"

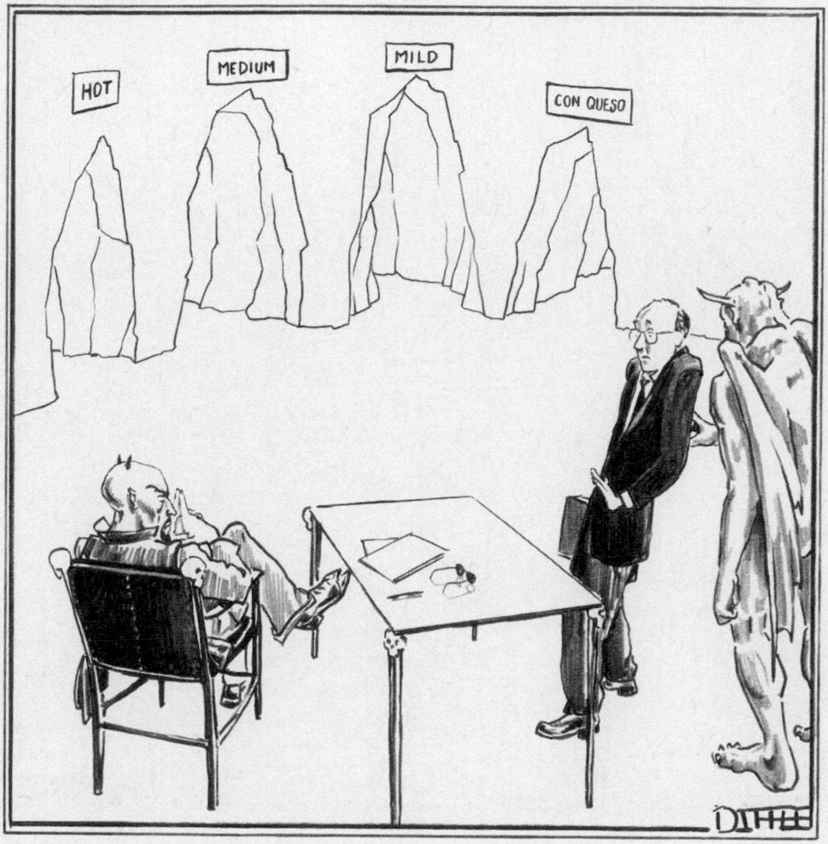
HOT
MEDIUM
MILD
CON QUESO
DITTEE

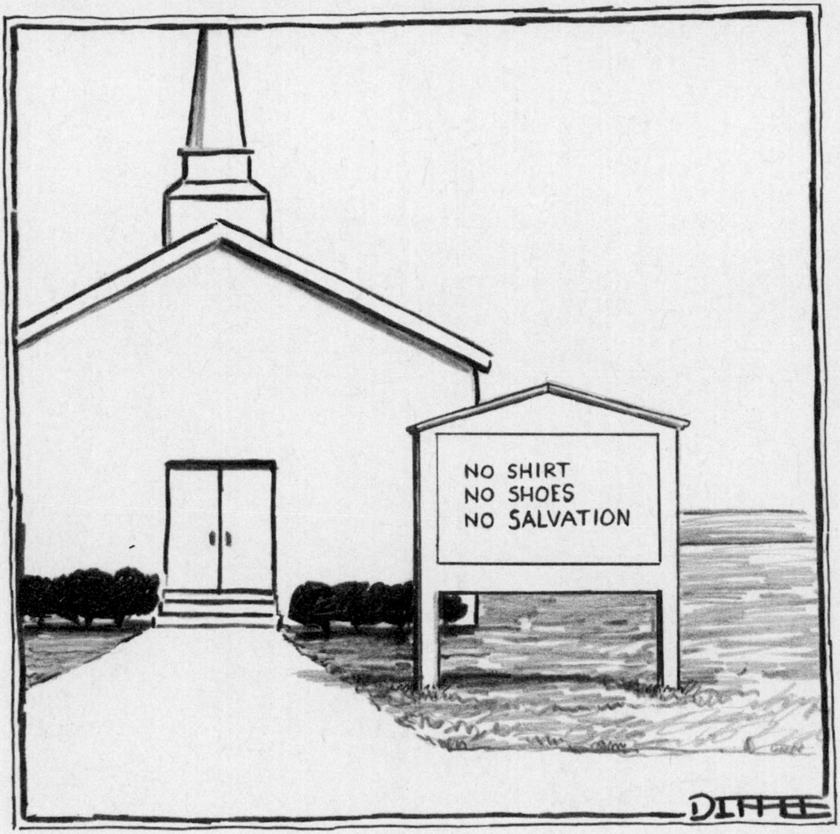
NO SHIRT
NO SHOES
NO SALVATION
DIFFEE

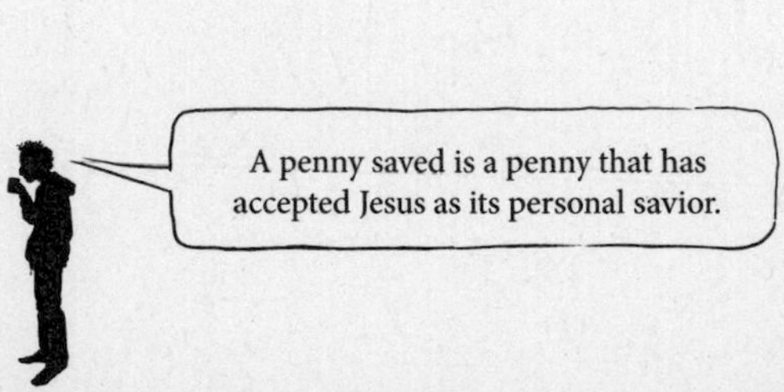
A penny saved is a penny that has accepted Jesus as its personal savior.

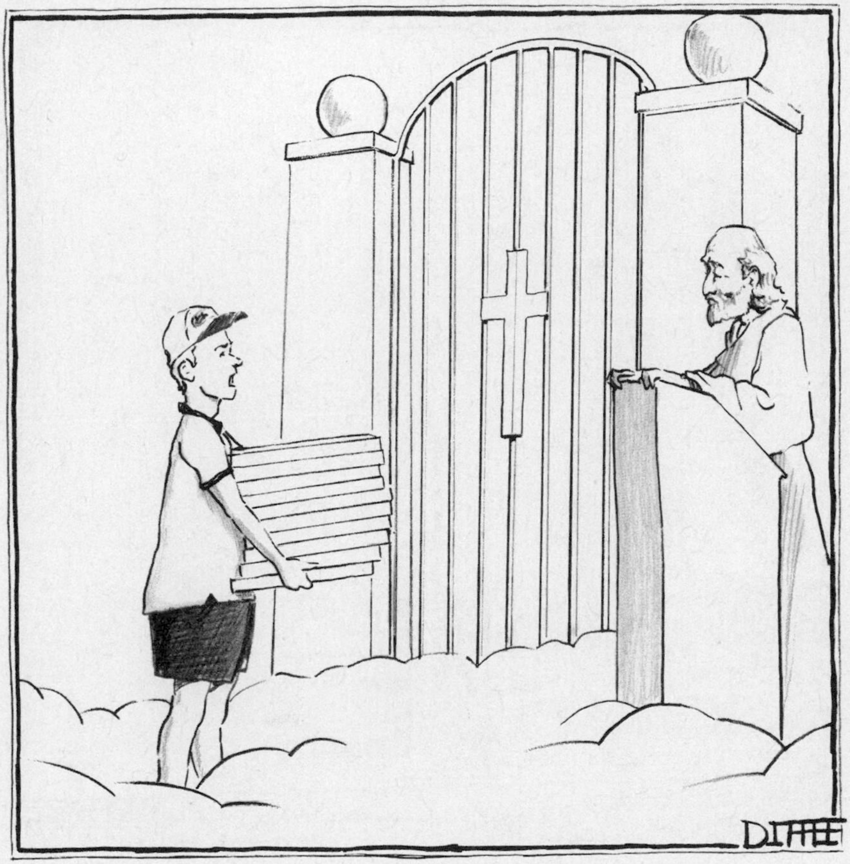
DIFFEE

"Wiles of the Devil or not, someone's gotta pay for these pies."

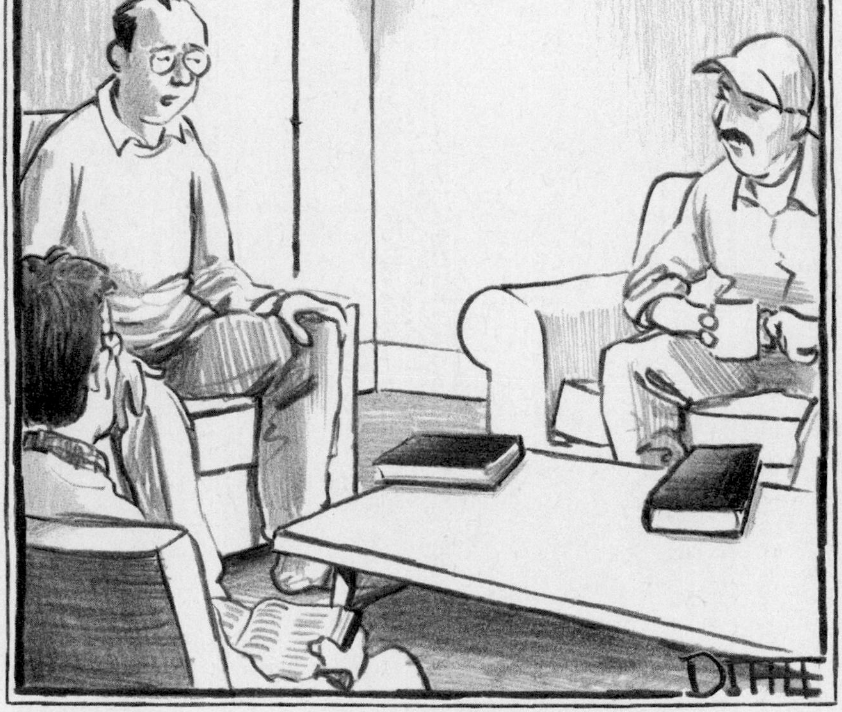
DIFFEE

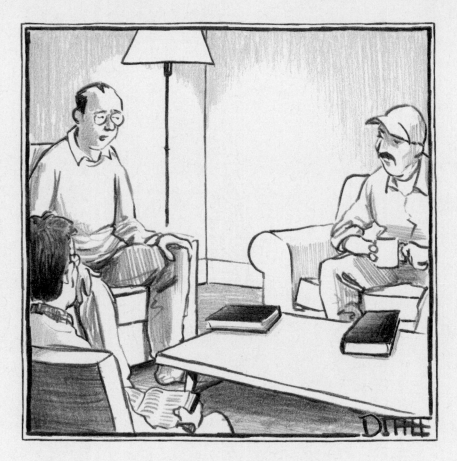

"O.K., the first rule of Bible Club is: always talk about Bible Club."

Wade Greenberg, wearing his hemp blazer, inadvertently became the life of the party when he stood too close to the menorah.

DEFFEE

MOSES: THE TEEN YEARS

CHAPTER THIRTEEN

FOR SMART ATTRACTIVE WEALTHY PEOPLE

What do you get the man who has everything except a key scratch on his Bentley?

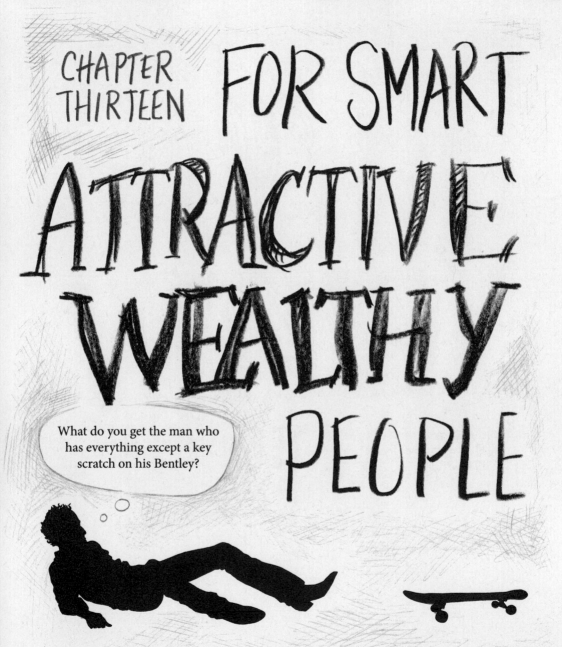

THE WEALTH DISPARITY IN AMERICA IS GETTING OUT OF HAND. THERE ARE PEOPLE WHO HAVE WRISTWATCHES THAT COST MORE THAN MY YACHT. SO UNNECESSARY. I MEAN, DOES ANYONE REALLY NEED A WRISTWATCH? AND WHEN IS ENOUGH ENOUGH? THE RICH WANT TO BE SUPER RICH AND THEN FILTHY RICH AND THEN CRAZY RICH. WHY IS IT THAT THE RICHER YOU GET, THE MORE YOU SOUND LIKE A HOMELESS PERSON? I MISS THE DAYS WHEN PEOPLE JUST WANTED TO BE MILLIONAIRES. SIMPLER TIMES.

YOUNG BILLIONAIRES SHARE THEIR SECRETS

"I'm a bed wetter."

"I'm only a fifty millionaire. And I'm forty-six."

"My Picasso is a Braque."

OF COURSE, THERE'S MORE THAN ONE KIND OF WEALTH. YOU CAN HAVE A WEALTH OF KNOWLEDGE OR A WEALTH OF EXPERIENCE OR YOU CAN HAVE A WEALTH OF MONEY. THAT LAST ONE'S PROBABLY THE BEST BECAUSE THEN YOU CAN HIRE PEOPLE WITH KNOWLEDGE AND EXPERIENCE.

A RICH FATHER'S ADVICE

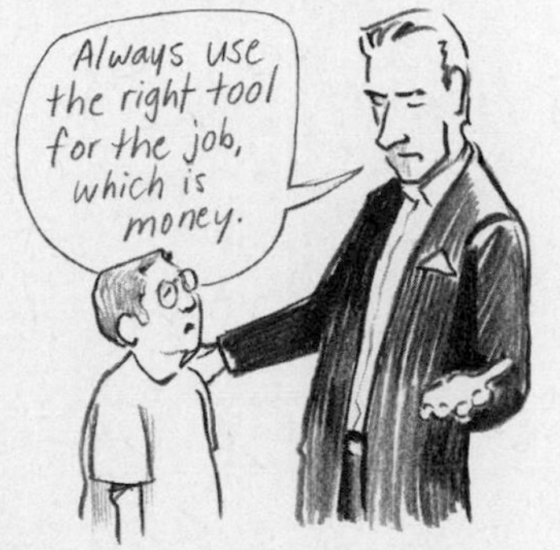
Always use the right tool for the job, which is money.

IT'S EASY FOR US WITHOUT WEALTH TO CAST STONES OR MOLOTOV COCKTAILS, BUT IT MUST BE TOUGH BEING RICH. YOU'RE CONSTANTLY TRYING TO KEEP UP WITH THE GATESES. STRUGGLING TO REMEMBER THE NAMES OF ALL YOUR BUTLERS AND WHICH ONE IS IN WHICH HUGE HOUSE. WORST OF ALL, YOU NEVER KNOW FOR SURE IF PEOPLE LIKE YOU FOR THE RIGHT REASONS.

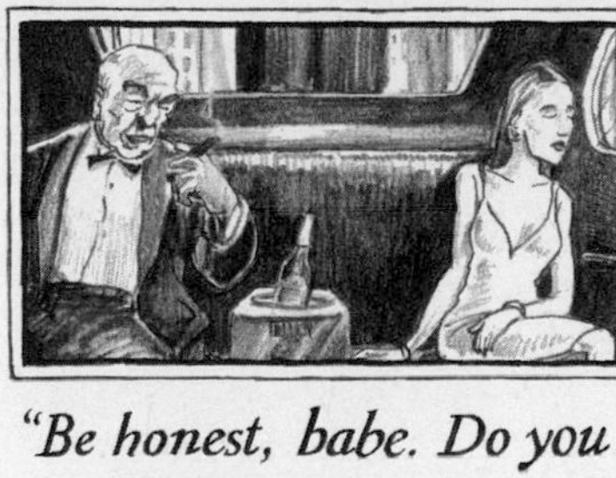

"Be honest, babe. Do you still find me rich?"

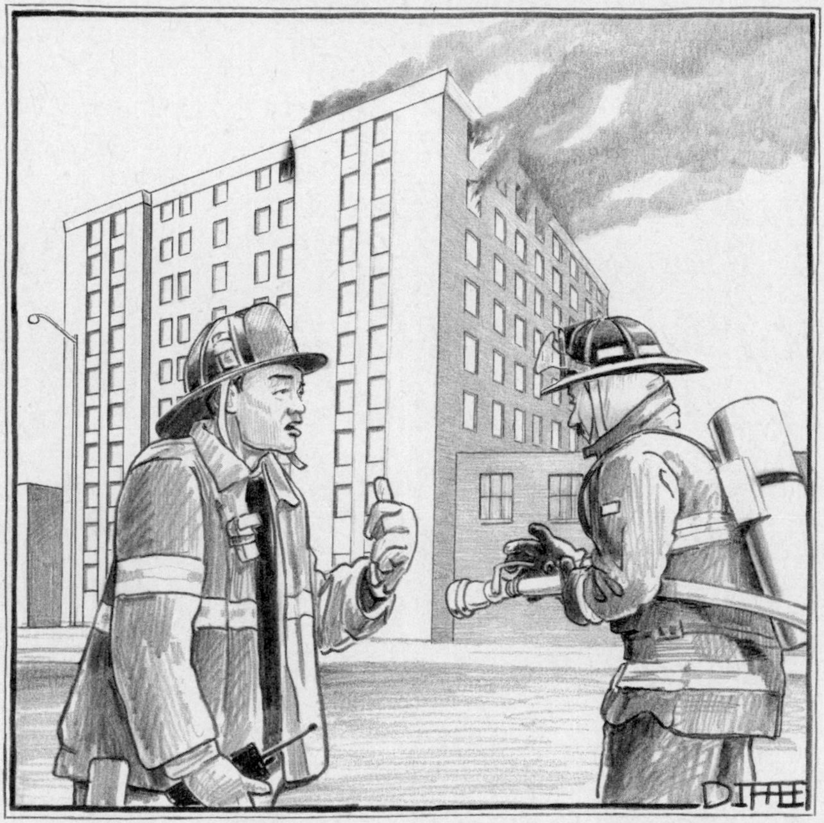
DIFFEE

"These are luxury apartments, so use the good water."

"I have a terrible fear of flying coach."

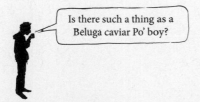

Is there such a thing as a Beluga caviar Po' boy?

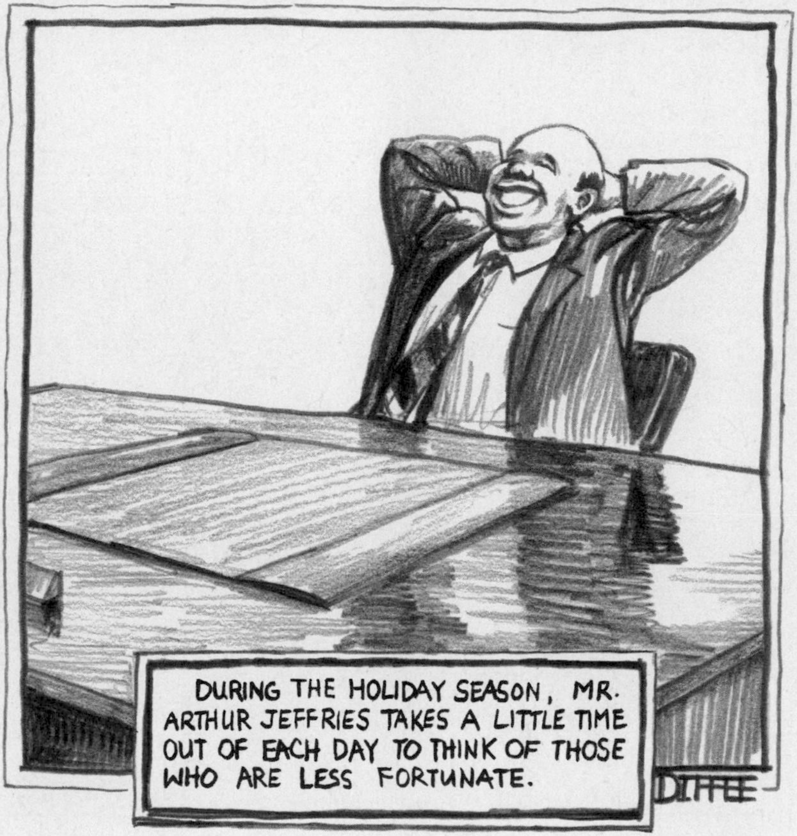
DURING THE HOLIDAY SEASON, MR. ARTHUR JEFFRIES TAKES A LITTLE TIME OUT OF EACH DAY TO THINK OF THOSE WHO ARE LESS FORTUNATE.
DIFFEE

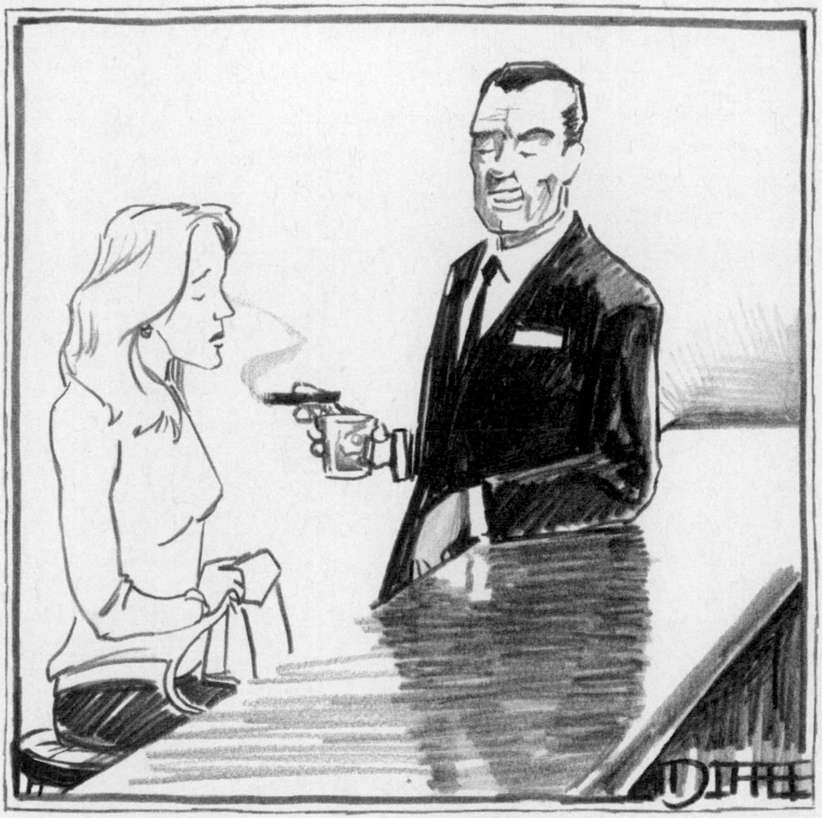
DIFFEE

"Can I buy you a house?"

The Whines of

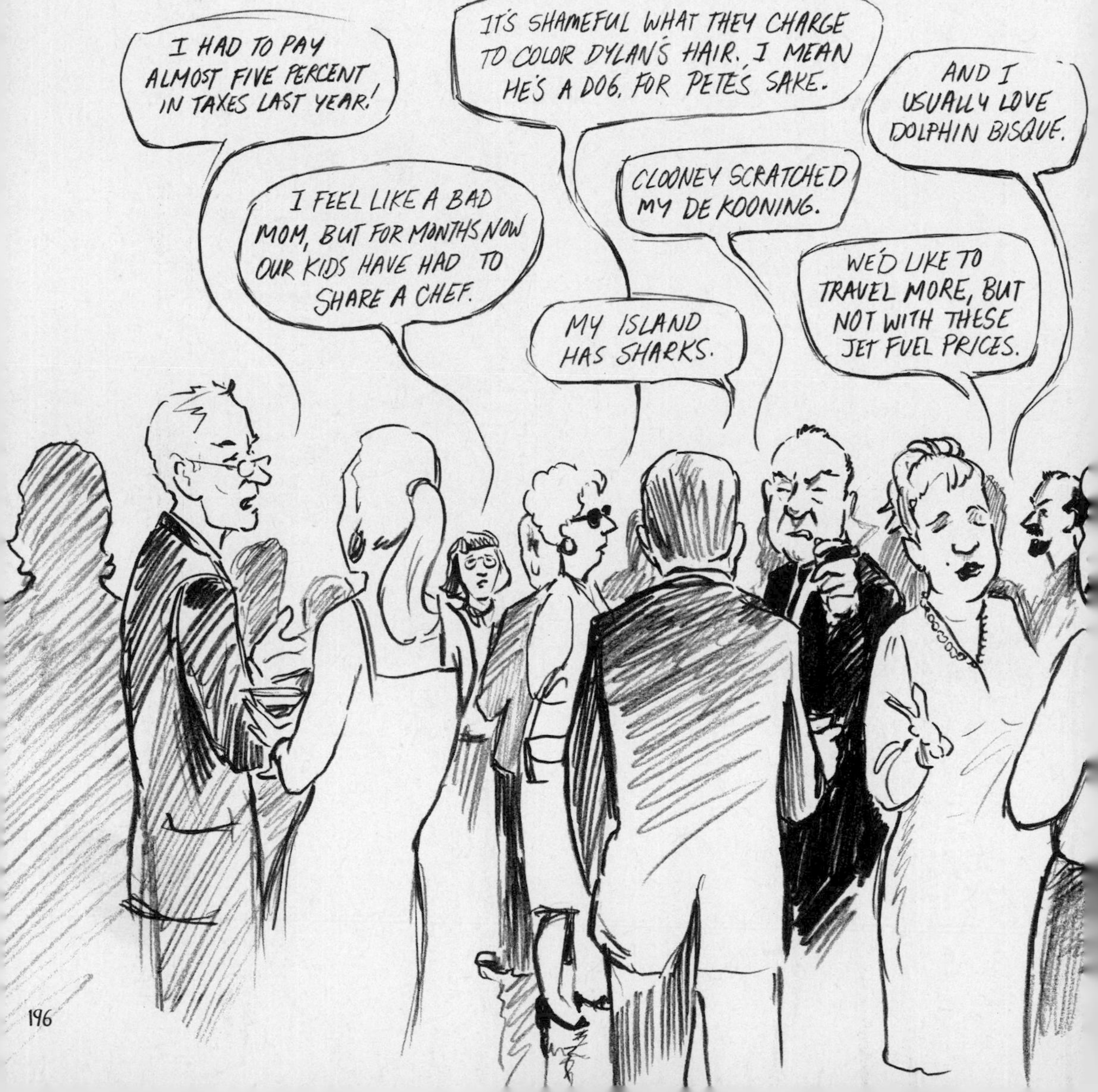

I HAD TO PAY ALMOST FIVE PERCENT IN TAXES LAST YEAR!
I FEEL LIKE A BAD MOM, BUT FOR MONTHS NOW OUR KIDS HAVE HAD TO SHARE A CHEF.
IT'S SHAMEFUL WHAT THEY CHARGE TO COLOR DYLAN'S HAIR. I MEAN HE'S A DOG, FOR PETE'S SAKE.
MY ISLAND HAS SHARKS.
CLOONEY SCRATCHED MY DE KOONING.
AND I USUALLY LOVE DOLPHIN BISQUE.
WE'D LIKE TO TRAVEL MORE, BUT NOT WITH THESE JET FUEL PRICES.

the One Percent

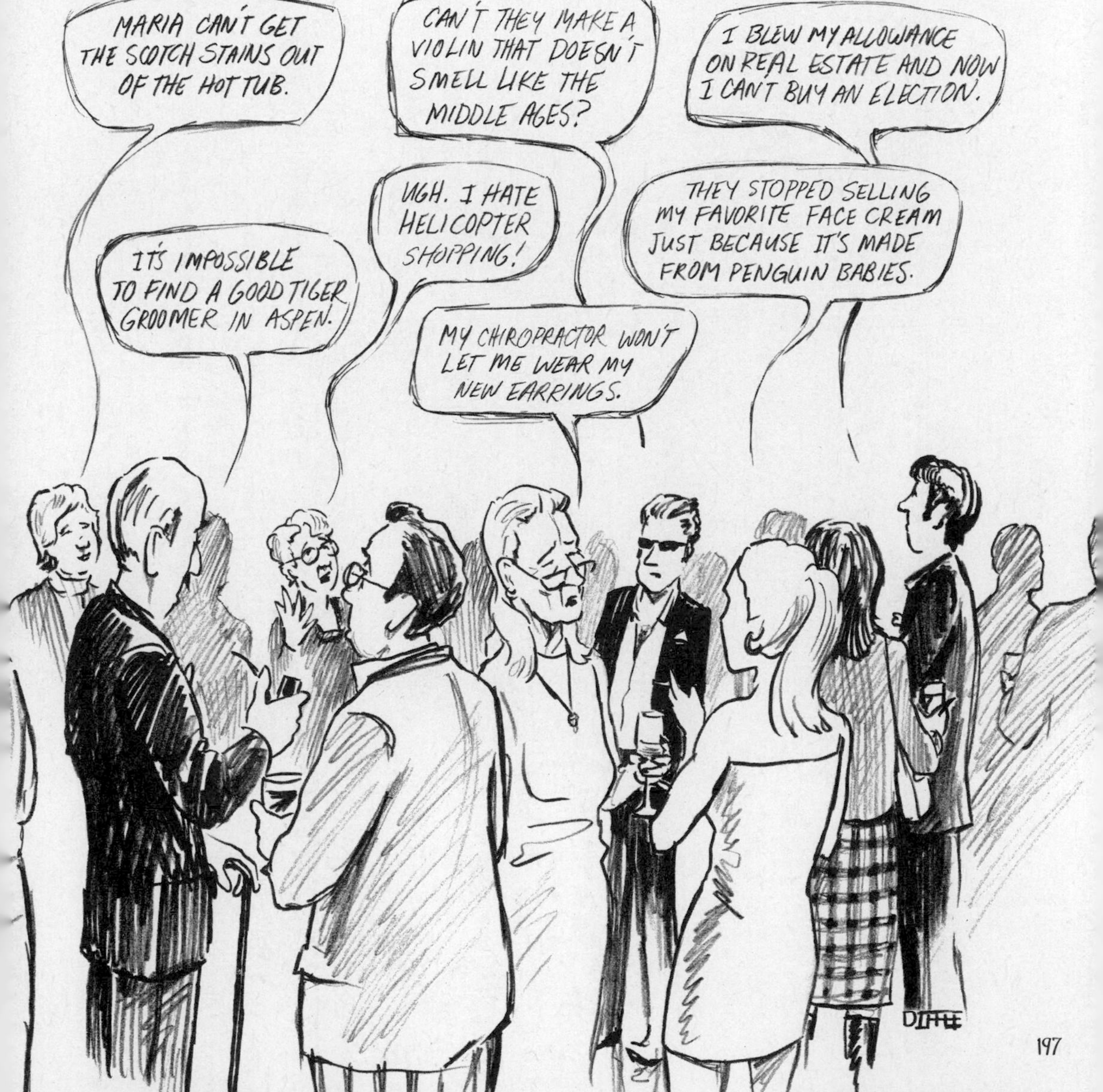

MARIA CAN'T GET THE SCOTCH STAINS OUT OF THE HOT TUB.
CAN'T THEY MAKE A VIOLIN THAT DOESN'T SMELL LIKE THE MIDDLE AGES?
I BLEW MY ALLOWANCE ON REAL ESTATE AND NOW I CAN'T BUY AN ELECTION.
UGH. I HATE HELICOPTER SHOPPING!
THEY STOPPED SELLING MY FAVORITE FACE CREAM JUST BECAUSE IT'S MADE FROM PENGUIN BABIES.
IT'S IMPOSSIBLE TO FIND A GOOD TIGER GROOMER IN ASPEN.
MY CHIROPRACTOR WON'T LET ME WEAR MY NEW EARRINGS.

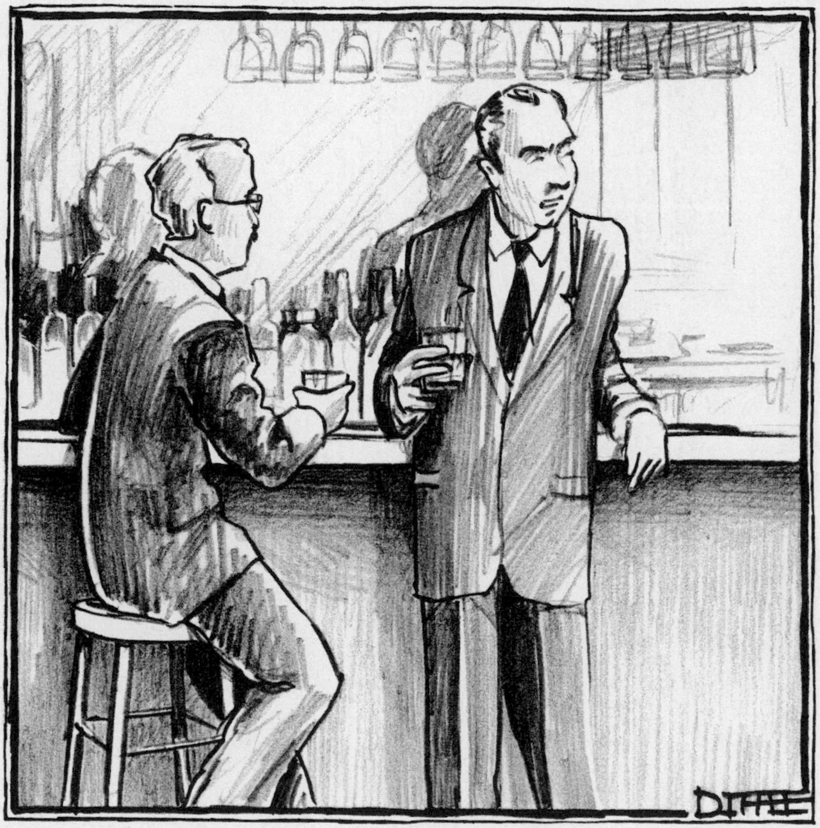
DIFFEE

"I've got a trophy wife, but she isn't what you'd call first place."

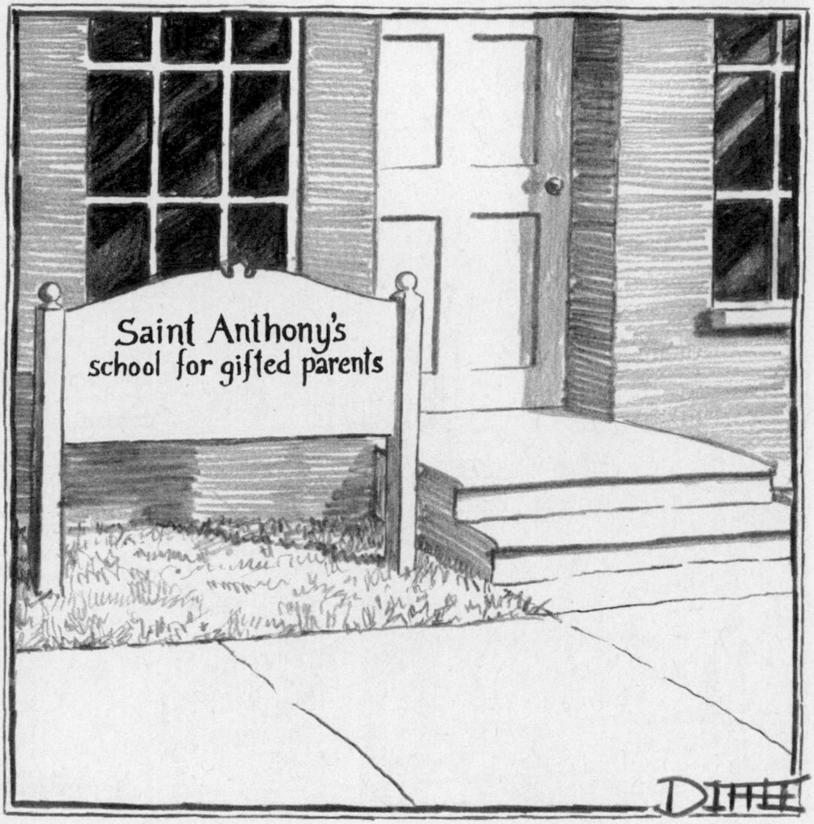
Saint Anthony's
school for gifted parents
DIFFEE

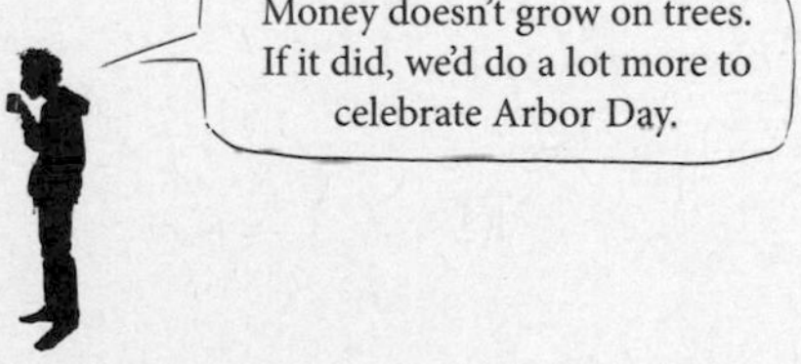
Money doesn't grow on trees. If it did, we'd do a lot more to celebrate Arbor Day.

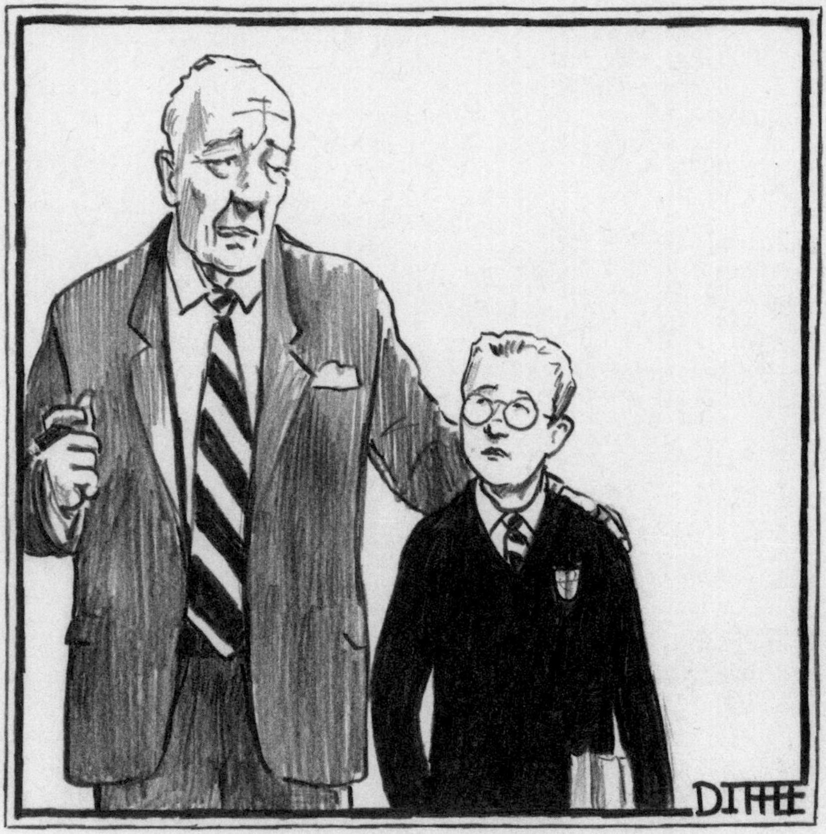
DIFFEE

"The best things in life are free. The worst are $19.95."

"I've spent so much time with family that I've started to lose sight of what really matters."

"This is my last day. My parents found a more expensive school on the East Side."

CHAPTER FOURTEEN FOR SMART ATTRACTIVE PEOPLE WHO LOVE OR HATE CHILDREN

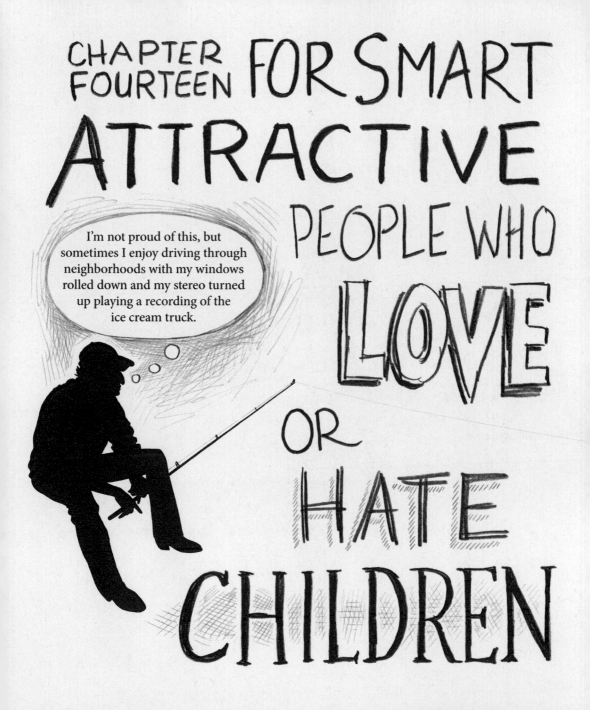

I'm not proud of this, but sometimes I enjoy driving through neighborhoods with my windows rolled down and my stereo turned up playing a recording of the ice cream truck.

I USED TO THINK THE WORST THING IN THE WORLD WAS A SCREAMING BABY ON A PLANE, BUT IT'S ACTUALLY FOURTH. BEHIND CANCER, WORLD POVERTY AND A SCREAMING ADULT ON A PLANE.

PARENTING SEEMS REALLY HARD, BUT STILL, YOU SEE AN AWFUL LOT OF PEOPLE DOING IT. I GUESS THERE MUST BE SOMETHING GREAT ABOUT IT. MY FRIENDS WITH KIDS TELL ME THERE'S A DEEP SOUL-SATISFYING JOY THAT COMES ONLY WITH HAVING CHILDREN. I TELL THEM THAT THERE IS A SHALLOW, BUT PRETTY SWEET JOY THAT COMES WITH SLEEPING IN AND HAVING NICE THINGS THAT AREN'T ALL STICKY.

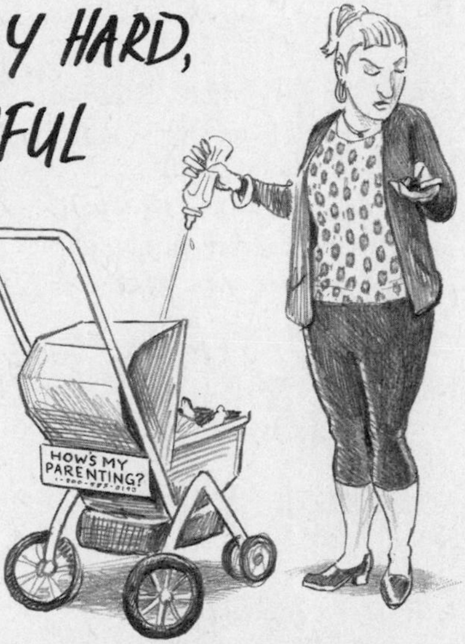
HOW'S MY PARENTING?

ALL THAT BEING SAID. I MIGHT HAVE KIDS AT SOME POINT. AS SOON AS I GROW UP.

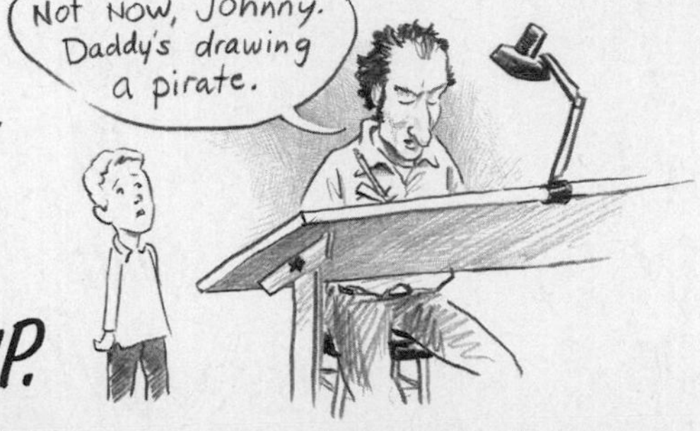
Not now, Johnny. Daddy's drawing a pirate.

I FIGURE HAVING KIDS IS LIKE HAVING A SERIOUS CAR WRECK, EVENTUALLY IT HAPPENS TO ALMOST EVERYBODY, IT'S USUALLY EXPENSIVE, AND YOU JUST HOPE YOU MAKE IT OUT ALIVE.

SOMETIMES I WONDER WHAT KIND OF PARENT I'LL BE.

PROBABLY THE KIND THAT BUILDS A TREEHOUSE WITH THE KIDS, AND THEN LIVES IN IT BY HIMSELF.

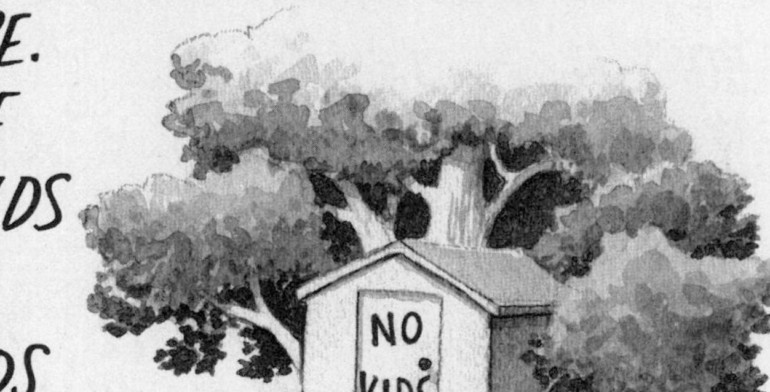
NO KIDS

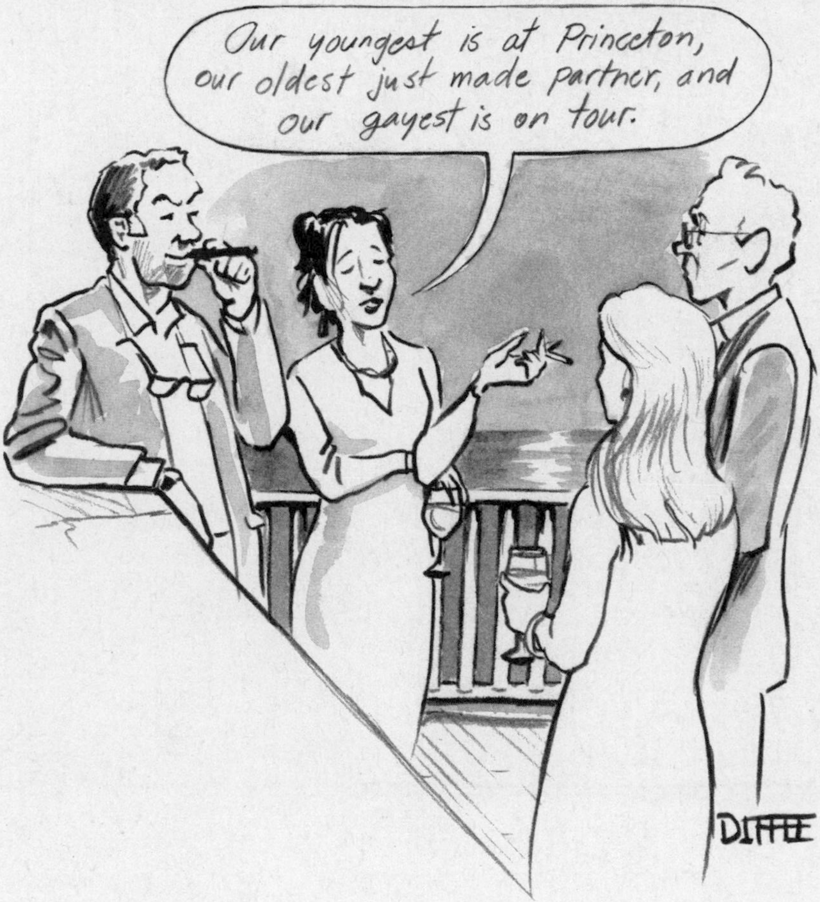
Our youngest is at Princeton, our oldest just made partner, and our gayest is on tour.
DIFFEE

"Before we begin this family meeting, how about we go around and say our names and a little something about ourselves."

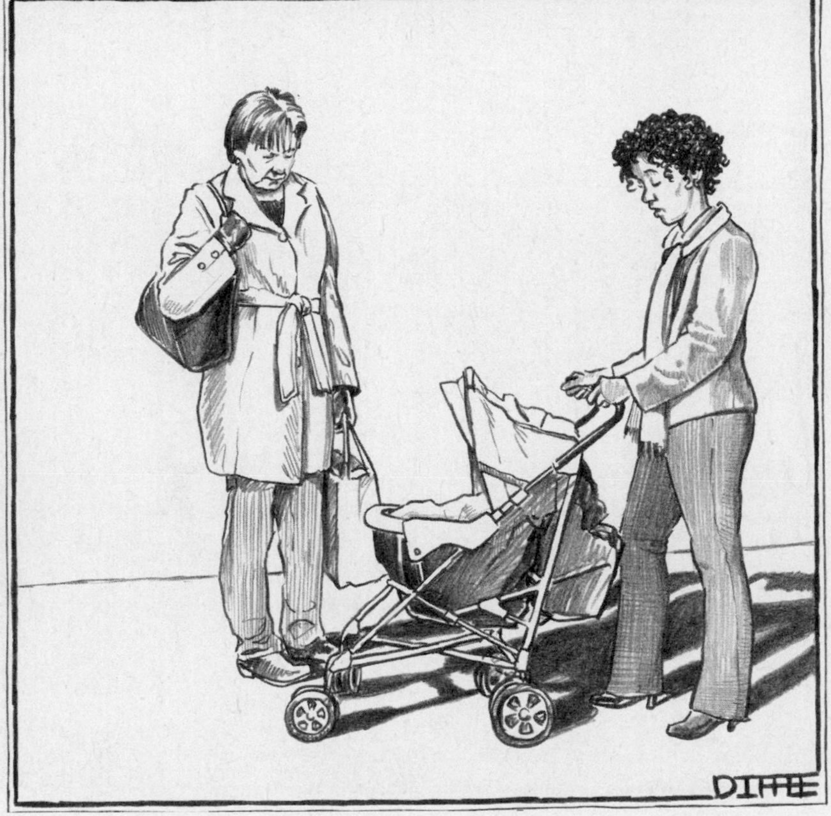
DIFFEE

"Sorry. He's been cursing like that ever since we put him in that little sailor suit."

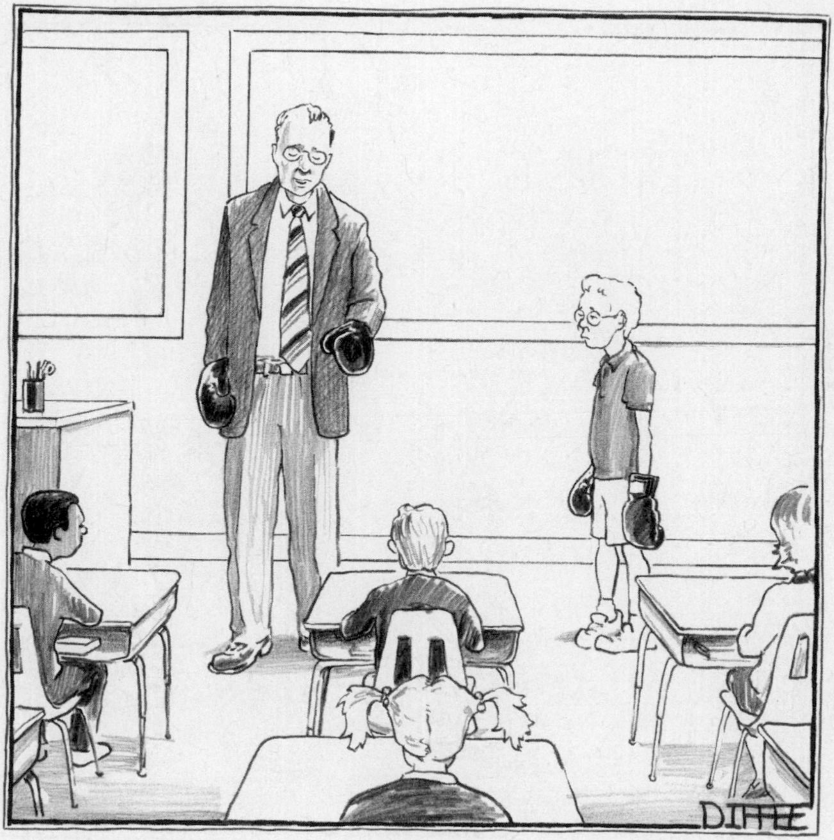
DIFFEE

"O.K., class, today we're gonna learn about survival of the fittest."

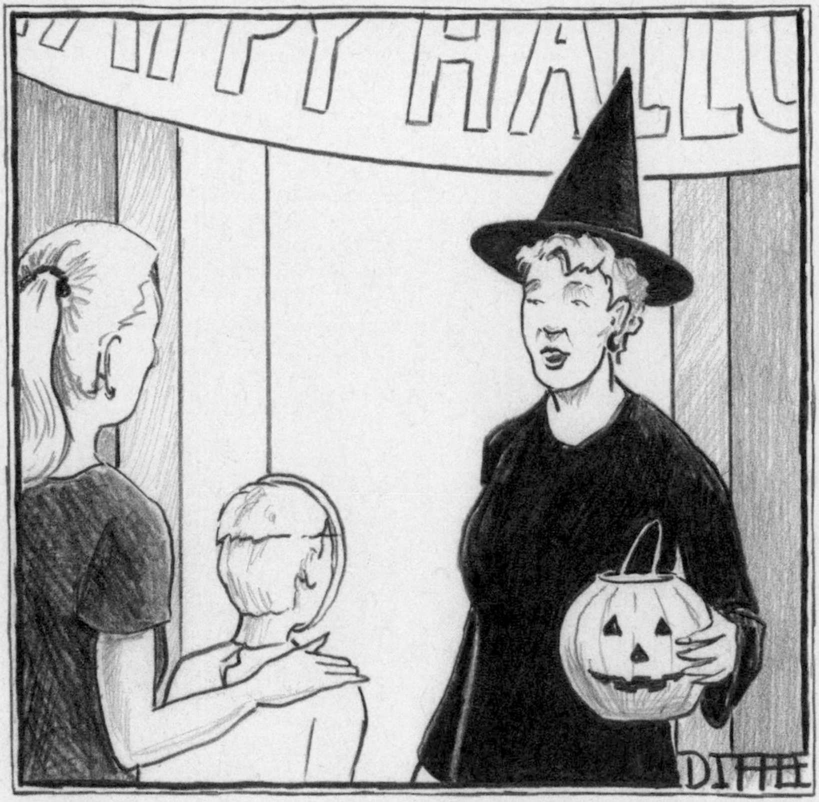
DIFFEE

"Come on in. The kids are in the backyard bobbing for pinkeye."

"Daddy, can I have a pony killed?"

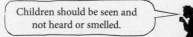

Children should be seen and
not heard or smelled.

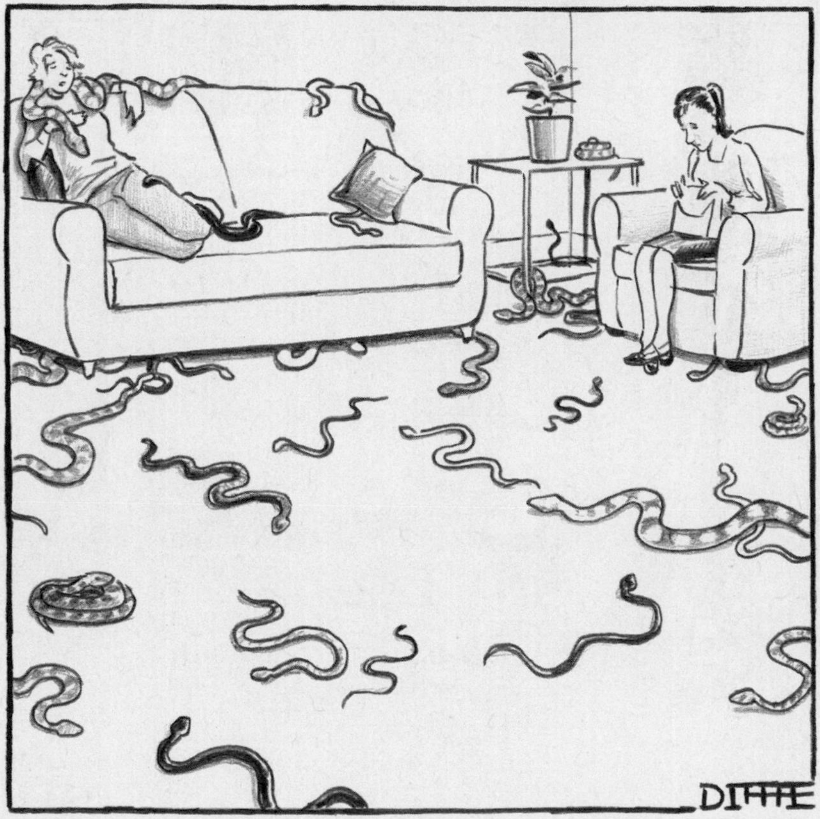
DIFFEE

"It's different when they're yours."

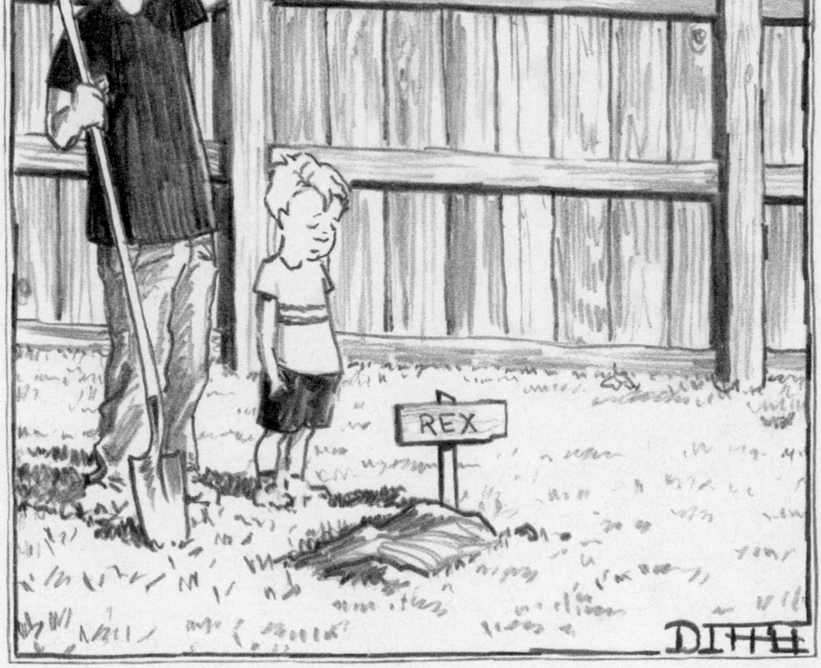
REX
DIFFEE

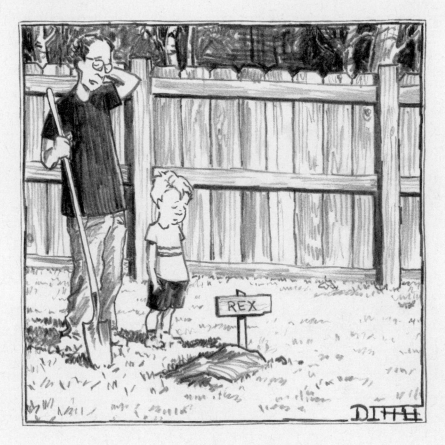

"Uh, sure. Unless, of course, he's in doggie Hell."

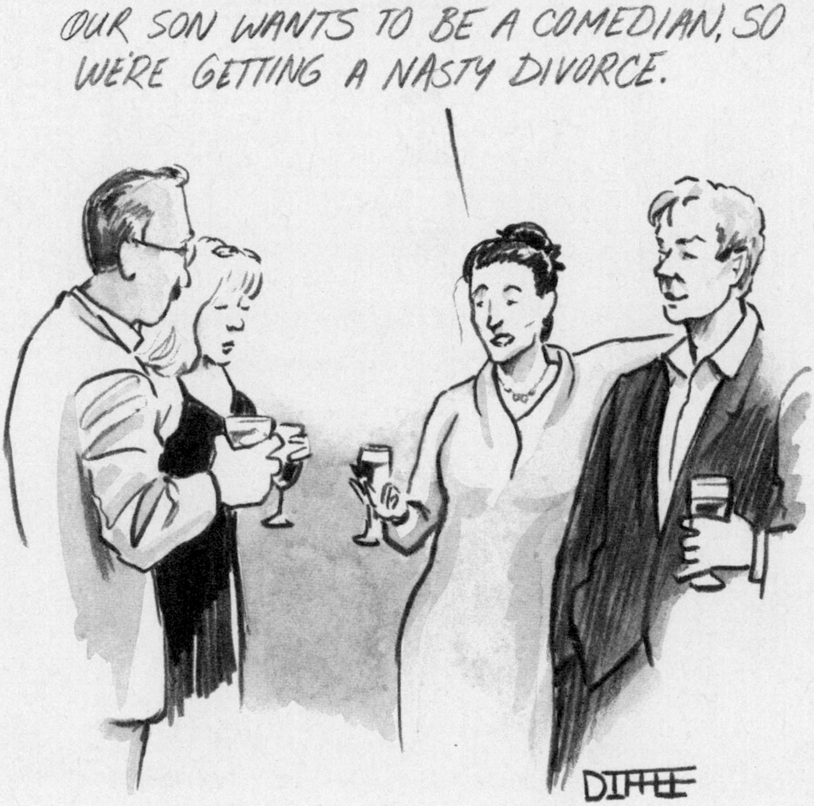
OUR SON WANTS TO BE A COMEDIAN, SO WE'RE GETTING A NASTY DIVORCE.
DIFFEE

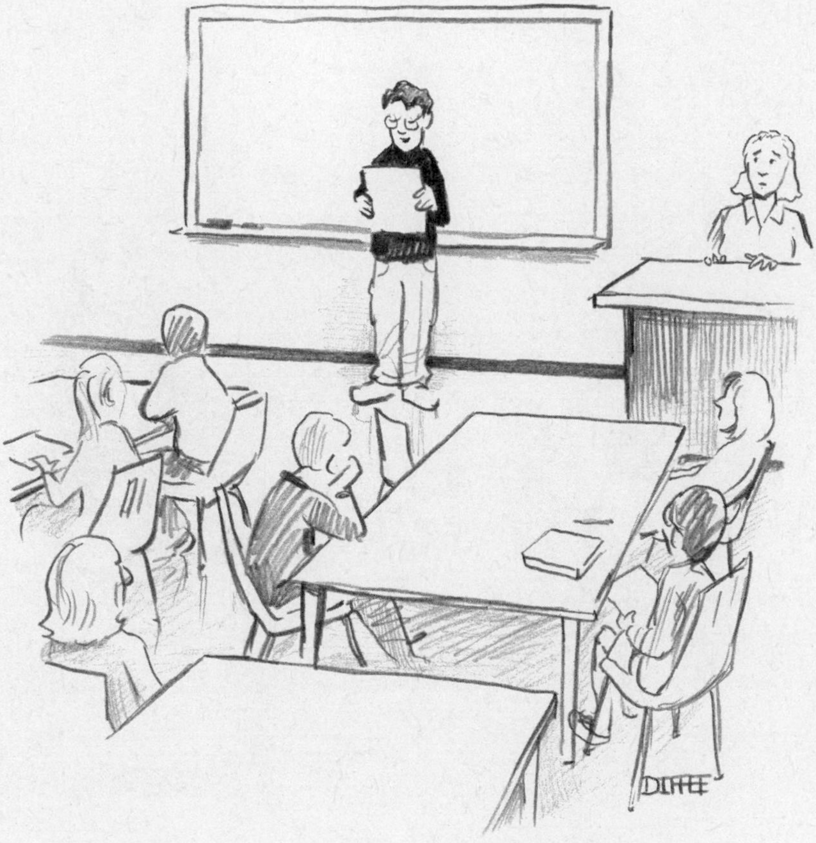
DIFFEE

"What I did over Summer Vacation with Miss Simmons."

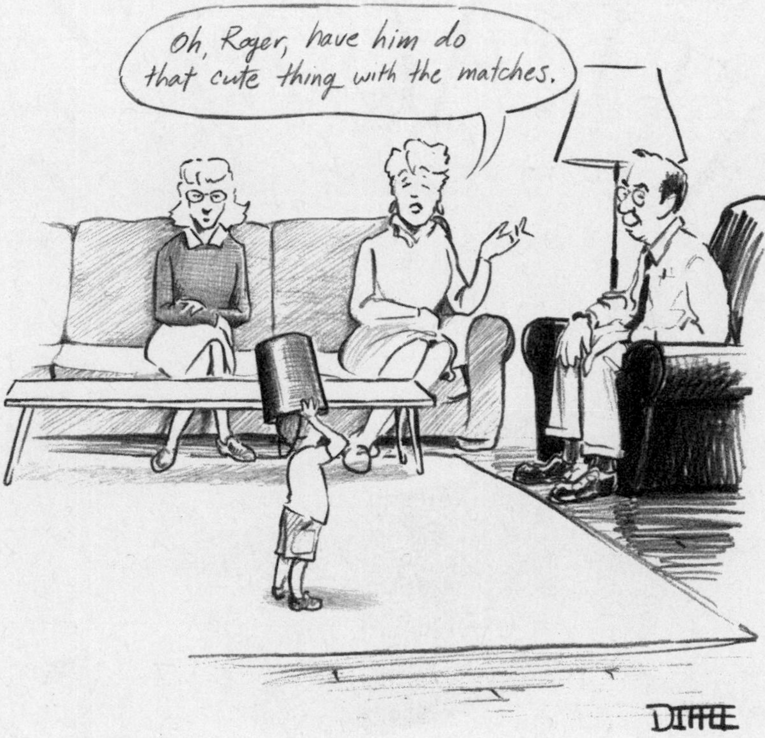
Oh, Roger, have him do that cute thing with the matches.
DIFFEE

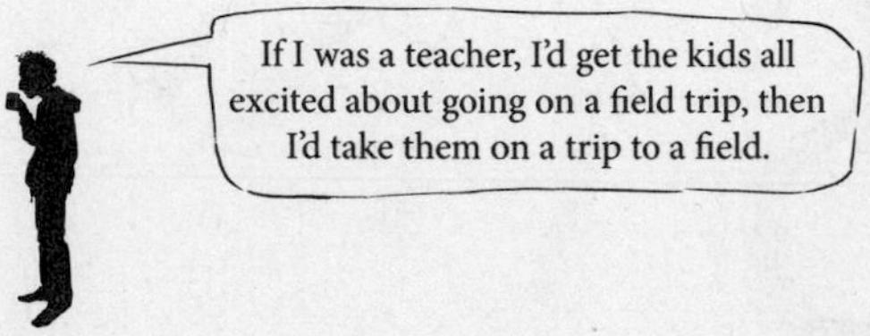
If I was a teacher, I'd get the kids all excited about going on a field trip, then I'd take them on a trip to a field.

CHAPTER FIFTEEN

FOR SMART ATTRACTIVE SPORTS FANS

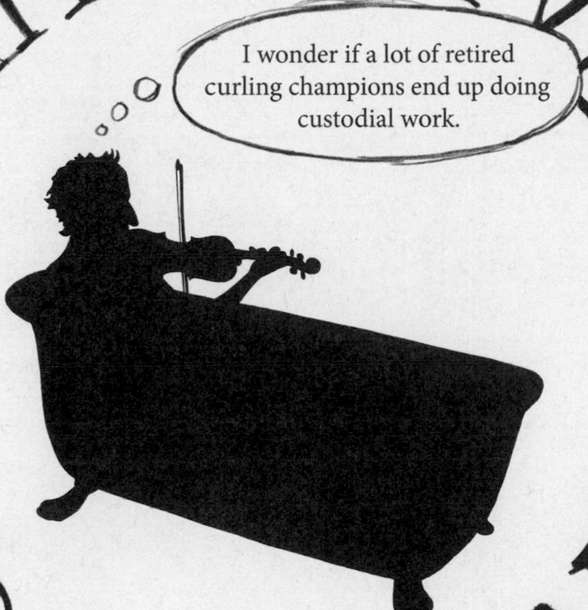
I wonder if a lot of retired curling champions end up doing custodial work.

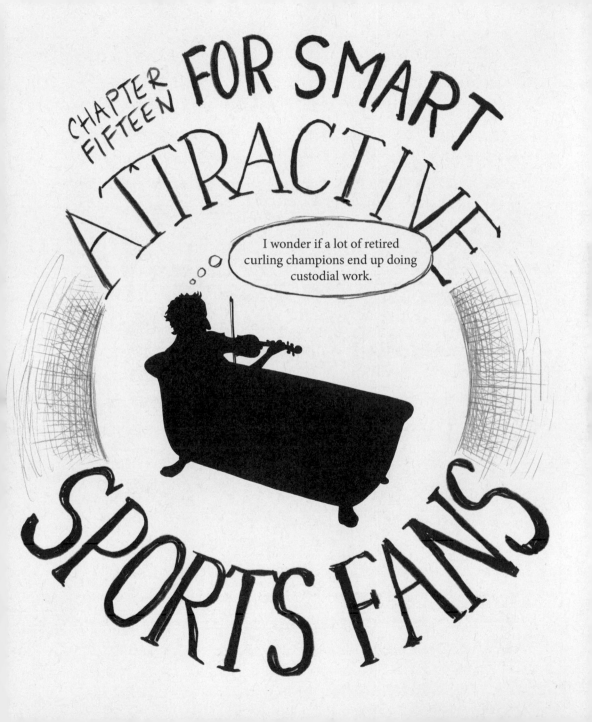

Believe it or not, there was a time when sports didn't exist. They were invented on a beautiful spring day in Penobscot, Maine, in 1871. Two young couples, fresh from berry picking, were enjoying a picnic when suddenly one of the young men, Chester Evans, enraged by cheese, hurled a walnut straight at the eye of the other young man,

one Gabe Cloverton. Reacting quickly, Gabe yanked a picket from a nearby fence and whacked the walnut high into the air, where it landed quite miraculously in an apple basket hung from a tree to evade the varmints. The girls cheered. Emboldened, Gabe skipped the perimeter of the glen, touching the trunk of every birch he passed (there were only three), before returning home to the blanket with a hearty slide and thus dusting Chester's cheese plate. Peeved, Chester challenged him to fisticuffs, which promptly commenced and continued for sixteen rounds. The ladies, feeling a need for some distraction, endeavored to keep a raisin aloft between them with the clever use of two flyswatters.

After this they were famished but had only one loaf of pumpernickel left. Chester, still sore over the walnut incident, seized the bread and sprinted for the sea. They all ran pell-mell after him, trying to force him to the ground and hold him there for three seconds. Reaching the beach and seeking closure, Chester slammed the loaf hard onto the sand and began to dance. One of the women, Claire Tarkinton, seeing the loaf had been soiled, kicked it into a fisherman's net. She then rolled in the sand, holding her ankle, while the others tried to "ride" the waves atop driftwood planks. Chester, who was later revealed to be a Satanist, found a piece of charcoal and scrawled "Go Devils" across his face. As the sun began to fade, the weary troupe packed up their belongings and walked back to their parked buggy. Sipping a salty lemon-lime rickey, Miss Tarkinton said, "We should do this again sometime, maybe with matching shirts." And do it again with matching shirts sometime they did.

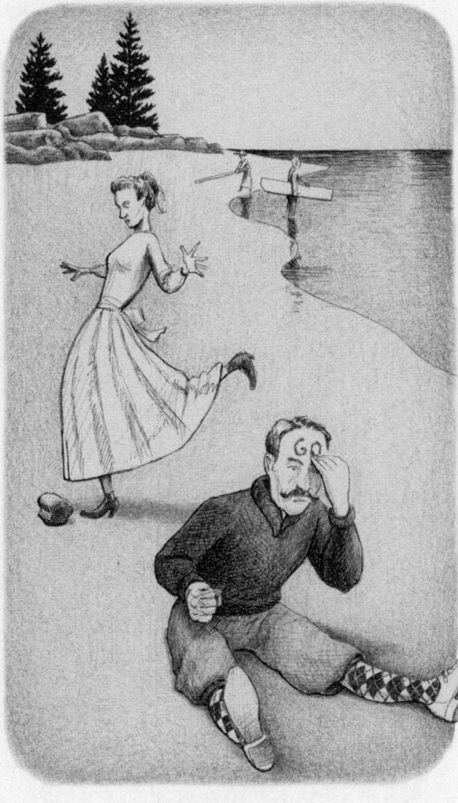
GO

"*O'Brian here has written us a new play.*"

"The postseason coverage ended yesterday. This is the preseason coverage."

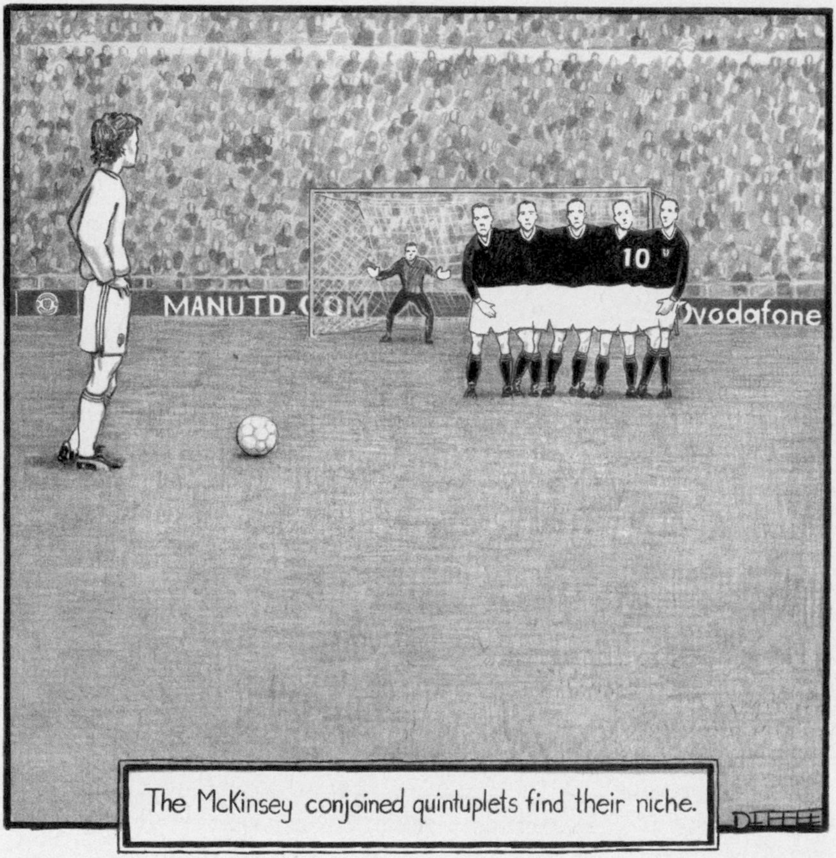
MANUTD.COM
vodafone
10

The McKinsey conjoined quintuplets find their niche.

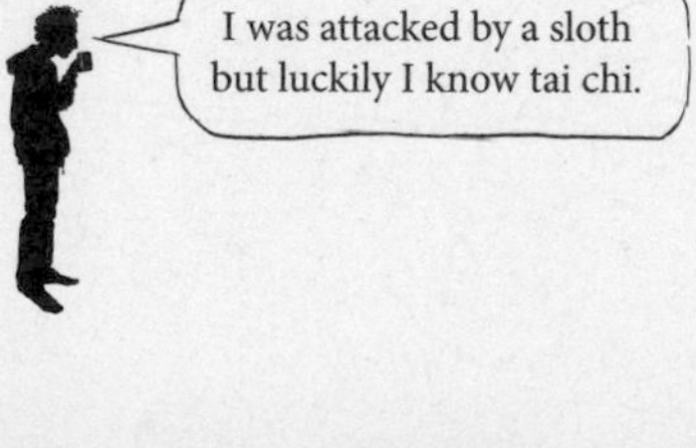
I was attacked by a sloth but luckily I know tai chi.

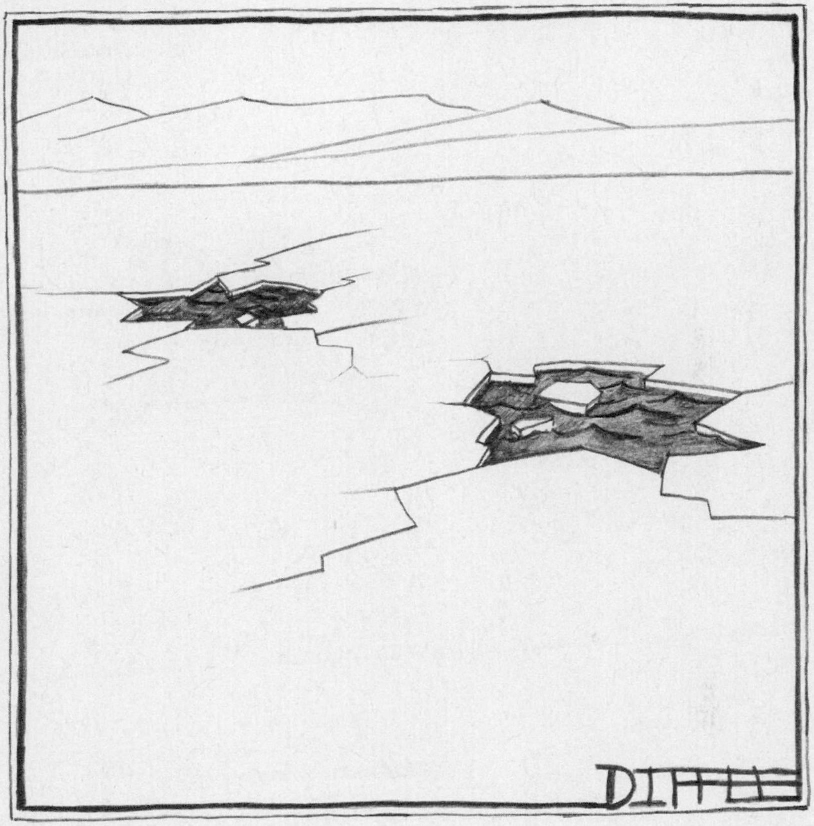
DIFFEE

"Sumo on Ice."

3 WAYS TO MAKE TRACK AND FIELD BETTER

STRIPPER
POLE VAULTING

JAVELIN CATCH

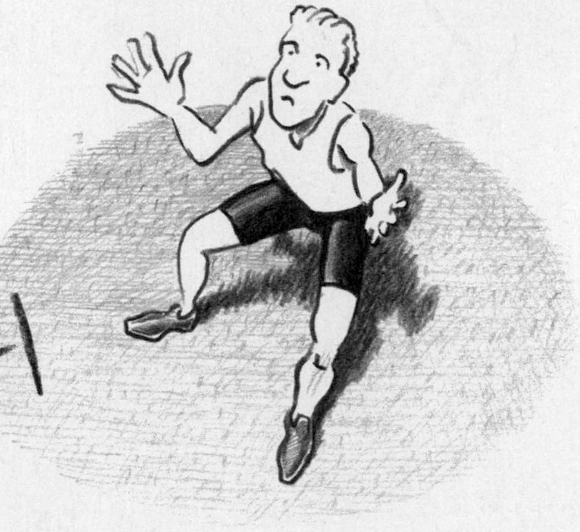

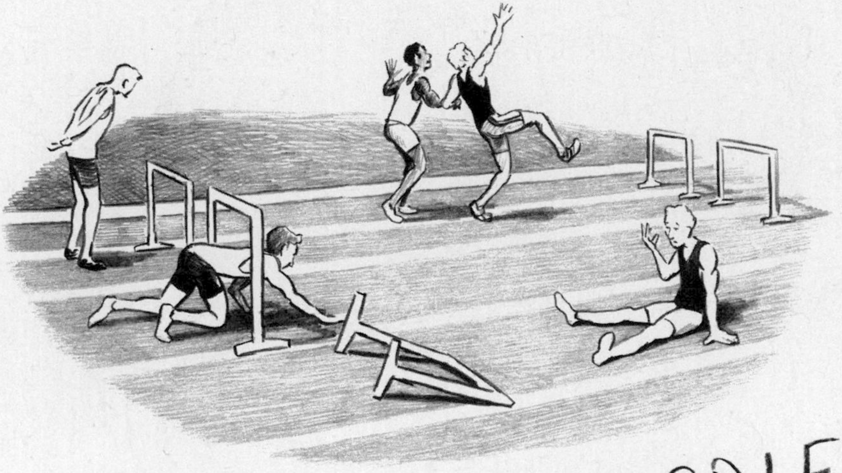

TOTALLY HIGH HURDLES

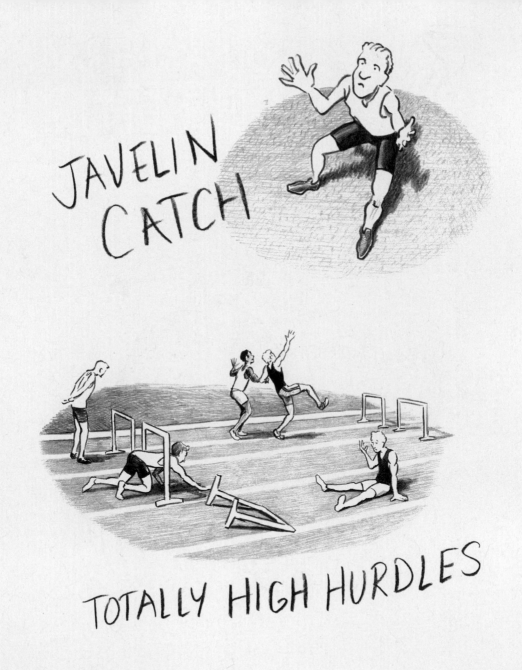

"But what if we're attacked in the press?"

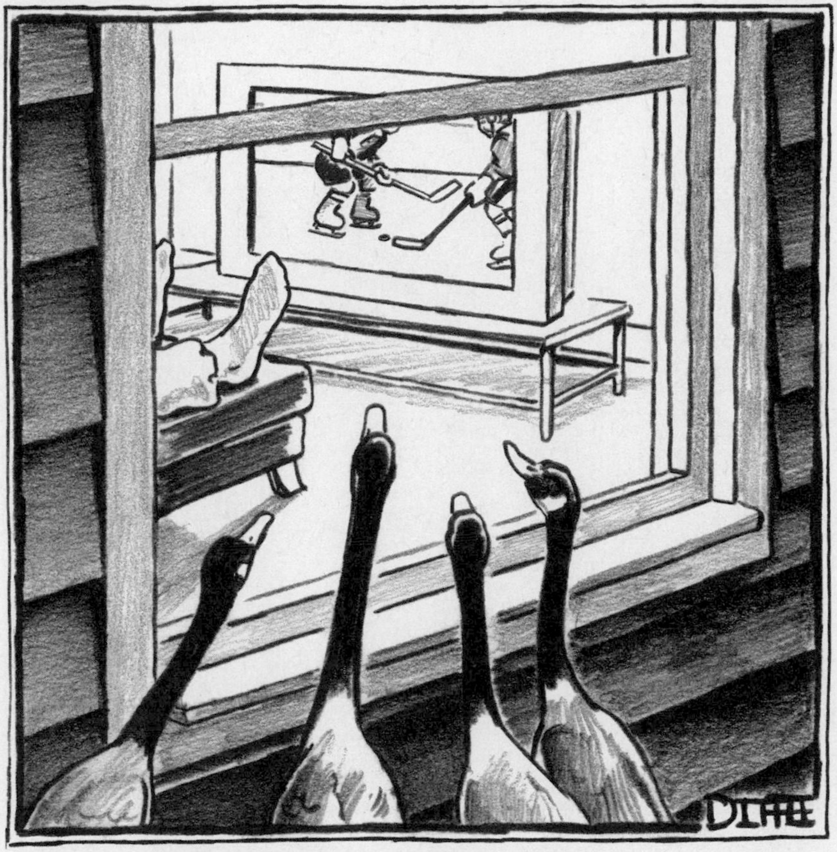
DIFFEE

CANADA GEESE

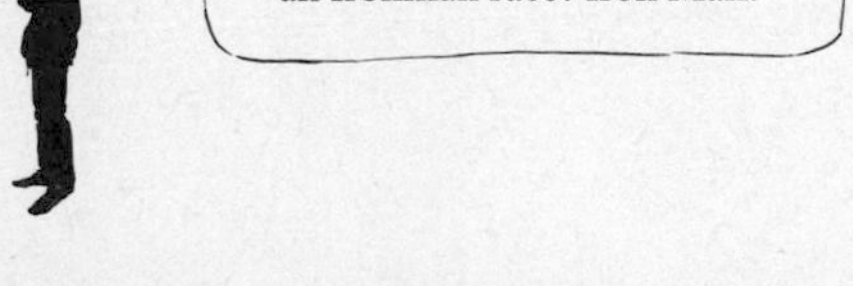
You know who wouldn't do well in an Ironman race? Iron Man.

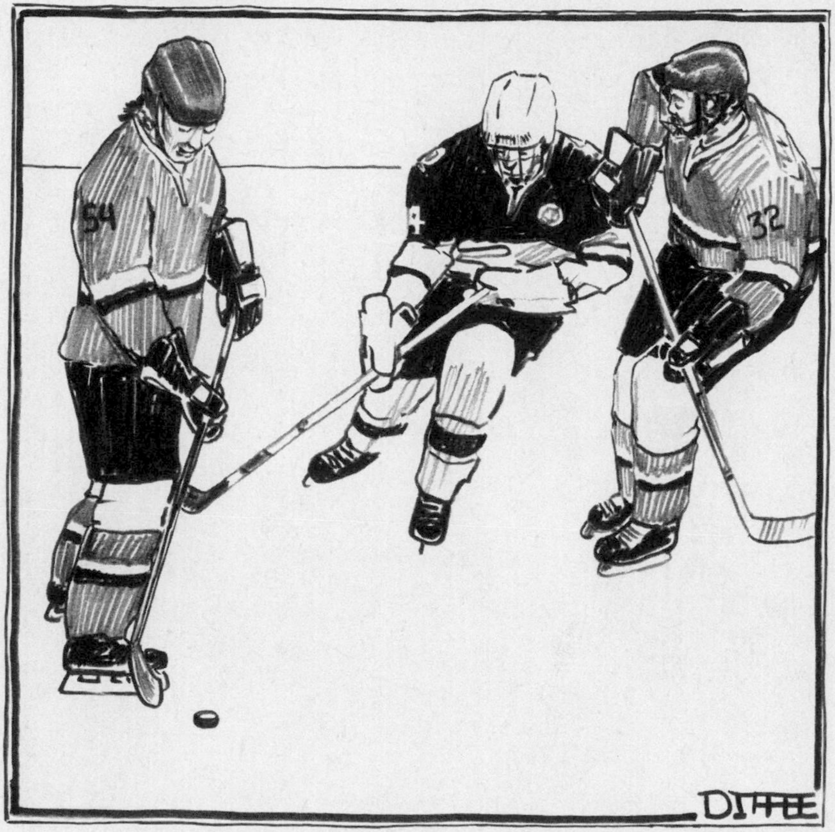
54
32
DIFFEE

"Hang on, I think we've got a Ring Ding here."

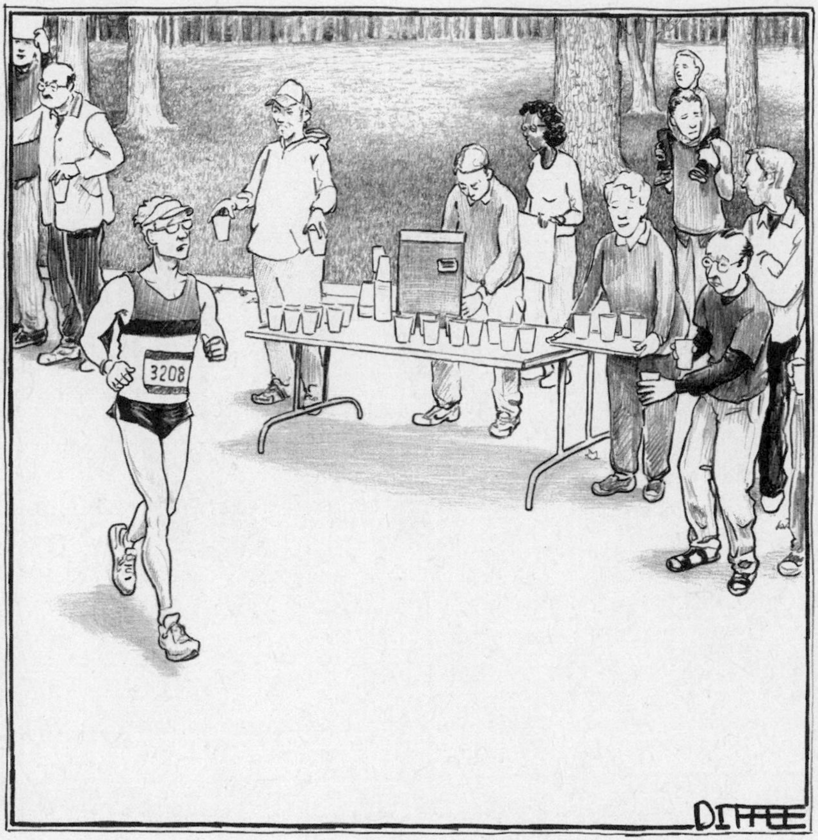
3208
DIFFEE

"Thanks, but what I really need is some bigger shorts."

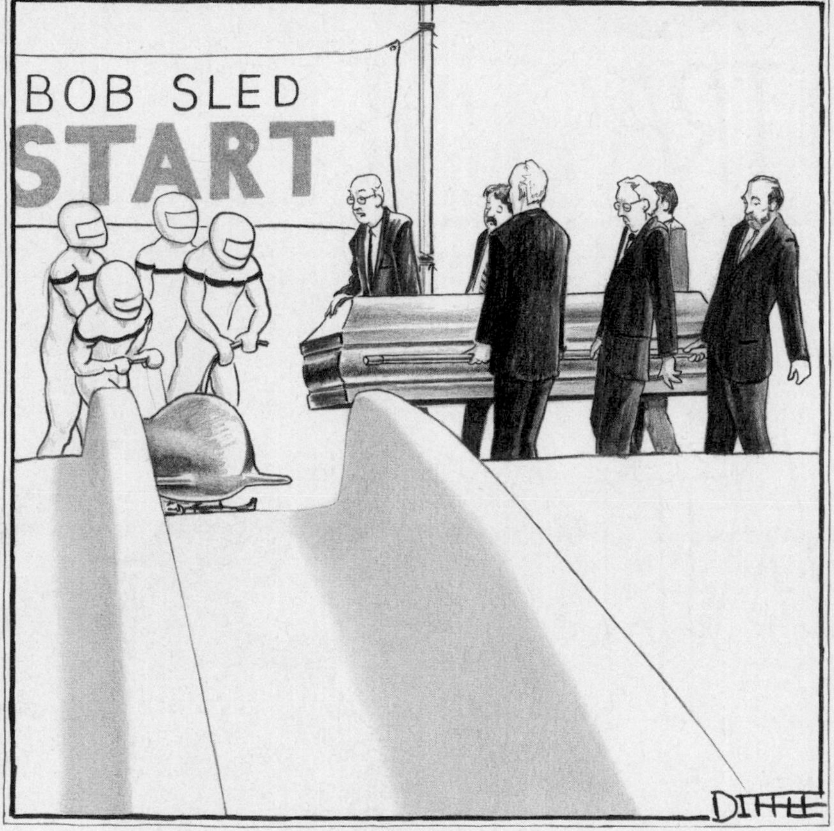
BOB SLED
START

"Hope you don't mind—it was his last request."

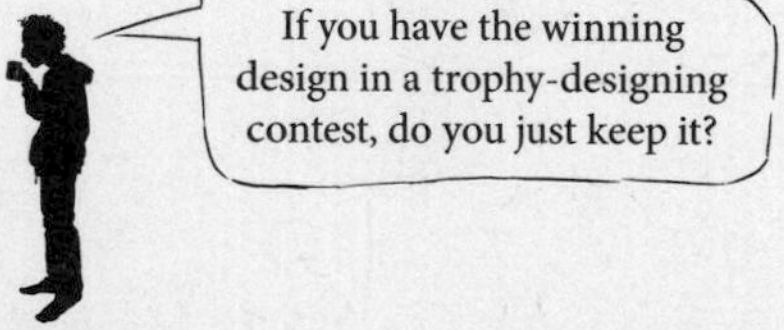
If you have the winning design in a trophy-designing contest, do you just keep it?

CHAPTER SIXTEEN

FOR SMART ATTRACTIVE PEOPLE WITH TATTOOS

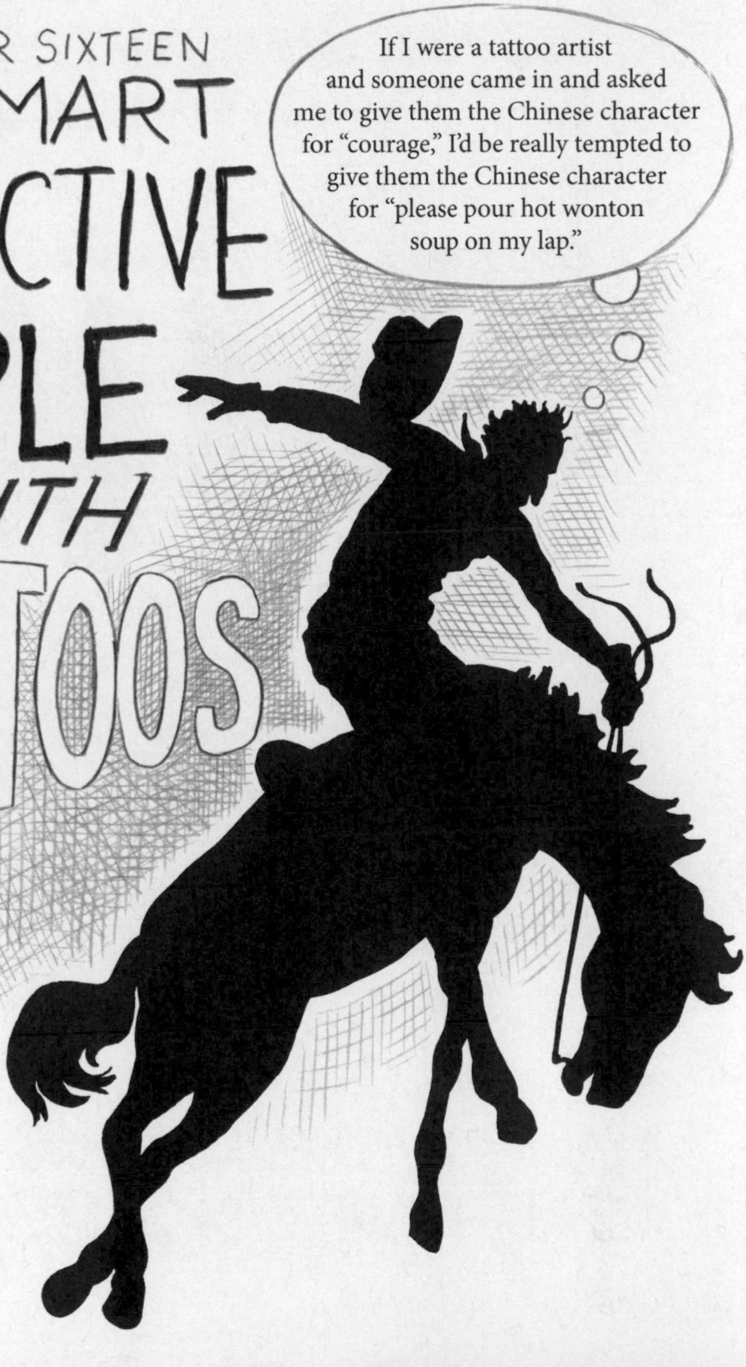

A FRIEND ONCE TOLD ME THAT I OVERTHINK THINGS. AFTER I THOUGHT AND THOUGHT AND THOUGHT ABOUT IT, I REALIZED THAT HE WAS WRONG. IT'S PROBABLY WHY I DON'T HAVE ANY TATTOOS. I'VE THOUGHT ABOUT IT, A LOT. BUT GETTING A TATTOO, TO ME, IS SORT OF LIKE EATING EGGS. THE MORE I ACTUALLY STOP AND THINK ABOUT IT, THE LESS LIKELY I AM TO DO IT.

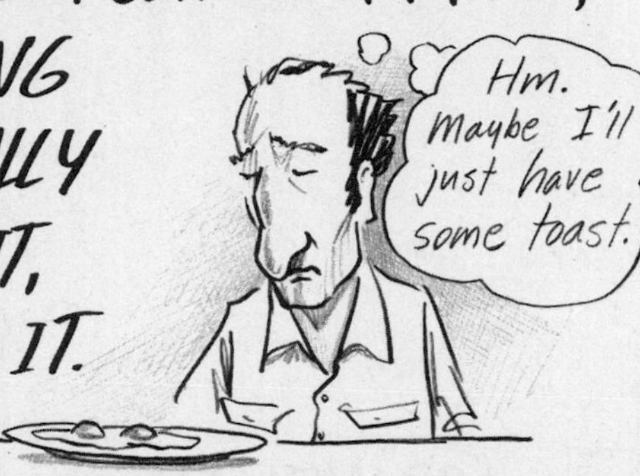
Hm. Maybe I'll just have some toast.

TATTOOS AREN'T RATIONAL. THAT'S HALF THE POINT. TATTOO PEOPLE FOLLOW THEIR HEARTS, NOT THEIR HEADS. THEY WON'T BE RULED. THEY ARE NONCONFORMISTS, JUST LIKE 38% OF AMERICANS BETWEEN THE AGES OF 18 AND 29. IF TATTOOS WERE RATIONAL, PRACTICAL DECISIONS, WE'D SEE A LOT MORE PEOPLE WITH TATTOOED LISTS OF WORDS THAT ARE HARD TO SPELL.

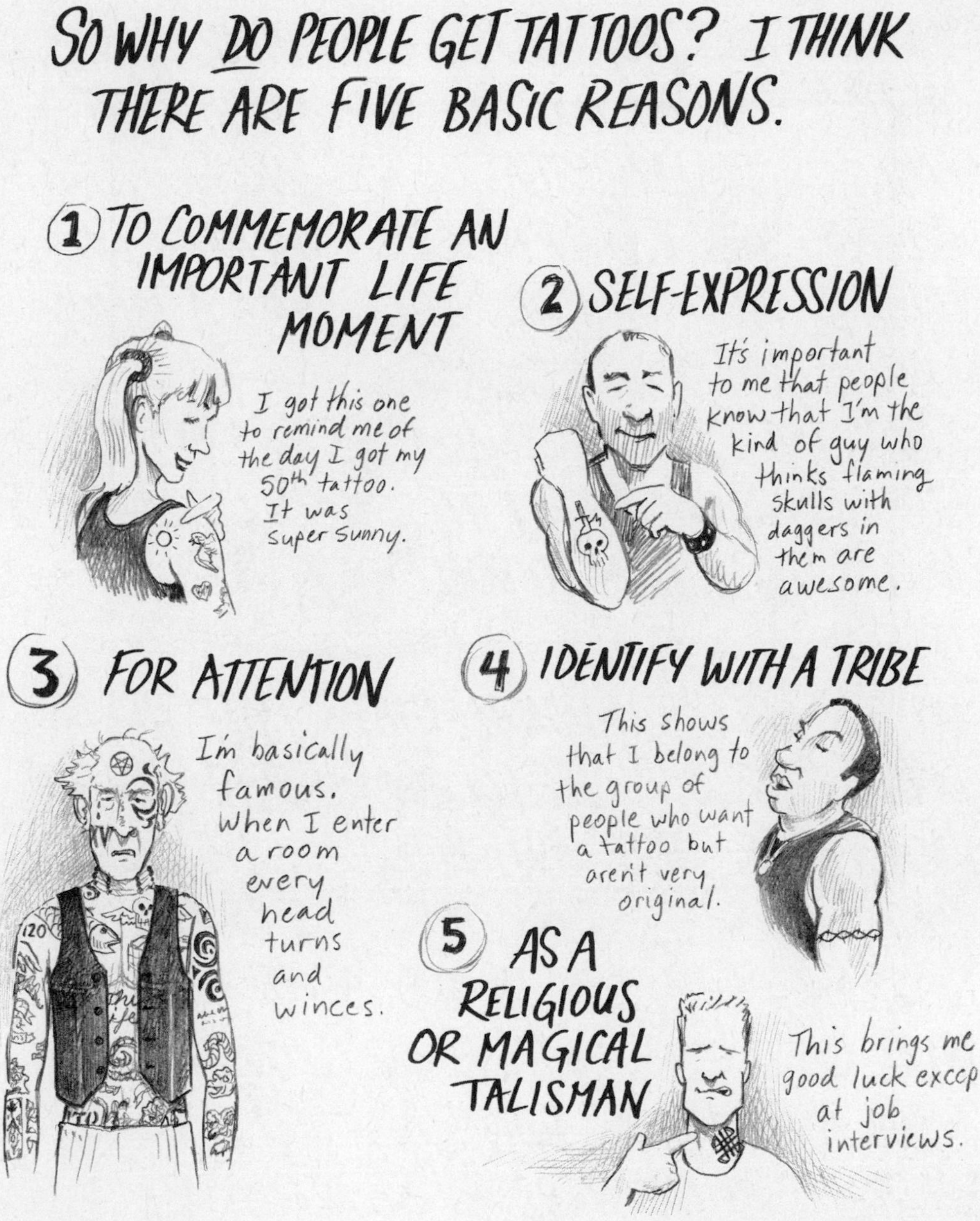

SO WHY DO PEOPLE GET TATTOOS? I THINK THERE ARE FIVE BASIC REASONS.
1 TO COMMEMORATE AN IMPORTANT LIFE MOMENT
I got this one to remind me of the day I got my 50th tattoo. It was super sunny.
2 SELF-EXPRESSION
It's important to me that people know that I'm the kind of guy who thinks flaming skulls with daggers in them are awesome.
3 FOR ATTENTION
I'm basically famous. When I enter a room every head turns and winces.
4 IDENTIFY WITH A TRIBE
This shows that I belong to the group of people who want a tattoo but aren't very original.
5 AS A RELIGIOUS OR MAGICAL TALISMAN
This brings me good luck except at job interviews.

"*A little advice. Make sure the image is in the public domain.*"

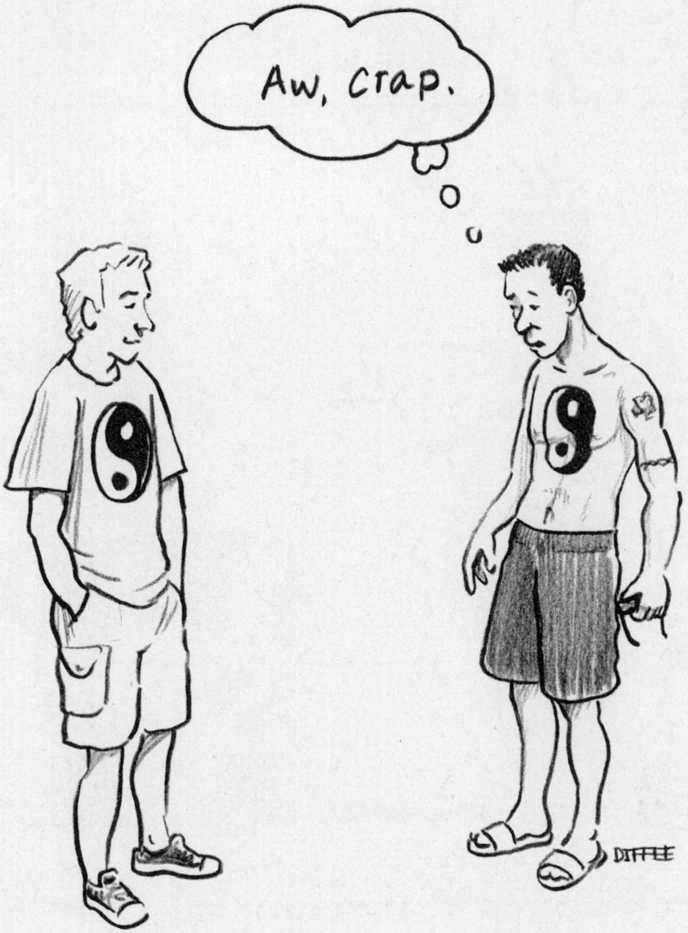
Aw, crap.
DIFFEE

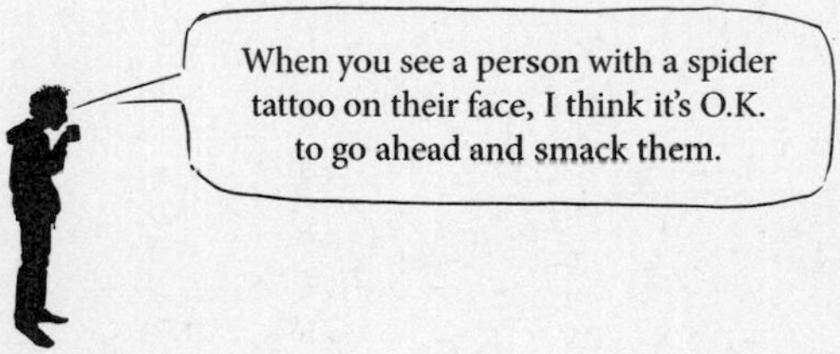
When you see a person with a spider tattoo on their face, I think it's O.K. to go ahead and smack them.

Knuckle Tats You'll Never See

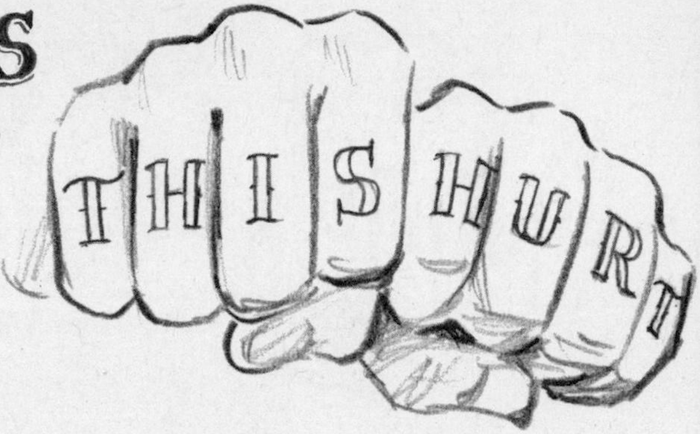
THIS HURT

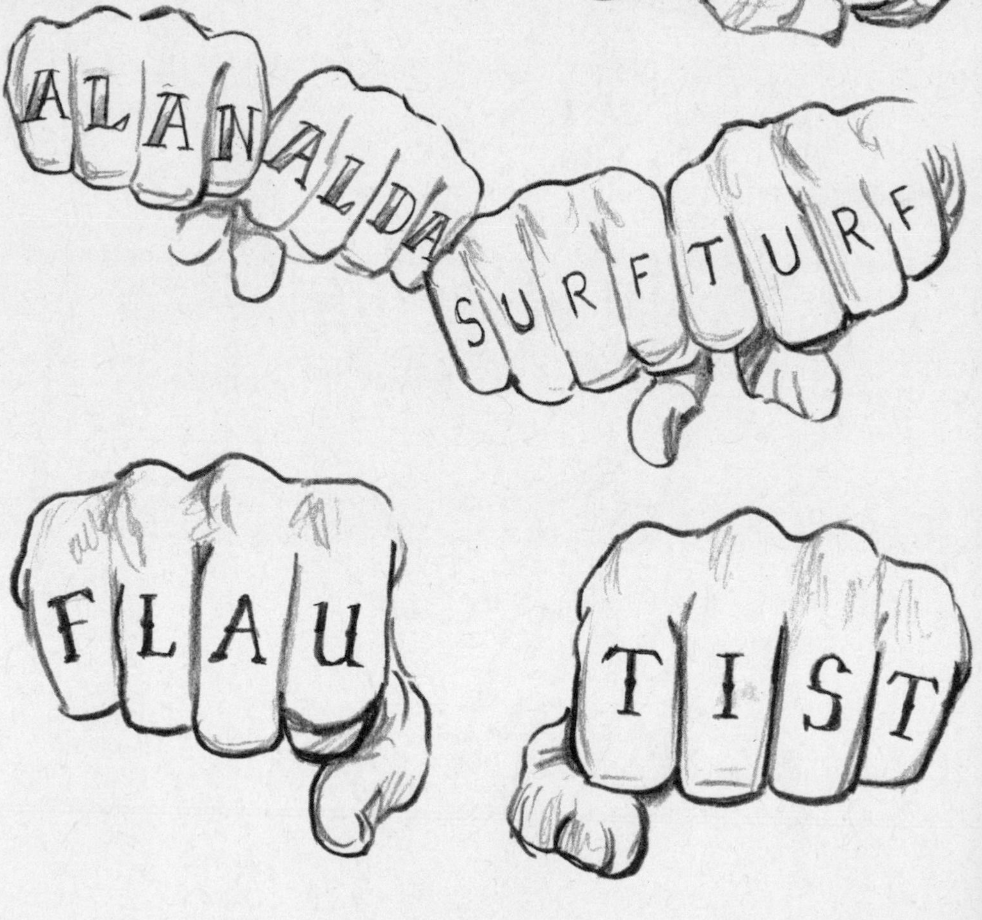
ALAN ALDA
SURF TURF
FLAU TIST

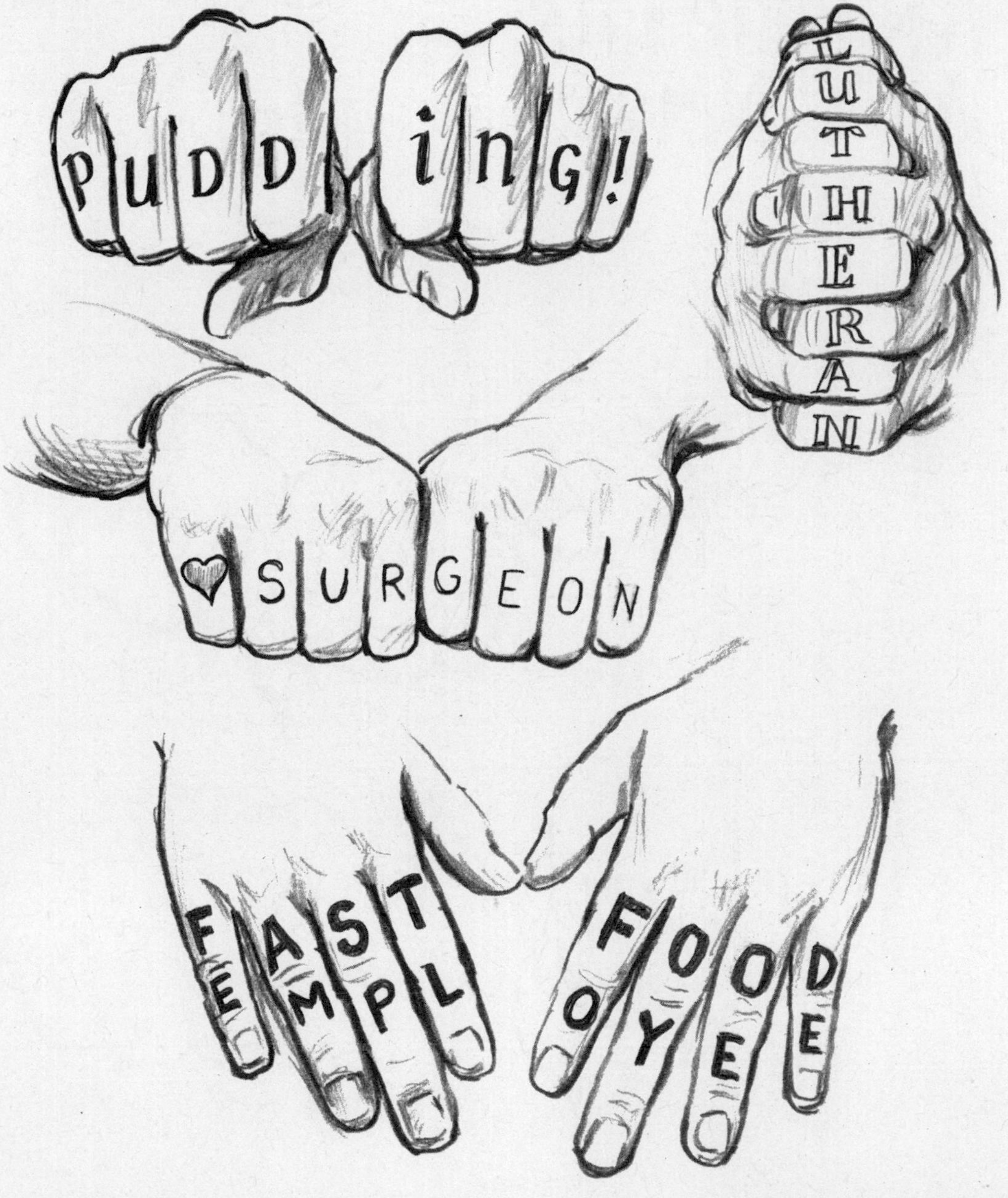
PUDDING!
LUTHERAN
SURGEON
FAST FOOD
EMPLOYEE

NICE SAVE
BORN TO RAISE HELL
BORN TO RAISE SHELLY
THEN
NOW

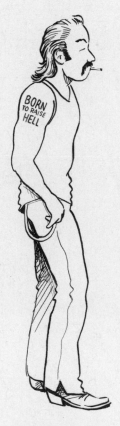

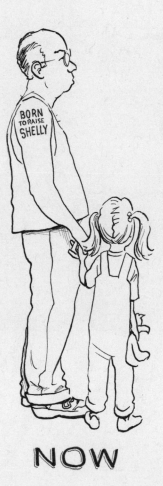

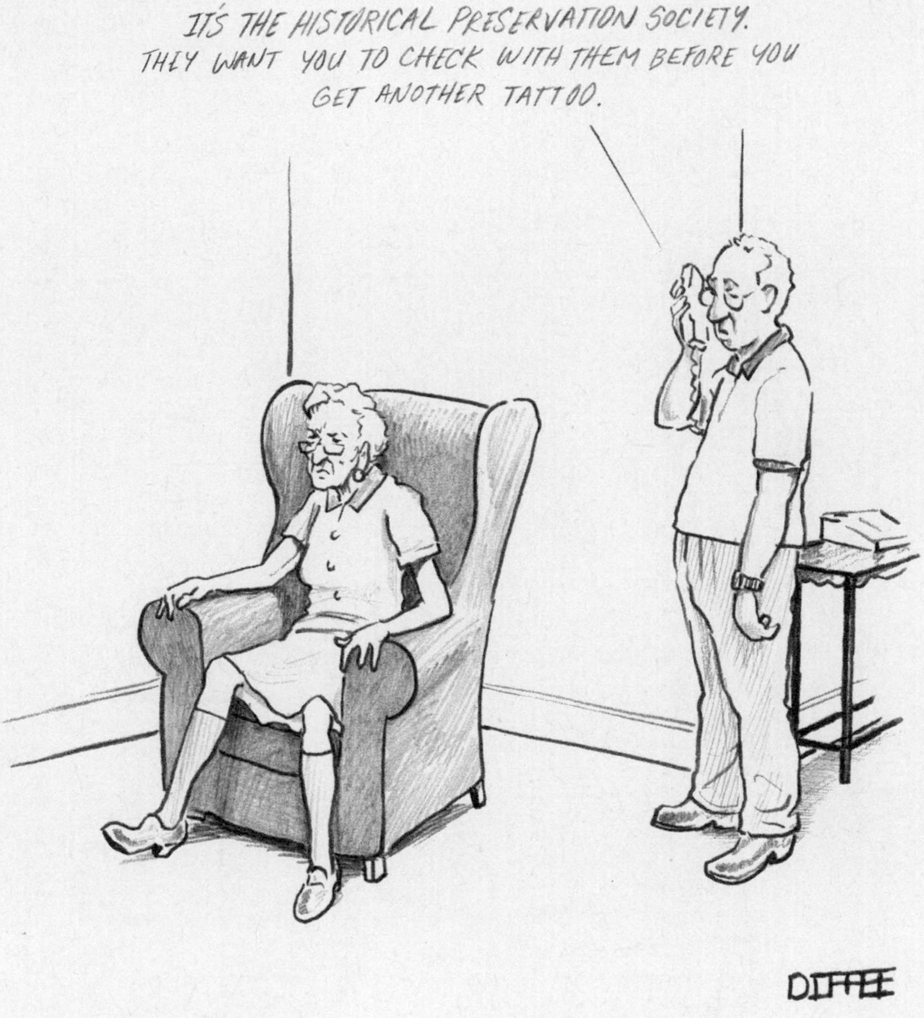
IT'S THE HISTORICAL PRESERVATION SOCIETY.
THEY WANT YOU TO CHECK WITH THEM BEFORE YOU
GET ANOTHER TATTOO.
DIFFEE

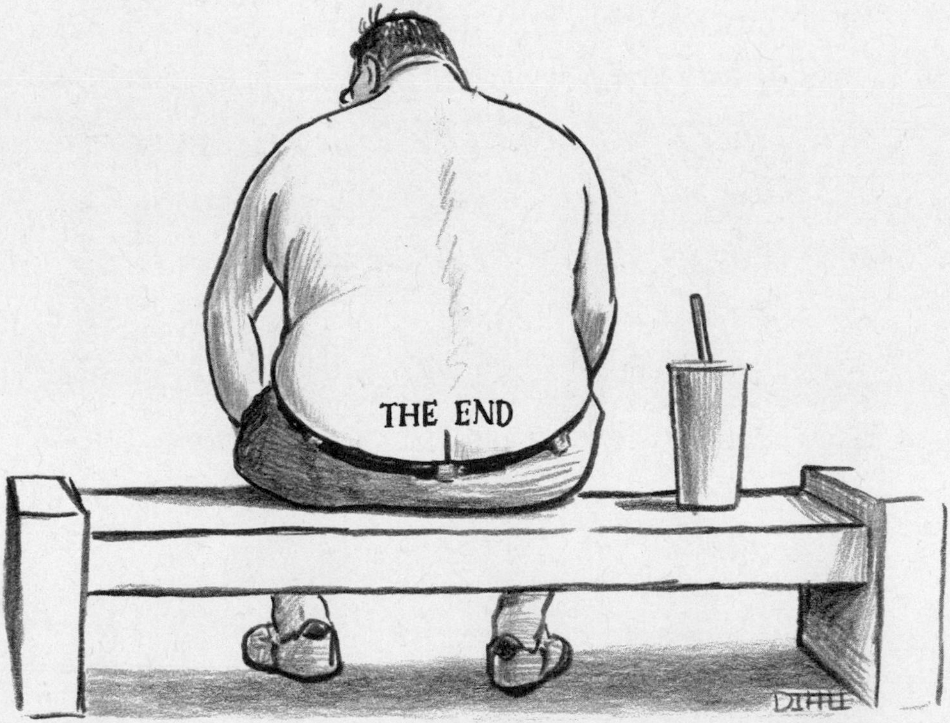
THE END
DIFFEE

ACKNOWLEDGMENTS

Big thanks to Drew Dernavich, Tom Gammill, Liam Francis Walsh, Paul Noth, Glen LeLievre, Jack Burgess, Yoni Brenner, and Jake Tilove, who looked at this when it was way too long and helped me make it shorter. To the whole team at Scribner, especially Nan Graham and my editor, Brant Rumble, who has the name, but also the reflexes and nimble control of a rodeo clown. To Bob Mankoff and David Remnick at The New Yorker, who gave most of these jokes their first life. To Jake Silverstein and TJ Tucker, who let me do things in Texas Monthly that opened up my possibilities. To Spencer Ramsey for his digital wizardry. To my agents, David Kuhn and Nicole Tourtelot. To the fine folks with "Diffee Doodles" on their walls, the readers of my Diffeeville Dispatch for their constant support and encouragement. And finally, to Tanya Erlach, the smartest and most attractive of all.